The ways out

International Library of Sociology

Founded by Karl Mannheim

Editor: John Rex, University of Warwick

Arbor Scientiae
Arbor Vitae

A catalogue of the books available in the **International Library of Sociology** and other series of Social Science books published by Routledge & Kegan Paul will be found at the end of this volume.

The ways out:
Utopian communal groups in an age of Babylon

John R. Hall
Department of Sociology
University of Missouri, Columbia

Routledge & Kegan Paul
London, Henley and Boston

First published in 1978
by Routledge & Kegan Paul Ltd
39 Store Street,
London WC1E 7DD,
Broadway House,
Newtown Road,
Henley-on-Thames,
Oxon RG9 1EN and
9 Park Street,
Boston, Mass. 02108, USA
Printed in Great Britain by
Redwood Burn Limited
Trowbridge & Esher

British Library Cataloguing in Publication Data

Hall, John R

The ways out. – (International library of sociology).
1. Collective settlements – United States
I. Title II. Series
301.34 HX654

ISBN 0 7100 8807 8

Contents

Preface vii

1 Introduction 1

A socio-historical model of countercultures 4
The comparative analysis of communal groups 7

2 Beginners 19

People 19
The group myth 22
Initial collective life 27
Early failure 34

3 Time and communal life 39

Time in the established order 40
On the phenomenology of time 43
Time orientations in communal groups 51
The diachronic worldly utopia 54
Synchronic time in communal groups 58
Apocalyptic time in communal groups 68
The end of history and utopian times 79

4 The social enactment of communal life 83

Attention, meaning and the enactment of communal life 83
The natural communal world 87
Produced communal worlds 91
Transcendental engagement in the phenomenal world 113
Summary 117

5 Needs, want satisfaction and work 120

Old and new bases of want satisfaction 121
Time, social enactment and want satisfaction 128
Strategies of resource acquisition 134
Labor substitution and production of goods 142
Organization of work 143
Work discipline and legitimation 152
Efficiency and effectiveness 156

6 Government 162

Sources of governing formations 163
The political process 169
Communal governments and crises of legitimacy 183
Summary 192

7 Conclusion 195

Domination and meaning in the established order 196
Communal groups: emergences and ideal types 200
Communal groups and utopian diffusion 208
Some speculations on the contemporary situation 218

Appendix 1 Some theoretical and methodological considerations 223

Appendix 2 Descriptions of communal groups included in the study 236

Appendix 3 Methods of research 244

Bibliography 252

Index 260

Preface

In order to live communally, people develop situationally new ways of relating to one another, ways which would not always make much sense to other people, just as the concerns, expectations and sensibilities of people in society-at-large are often quite out of place in communal groups. In fact, many of the people who have begun to live communally within the last dozen years or so have done so in an explicit rejection of the established social order. People in communal groups have set up alternative arenas where the hope is to forge, personally and collectively, more meaningful and fulfilling ways of life. Some communalists seek to change the world as well.

In being concerned with fulfillment and with change, communalists are not so different from other people who are willing to examine the conditions of human existence. The difference is simply this: in communal groups, the absolutes of living under one or another ideal of society are often intentionally or unintentionally drawn out; it is thus possible to see 'the thing itself' which is more mysteriously woven into less uncompromisingly 'idealistic' situations. The study of communal groups is thus a concentrated study of developments which transpire in more diffuse countercultures and social movements as well. Moreover, communalists do not take on the problem of utopia simply as an impracticable wish for a perfect society, but as lived reality. The concerns of communalists with ways of surviving, with ethical problems, with problems of organization, power and justice, with love, war, freedom and communion are not simply concerns of communalists; they are human concerns. And, like other people, communalists are flawed, so that for all the drive toward an ideal, tragedy and pathos and triviality find their ways into communal life. This study is concerned with communalists, but in more than one respect, what happens in communal groups bears resemblance to what happens elsewhere. For the most part, I have not tried to make these connections explicit; I leave it to readers to do so as they may.

When I first became interested in communal groups in the middle 1960s, I was impressed with a simple observation: even though people in communal groups seem to broadly share rejection of established ways of life, the new solutions which people choose to embark on often bear little resemblance to one another. This book is the result of an attempt on my part to come to terms - both personally and intellectually - with that first impression. In order to live communally, I sought a deeper understanding of communalism. In turn, that search led me to experience communal ways of life which were not my own. This book is therefore a comparative study of alternative contemporary communal groups. Though I have used some cited secondary sources, the study is for the most part based on my own first-hand knowledge of communal groups from 1970 through 1976. It is a dialogue between my lived experiences and my interests in sociological theory.

Specifically, I have sought to study the situated sociology of knowledge in alternative communal groups; I have tried to discern the alternative ways in which people know about the world they live in. This focus has led me to employ a sociological approach based on mundane phenomenology; the approach looks to people living in unfolding time and paying attention to the world according to one or another scheme of interpretation. To the degree that I have interpreted social action in alternative cognitive communal worlds in terms of sociological categories, I have relied substantially on the perspective which Max Weber described - that of 'Verstehen,' or subjective understanding. In other words, I have sought to understand action as the actors themselves stood in relation to it. In terms of sociological theory, then, the present study draws out the lifeworldly connections in communal groups between the a priori mundane phenomenology of Alfred Schutz and Weber's categories of interpretive sociology. Sociologists may well regard the perspective and the categories I employ to be of general interest, over and above the specific concern of this book with communal groups. The theoretical concerns focus the study to a considerable degree; I am more concerned with cognitive orientations than with material accomplishments and more concerned with the subjectively meaningful basis of action than with specific 'contents' of action. I have proposed a set of ideal types which seem to me to summarize configurations of communal association. More generally, these types may be regarded as an attempt to get at the cognitive status of one or another type of social action.

In these sociological concerns I have different purposes than those of most communalists. Thus, even though I have tried to understand communal ways of life from the points of view of the actors involved, communalists at The Farm (a spiritual community in Tennessee) who read portions of the manuscript do not agree with what I have written: 'It sounds staged and not very real.' In part this kind of problem stems from my sociological purposes; in part it derives from the difference between my comparative perspective and the everyday perspectives of people at The Farm who do not experience themselves within such a framework. In part the problem is one of a lapse in time between my visits to communal groups and the occasions when communalists had opportunities to read drafts of what I had written. Thus, Serious Israel (an elder in the Love Family) told me this summer that what I had written about the Love Family is a reflection of three years ago. He emphasized that Love Israel, the founder of the group, is no longer such a separate authority: 'We've been learning to live in the one mind of God.' He acknowledged that 'In the early years we had a vision of it and how it's supposed to be, and we tried to impose it on ourselves. But it didn't work. Now we are finding out that we can let it become, grow into it.' Similarly, a person at The Farm says, 'we have matured and grown as a community over the years - what was characteristic then is not necessarily so now.'

This book is based on the field research at the times when it was done; I have corrected any inaccuracies which communalists found in the draft, but I have not tried to update the account, and I will have to live with the honest disagreements of emphasis and interpretation between myself and other communalists. The analysis represents my attempt to come to terms with different types of communal association; it does not claim to trace historical developments subsequent to the period during which most of the visits to communal groups were made (1972-3). In all of this it is important to recognize that life continues, that a group which once approximated one type of communal association may now be something quite different. The new communal groups which have survived so far are quite young; some of them will unfold in ways which will surprise all of us. Indeed it is that very process for which the present study may provide benchmarks of interpretation in future analyses. In the present study, I have sought to depict the alternative tendencies of the utopian dialectic. In the end, it may all come to 'a mere average' of the new concerns, as Frederick Engels suggested for primitive Christianity (1964b:207). Or, as communalists of various persuasions are given to saying, 'It is all one.'

Social life is manifold, and no truly empirical sociology can claim to be anything but exploratory. For there is a certain paradox of our experience: the immediacy of it is immensely rich in content and unceasingly emergent, and the attempt to capture it with words can only be reflective and incomplete. I am especially grateful to those innumerable communalists who have contributed to the substance of the study by letting me experience and helping me understand their ways of being in the world. In so far as the study represents a meaningful portrayal of communal life, it has depended on the openness and cooperation of communalists. In this sense I have only acted as a vehicle - people in communal groups have been the compelling inspiration.

I wish to thank my friends and colleagues for their principled support of inquiry grounded in intellectual freedom. My deepest appreciation goes to Guenther Roth for his scholarship and his humanity, and to H. Stith Bennett for his spiritual counsel. I also want to thank Michael Hechter, Kathleen Ritter, Rodney Stark and Pierre van den Berghe of the Department of Sociology, Pamela Amoss of the Department of Anthropology, Margaret Levy of the Department of Political Science - all at the University of Washington - William Kornblum of the City University of New York, and George Primov of the University of Missouri, for the insightful contributions each has made to various aspects of the study. Anonymous readers, people at The Farm, Serious Israel of the Love Family, and David Ruth of Twin Oaks made comments and suggestions about the original draft, and I am grateful for their critiques and encouragement.

The research has been supported in part by the National Institutes of Mental Health. Hans Hoffman of Arlington, Washington, helped by allowing me the use of a cabin in which to write. I am also most grateful to Margaret Smart and Paula Malin for secretarial assistance.

Though I would never have been able to complete this study without 'a little help from my friends,' I alone take responsibility for its contents.

Columbia, Missouri
November 1976

JRH

1 Introduction

Something's going on,
But you don't know what it is,
Do you, Mr. Jones?

Bob Dylan

In so far as radical social change - the emergence of situationally new forms of association - does not derive solely from technological advancements, utopian communal groups have played perennially significant roles. These associations of persons, in the course of coming to grips with certain cultural problems of their era, enact situationally new, 'deviant' forms of ethical and exemplary conduct. Even when, in commonsense fashion, the communal groups may be considered secular, they bear a religious character. As Engels (1964b:206) recognized, socialist sects, like primitive Christians, seek to 'get hold of the masses'; whether rhetoric draws on religious or political images, the associational form is that of a band of true believers. Even when communal association is based simply on friendship, in so far as it involves a critical rejection of social and cultural possibilities within an established order, it may be considered utopian.

Communalism may well have been the organizing principle of all early human life, as both bourgeois (Heusler, 1886) and revolutionary (Kropotkin, 1914; Kautsky, 1966) social theorists of the nineteenth century came to suggest. But with the rise of civilizations, communalism especially becomes a vehicle of deviance from prevailing socially ordered ways of life. In sharing a deviant perspective, those who live communally assert a charismatic legitimacy for their actions. As Peter Berger and Thomas Luckmann (1966:106) have observed, a deviant group objectivates an alternative definition of reality: what would have been simply a case of either individual 'sin' or widespread anomie becomes a matter of 'heresy.'

Deviant groups seem to have been ever-present features of civilizations (cf. Knox, 1956). Yet at certain points in history, a variety of communal groups and other bearers of deviant perspectives emerge almost simultaneously. It then becomes appropriate to speak of a more general counterculture.

Since the middle 1960s, such a countercultural emergence has taken place in a number of industrialized countries (Fairfield, 1972; Rigby, 1974). In the USA, sizable numbers of youth have in one way or another 'dropped out' of society. During the 1950s, generations of youth had found themselves in times of 'peace and prosperity'; their initial career choices were largely ones of conformity to available social options. But subsequent youth generations came of age in times of assassinations, war, protest, governmental and business scandals, and economic crisis. In searching for personally satisfying lives, many youths have denigrated participation in the ongoing social order. Rather than accept any liberalized or therapeutic adaptation to existing institutions, they chose to participate in various countercultural activities - often simply ignoring the dominant order so far as possible, sometimes cloaking their own actions in utopian visions of perfectible community or large-scale social change. The result has been the proliferation of communal groups, cooperatives, political operations and religious movements.

Of course countercultural communal groups such as those prevalent in the USA since the middle 1960s are simply among the more easily discernible aspects of pervasive shifts in social orientation among portions of a population. But they bear a special relationship to more diffuse countercultures and social movements: they are the core arenas in which fulfillment of the new values is most actively pursued. While political study groups, meditation groups, consumer cooperatives, work collectives and the like are significant countercultural institutions, it is especially in communal groups that the attempt is made to implement utopian visions as alternative and encompassing ways of life. Communalists must immediately come to terms with the tensions between utopian ideals and the difficulties of realizing those ideals in a real world. For this reason, the understanding of communal groups provides the possibility of coming to terms with more diffuse countercultures and their implications for the societies to which they offer critiques.

Communal groups are involved in what Max Weber (1968: 24) called value-rational action - action in pursuit of ultimate values, engaged in 'independently of its prospects of success.' Indeed, a workable definition of 'communal group' would have to emphasize the importance of values. Diversity among communal groups is good reason to avoid any narrow definition based on structural criteria such as absence of private property or a common source of income. Most of the new groups would not meet such criteria; yet they share a value-based turning away from other options in favor of a collective life. In its broadest sense then, a communal group may be taken to be a household or interrelated set of households inhabited by three or more adults engaged in attempts at value-achievement not available in society-at-large.*

Literally thousands of communal groups have been formed in the USA since the middle 1960s. Such groups have provided alternative ways of living which counter more conventional forms of household association - the nuclear family and 'singles' life. Many communal groups were transitory crash pads never intended to be permanent living sites. Others, begun with great optimism, did not survive long. Though the contemporary communal movement in the USA probably peaked in the early 1970s, a substantial number of groups are going concerns, and new ones

---

* This definition of a communal group is a modification of Jesse Pitts's (1973:351) definition of a utopian community: 'an attempt by three or more unrelated adults to organize into a total institution dedicated to the realization in the everyday life of its members of a higher level of value achievement than is apparently present in the society at large.' Pitts's definition is modified in three respects. First, a communal group need not be a total institution. Whether it can persist without so being is an empirical question. Second, efforts at value achievement may be directed to other arenas as well as to those of the everyday life of members. Third, 'higher order' implies a capability for grading values objectively, while in the present study, values are treated as representing no more than personal or shared preferred goal states. Though Abrams and McCulloch (1976:39) suggest that 'perhaps five is the minimum number required to break the conventions of monogamous pairing and private life,' St Benedict (1975:49) noted unpacified monks living together in twos and threes, 'unschooled by any rule.' So long as a value-rational orientation to action obtains, there would seem to be no basis for definitionally excluding cases of communal action on the basis of small size.

are still being started. Communal living has persisted independently of faddish cycles of media interest. But even a casual acquaintance with extant communal groups suggests that 'the' counterculture is not the unified phenomenon that Roszak (1969) depicted. Initial waves of countercultural enthusiasm during the middle 1960s evidenced a syncretic merger of cultural critiques and utopian ideals, perhaps symbolized best in the proverb, 'Make love, not war.' But by the 1970s, we hear a cacophony of voices proclaiming the ways out. The ethic of one way counters the ethic of another. While people of one persuasion promote spiritual enlightenment, others seek to bring about revolution. While some surrender to the ecstasies of the drug culture, others embrace asceticism. The seeds of reaction and those of social change are couched in similar utopian claims. And so millenarian religious sects (Ellwood, 1973), subsistence rural 'hippie' communes (Diamond, 1971; Mungo, 1970; Rabbit, 1971), urban cooperative households, and egalitarian behavioral communities (Kinkade, 1973) are in many respects as different from one another as they are from the society left behind by their participants (Houriet, 1971).

A SOCIO-HISTORICAL MODEL OF COUNTERCULTURES

The diversity among contemporary communal groups and their emergence at roughly the same time strongly parallel previous social movements in which various groups of people came to act in opposition to a prevailing order. The primitive Christian Church, for example, was but one of a number of known communal responses to the established Roman dominion and Judaic subservience. Similarly, the Christian Church of the Middle Ages was sporadically confronted with alternative communal religious movements, some of them heretical, others not. Though the preconditions, forms and outcomes of communal organization differed substantially, both frontier America (Bestor, 1970) and Germany in the 1920s (Laquer, 1962; Zablocki, 1971) witnessed waves of communal enactments.

Among other social theorists, Karl Mannheim, Frederick Engels and Norman Cohn have each considered such phenomena of countercultural deviance. While each theorist gives a somewhat different theoretical interpretation, consideration of their views on countercultures may serve as a basis for describing a socio-historical model - in Guenther Roth's (1975) terms, a set of generalizations which emphasizes the repetitive elements in various historical occurrences. The socio-historical model of countercultural deviance will indicate the range and character of parallel phenomena, and place the contemporary emergence of communal groups in the context of previous social theory. I will then describe the approach of the present study.

In 'The Pursuit of the Millenium' (1970), Norman Cohn has described mystical, anarchist and millenarian groups of the European Middle Ages. His research suggests a marked uniformity: some parts of Europe never experienced rebellious challenges to the feudal and Christian establishments; those which did were areas beset with overpopulation and rapid social and economic change. In the latter areas, people who, in Cohn's (1970:59) words, 'could find no recognized place,' were frequently ready to embrace any alternative to their frustration. Where hopelessness and futility abounded, one or another prophet would appear. 'On the strength of inspirations or revelations for which he claimed divine origin, this leader would decree for his followers a communal mission of vast dimensions and world-shaking importance' (1970:60). Those who became followers could pull themselves out of the netherworld into a status group which sought to transform the world.

The directions of revolutionary millenarianism seem to have been as varied as its preconditions were similar. There were the flagellants, as well as people of the Free Spirit, the movement behind Thomas Münzer, and a host of other occurrences.

These heretical challenges to the established order at times had tremendous appeal to people who came in contact with them, and this appeal did not go unnoticed by those committed to maintaining the status quo. For its part, the Christian Church attempted, sometimes with considerable success, to channel asceticism (Cohn, 1970:158; Weber, 1968:1169). But this strategy failed in the long run. The ethic of methodical conduct developed in the monasteries later formed the basis of both Calvinist asceticism (Weber, 1968:1200) and the rationally ordered work organization which is at the heart of the spirit of capitalism (Weber, 1968:1169). Both heretical and monastic emergences were consequential in sweeping away the old feudal order.

Frederick Engels regarded occurrences such as the Reformation, medieval heresies, and the primitive Christian Church as conflicts of class interest 'carried out under religious shibboleths' by those who 'stood outside the existing society' (1964a:98). Max Weber (1968:1180) has disputed any necessary class basis of religious revolutions, since they usually involved the déclassé - former members of various classes. But for Engels, religious movements with their sectarian bases represented antecedents to the modern secular communist movement. Various sects with somewhat different ideals - all in opposition to the established powers - embody the vehicle of social change in both religious and secular revolution. Though the theology of primitive Christianity was later modified and adopted as part of a state religion in Rome, primitive Christianity itself had been spawned (Engels, 1964b:207)

> at a time when new sects, new religions, new prophets arose by the hundred. It is, in fact, a mere average, formed spontaneously out of the mutual friction of the more progressive of such sects.

In Engels's view, such sects, like socialist sects of the nineteenth century, were involved in a 'Darwinistic struggle for ideological existence' (1964c:204). They shared opposition to the established order and embraced a utopian dialectic which seemed to provide a new direction for history. In this formulation, Engels's perspective is not antithetical to Weber's analyses which stress the religious innovativeness of marginal groups.

While Cohn mainly concerned himself with historical analysis and Engels sought to interpret history in terms of a materialist theory, Karl Mannheim specifically proposed a theoretical model of alternative and competing viewpoints of an era. For Mannheim (1952:309), just as for Cohn, rapid change is a precondition for the emergence of a new generational style - what he called an 'entelechy.' With Engels, Mannheim noted that the various groups may hold alternative new accounts of the times. But Mannheim suggested that, whether its causes be economic or cultural, the split in worldviews is a generational phenomenon. In his view, members of older generations have typically found their places in the social order and rarely subscribe to new accounts. Instead, they watch the bearers of the new accounts come to predominate in their midst, helpless to stem them. In conditions of rapid change, members of succeeding generations experience events quite differently from their predecessors; the old wisdoms therefore no longer seem relevant.

But the supposedly shared style of an emerging generation is not held by the generation as a whole. Rather, various 'units' of the same generation (as Mannheim called them) may differ in many respects. Within each unit there exists 'an identity of responses, a certain affinity in the way in which all [individuals] move with and are formed by their common experiences' (Mannheim, 1952:306). Such generational units do not arise simply as parallel responses of individuals to personally experienced external events; they occur within 'concrete groups' (e.g. student associations) where 'integrative attitudes' may be developed (1952:318):

> Once developed in this way, however, these attitudes and formative tendencies are capable of becoming detached from the concrete groups of their origin and of exercising an appeal and binding force over a much wider area.

Since alternative new worldviews coexist and compete, no epoch is totally of one style or another. Nevertheless, it may be stamped as such by the literati, who are unattached and therefore seek to come to grips with what they discern to be the dominant style of their epoch (1952:318).

Cohn, Engels and Mannheim each provide somewhat different interpretations of emerging alternative viewpoints in conflict with an established order. Yet the differences are more a matter of emphasis than of contradiction. A socio-historical model which synthesizes their views suggests that rapid social and economic change creates a situation in which certain people, marginal to the established order, perceive glaring inadequacies in previous 'recipes' and legitimations concerned with participation in the social order. Under these conditions, people who seek survival or a new meaningful relation to the world form groups under the aegis of one or another utopian vision. Whether these visions be secular or religious, they may be said to be prophetic in so far as they promise this-worldly or other-worldly salvation based on new missions (cf. Weber, 1968:448-50). Such groups, though spawned out of a common set of circumstances, are subject to both internal conflict and conflict with other, antagonistic groups. Individuals marginal to the established order may come under the influence of one or another group's vision of reality. The competition between new groups which share an opposition to the established order therefore marks a dialectical process, the outcome of which may affect the direction of social change.

THE COMPARATIVE ANALYSIS OF COMMUNAL GROUPS

The value-rational orientations of contemporary communal groups indicate the relevance of the socio-historical model sketched above to understanding today's counterculture. Given the dialectical competition of alternative new groups opposed to the established order, what becomes interesting for any developmental theory of long-term social change is the nature of the new, collectively deviant groups and their avenues of effect on society-at-large. As forms of association which have emerged outside of society-at-large, communal groups bring into being alternative forms of consciousness, interpretations of the meaning of social existence, and ethics of association. As has happened in the past, one or another of these groups - perhaps one which approaches what Engels called 'a mere average' of the new concerns - may become a decisive vehicle of social change. Communal groups are of importance for their innovative approaches to the questions of how, and for what, to live. It is therefore the purpose of this study to examine the new communal groups in these terms, that is, as cognitively-based attempts at reconstruction of social reality (cf. Ogilvy and Ogilvy, 1972).

This approach to understanding communal groups is purposely acausal. It does not entail an attempt to unmask external, latent, historic, functional or psychological determinants of various forms of collective life. Instead of seeking out the causes of the countercultural emergence, I treat alternative communal groups as situationally new, socially shared meaning configurations.

The attempt to understand the cognitive character of communal life is also necessarily an attempt to resolve a more general epistemological problem of sociology. Sociologists tend to undercut the meaningfulness of social phenomena to the people involved by 'explaining' actions in ways which have little to do with the purposes of the people involved. This problem becomes especially pronounced in the study of communal groups. There may be considerable divergence between the meanings of communal groups as lived realities and as objects of sociological inquiry. Many communalists are quick to display their aversion to 'conceptual knowledge' in general and sociology in particular. Such people have come to regard sociology as part and parcel of the social order which they reject. As Abrams and McCulloch argue in their study of what they call 'secular family communes,' the dualism of Western civilization runs head-on into serious communal attempts at monism: whereas sociology typically involves the construction of abstractions detached from reality, people in communal groups seek to assert new ways of connecting thought and action as praxis. Thus, sociology would destroy the meaningfulness of communal life by placing an account of it within an alien matrix of inquiry

- one which interprets social life according to a legitimated body of social theory, while communalists are developing new and lived social theories. Abrams and McCulloch (1976:7) are left to wonder: 'Are the two orders of reality perhaps so far apart as to make a sociological understanding of communes a contradiction in terms?'

Such a question cuts to the core of a persistent sociological dilemma: if sociology (in any of a variety of paradigms) is claimed to have a higher order, somehow 'objective' viewpoint, this viewpoint itself bears an ideological character; it becomes a form of cultural imperialism. On the other hand, if it is acknowledged that sociology, as one or another conceptual ordering of typified social phenomena, has no epistemological priority over other universes of discourse, then the relativity of social knowledge is admitted, and the status of the sociological enterprise becomes, at best, tenuous. We are faced, quite simply, with a problem of what Alfred Schutz (1973:207ff) termed 'multiple realities.'

In its theoretical concerns and methodological approach, the present study is an attempt to confront the problem of multiple realities by offering an analysis based on participant-observation which explores in comparative fashion the alternative cognitive constructions and objective economic and organizational correlates which obtain in various communal groups. In approaching the problem of cognitive world construction - what might be called the situated sociology of knowledge (cf. Berger and Luckmann, 1966:14ff) - I draw extensively on the sociological legacies of Max Weber and Alfred Schutz. Weber (1968:8ff) approached sociological analysis as a problem in 'Verstehen,' or subjective understanding. Alfred Schutz (1967) sought to clarify the epistemological presuppositions of Weber's sociology, in part by offering a 'mundane' phenomenology of the essential structures of everyday life (i.e. what Schutz termed the lifeworld). But though Schutz provided a conceptual framework for understanding the world of everyday life, he did very little in the way of comparative lifeworldly analysis. And though Weber undertook a comparative sociology based on 'Verstehen,' his analyses were typically concerned with abstractions (e.g. ethics) detached from the lifeworldly situations wherein subjective meaning is constituted. It is thus reasonable to inquire through empirical investigation what, if any, connection there might be between Schutz's description of the essential structures of the lifeworld and Weber's interpretive typifications of social phenomena. An analysis of communal groups in mundane phenomenological and interpretive terms provides an opportunity to examine the utility of both Weber and Schutz for understanding extant lifeworlds. At the same time, such an inquiry may help surmount the problem of sociological dualism by delineating the cognitive statuses of alternative meaningful universes of discourse.* Of course the gap between sociological analysis and communal action can never be narrowed in this manner, but perhaps the subordination of communal 'alternative realities' (Rigby, 1974) to an 'objectifying' sociological universe of discourse can be mitigated. The hope is that a comparative sociology of lifeworlds can provide a meaningful understanding of communal groups as countercultural carriers of situationally new ways of life.

It is Karl Mannheim who especially took on this concern with a comparative understanding of what he called 'utopian mentalities.' As a basis for his analysis in 'Ideology and Utopia,' Mannheim argued that a utopian mentality can best be understood by reference to its sense of time (1936:209):

> The form in which events are ordered and the unconsciously emphatic rhythm, which the individual in his spontaneous observation of events imposes on the flux of time, appears in the utopia as an immediately perceptible picture, or at least a directly intelligible set of meanings. The innermost structure of the mentality of a group can never be as clearly grasped as when we attempt to understand its conception of time in the light of its hopes, yearnings and purposes.

In this emphasis on time, Mannheim grounded his analysis in a perspective akin to that of Alfred Schutz, who developed his mundane phenomenology based on time consciousness during about the same years - the late 1920s.

Significantly, Max Weber had earlier noted that as a force in cultural transformation, the Protestant ethic had as one of its most distinctive features an emphasis on personally managed rational and efficient use of time. But, as has already been noted, for the most part Weber chose to examine the Protestant ethic as a belief system; only in his essay on American sects (1946) did he examine actual conduct. Similarly, Mannheim (1952:307) identified 'concrete groups' such as student associations as carriers

---

* A more detailed discussion of objectivist sociology, Schutz, Weber and the epistemological problems entailed in the study of communal groups is included in appendix 1.

of utopian mentalities; he chose to describe utopias as wishful mentalities rather than as new forms of association. Thus, sociological theory about utopian groups, though emphasizing the significance of time, has been directed primarily to mentalities and ethics detached from everyday life wherein one or another subjective orientation toward time obtains.

At least in Mannheim's case, the analytic dissociation of a mentality from those who enact it as an encompassing way of life leads to a confounding of time with other aspects of social reality. On the basis of time as an organizing principle of utopian mentalities, Mannheim (1936:211-47) described four ideal typical utopian mentalities: 1 orgiastic chiliasm, in which the millennium is perceived to be upon the world, and dissociation from symbols and images is identified with a direct experience of 'absolute presentness' alone; 2 the liberal-humanitarian idea of goals projected onto the present from an indefinite future horizon 'whose function it is to act as a mere regulative device in mundane affairs,' thus giving rise to a linear and progressive experience of time; 3 the conservative idea of a natural world order which is as it should be, in which the 'here-and-now' is experienced not as an evil reality, but as the present embodiment of the highest timeless values and meanings; and 4 the socialist-communist utopia in which 'it is the social structure which becomes the most influential force in the historical moment,' and time is experienced as 'a series of strategical points.'

Mannheim's four utopian configurations actually encompass only three distinct modes of cognizing and socially constructing time. These may be distinguished from one another on the basis of the manner in which acts of immediately given perception, memory and anticipation occur in the stream of consciousness of an individual. In diachronic time, the given moment is experienced as one of a linear succession of moments, and immediately given meaning directs attention to remembered past events and an anticipated future as coordinates which contextualize action. In its social manifestation, diachronic time is typically evidenced by the employment of rationalized physical duration (clock time) as an organizing principle; time can thereby be spent or saved. A second possibility, synchronic time, involves the experience of durée, or accent on the subjectively experienced immediately given moment in and of itself, without a referencing frame of remembrance or anticipation, and without a linear succession of objectified units of time to order the flow of time (Bergson, 1960; Husserl, 1964; Schutz, 1967).

In its social manifestation, synchronic time involves the intersubjective (Schutz, 1967:97ff) episode of the 'here-and-now' as the locus of coordination. Third, apocalyptic time involves cognition of the last days of a prevailing order - the end of historical time (i.e. societal diachronic time) - giving way to a new, typically timeless world. Though this orientation thus contains both diachronic and synchronic elements, it is the juxtaposition of these elements in a focus on the end of one epoch and the beginning of another which makes it distinctive. The character of this millenial conception will vary according to whether the cognition is a pre-apocalyptic one of playing out the end of history, or a post-apocalyptic one of beginning a new world beyond the pale of the old order. Obviously, these distinctions are simply analytic, while cognitive modes of organizing time in daily life involve more complex admixtures.

Differences between Mannheim's four utopian mentalities are not based solely on the experience of time. Both the chiliast and the conservative converge on experience of the here-and-now, but the chiliast is dissociated from the meaningfulness of symbols in general, while the conservative seeks a resonant correspondence of ethical symbols with the 'natural order' of the world. As Alfred Schutz (1967) has suggested, the cognitive character of conscious participation in the lifeworld is set not only by the way in which time is experienced but also by the (e.g. 'taken-for-granted') assumptions an actor makes about the meaningful status of the perceived world. People may experience time in similar ways and still constitute meaning in ways which make their experiences quite different. And this is an aspect of social reality with which utopianists themselves have perennially tried to come to grips: their problem has been that of substituting a new way of cognizing the world for what was previously 'taken-for-granted.'

Cognitive assumptions and their relations to social action - what I will term cognitive modes of social enactment - thus provide a second basis for distinguishing among communal formations. Three broad possibilities obtain. In a natural mode, that which is experienced and the interpretations appended to experience are taken for granted as valid and real, existing 'out there.' Individuals both alone and in concert may subject events to scrutiny, analysis and reinterpretation, but no socially unifying philosophy, system of belief or set of ethics provides collectively legitimated rules for interpretation of experience. On the other hand, in a produced orientation to social enactment, daily conduct involves an attempt to live out a coherent, unified and comprehensive system of belief. The experiences of consciousness are mediated by preordained norms, values or ethics. Attention of consciousness is directed on the basis of socially legitimated themes of concern, and cognized events are evaluated according to perceptions of their congruence or incongruence with collectively established schemata of interpretation. Third, in a transcendental mode, taken-for-granted preconceptions about how the world 'is' and normative statements about how it 'should be' are bracketed or set aside.* In such a 'mystical' modification of attention, consciousness is immersed in immediately given phenomenal experience prior to meaningful interpretation, belief or ethical assessment.

Consideration of the modes of organizing time together with cognitive modes of social enactment yields a two-dimensional typology, in terms of which communal groups may be compared (see Table 1.1).** While derived from an

---

* This usage parallels Husserl's (1931:114) 'transcendental consciousness,' i.e. 'pure' consciousness with belief in the outer world suspended. As Husserl noted, bracketing or suspension may involve various steps: it may be more or less complete. I leave the issue of completeness of bracketing in a transcendental enactment to empirical analysis. In my definition, therefore, the term 'transcendental' is not held to strictly philosophical usage: the Husserlian phenomenological program which draws on a transcendental method is taken to be one approach to transcendence. The transcendental mode could be approached in alternative ways, for example, as a basis of meditation, a source of 'religious' insight, or a social organizing principle. But it should be emphasized that the category 'transcendental' is employed here and throughout the study in a specific phenomenological sense of consciousness through direct perception. The reader should abandon any commonsense definition of 'transcendental' as 'surpassing' in favor of a sense of 'passing across' episodes without recourse to judgment, interpretation or explanation.

** In this framework, Mannheim's liberal-humanitarian mentality may be said to represent a diachronic type; the conservative and chiliast mentalities involve synchronic conceptions of time, the latter of a transcendental enactment. The conservative idea, Mannheim suggested (1936:230), remains latent until challenged by competing utopias. It may thus be manifested as an identification with the established order, or more to

TABLE 1.1 Typology of utopian communal possibilities. Mode of organizing time and mode of social enactment as phenomenological dimensions of variation.

		Mode of organizing time		
		DIACHRONIC	SYNCHRONIC	APOCALYPTIC
Mode of social enactment	NATURAL			
	PRODUCED			
	TRANSCENDENTAL			

approach based on the mundane phenomenology of Alfred Schutz, both dimensions refer to various subjective orientations to the world of everyday life. We thus anticipate the possibility of alternative subjective orientations. However, the contents of these alternatives are not specified a priori. Instead, the typology is elaborated by reference to contemporary communal groups. As Weber (1968:213) noted in a similar context, the selection of a scheme of classification can only be justified by its results. And such results can be discerned, if at all, not by assertion of logical possibility, but through the application of comparative distinctions to empirically observed phenomena.

---

the point, with a particular way of life embodying values under that order. Ideological conservatism remains taken-for-granted, and its sense of time is bound up with existence in the ongoing society. The conservative communal utopia, on the other hand, would seem to involve a produced enactment in which the synchronic here-and-now comes to contain a reassertion of the old values, perhaps in a reaction to the demise of values within the established order, but transformed as well in a contemporary dialectic with other utopian impulses. Mannheim's fourth type, the socialist-communist utopia, involves a produced apocalyptic enactment. While the conceptual framework presented in Table 1.1 serves to clarify Mannheim's argument, it also points to logical possibilities which Mannheim did not discuss. In this regard, the quasi-utopian natural enactment represents an immediately obvious possibility, and as we shall see in the remainder of this study, the produced apocalyptic kind of enactment contains alternative possibilities, depending on where in time the apocalypse is placed.

The present comparative study of communal groups draws on information I obtained through participant-observation at over twenty-five communal groups, as well as from interviews with key informants, and from secondary sources. Appendix 2 contains brief descriptions of the groups included in the study.* While no special sampling techniques were employed for selecting groups for inclusion in the study, I have visited and lived with a wide variety of groups. They range in size from three to over eight hundred persons and include both urban and rural groups; political, apolitical and religious ones; some in which economic self-sufficiency is of little interest and others that are relatively independent of the wider economy.

While visiting and living in communal groups, I held in abeyance any tautological application of the framework described above; in Husserl's (1931:s.31) sense, I bracketed the thesis, setting it aside through the 'attempt to doubt' it. In general, I held to a mundane phenomenological method of what I will call free attention, in which I followed the unfolding cognitive themes invoked by participants in communal groups. This field research method, the biographical course of research, and the logic of data analysis are described in appendix 3.

Upon reviewing the information I had gathered while conducting field research, I found that seven of the communal groups closely approximated cells of the typology presented in Table 1.1. One of the groups - 'URON,' an urban communal group which also maintains a nearby farm - lacks any overarching ideology. I suggest it approximates a natural synchronic formation, which I term a 'commune' as an ideal type. Two other groups enact elaborated systems of belief directed at social reconstruction. At the Virginia behavioralist community, Twin Oaks, utopia involves a scheduling of labor through use of clock time, and I suggest it approximates a produced diachronic formation. Ideal typically, it may be considered a variant of 'intentional association.' The Tennessee spiritual community known as The Farm, on the other hand, is pre-eminently concerned with producing a way of life based on the 'here-and-now.' I have accordingly treated it as approximating a produced synchronic formation, referred to ideal typically as a 'community.' In that these latter

---

* Of the groups included in the analysis, some are widely known, and I have used their real names. In other cases, protection of the privacy of inhabitants is maintained through use of a consistent pseudonym placed in quotation marks.

two groups enact ways of life that their participants argue could be extended to society-at-large, I suggest that they represent 'worldly utopian' configurations.

Three other of the seven principal groups seek to enact unified sets of beliefs while maintaining an apocalyptic sense of time. One group (which I never visited), the Symbionese Liberation Army, has engaged in an apocalyptic struggle with the established order; in ideal typical terms, it may be considered an example of a 'warring sect.' The two other produced apocalyptic groups - the Love Family of Washington State (a primitive Christian group), and the organization for Krishna consciousness (ISKCON), represent 'other-worldly sects' - attempts to establish timeless heavenly kingdoms beyond the reaches of the secular world. Finally, at one communal group, 'The Cabin,' a primary involvement with the phenomena of the moment, prior to production of meaning, seemed to me to approximate a transcendental synchronic formation, typified as an 'ecstatic association,' and I have treated it as such.*

In the following chapters I describe the seven principal groups in the framework of the typology. This approach in no way 'proves' the typology; it simply serves as a methodological device of analysis. For each group, I construct a summary of lifeworldly constitutions on the basis of information derived from field research. While these summaries generally substantiate the classification of groups in one or another typological cell, I have intentionally sought out negative evidence for each case, which serves to distinguish it as a concrete communal group. Thus, each group is typified independently of its treatment as approximating one or another cell of the typology. Cases other than the seven which I treat extensively similarly serve to qualify the analysis and suggest transitional types and their conditions. Though the number of cases is small from any point of view concerned with statistical generalization, the phenomena described are not subject to such generalizations in any event. Instead, in so far as the analysis suggests the typology to be a useful scheme of interpretation, we may

---

* The empty cells of the typology stem from subsumption of other organizing time constructions within a synchronic mode. As will become apparent in chapter 3, a transcendental mode of enactment transcends all cognitive elaborations of time, while the commune as a natural synchronic formation involves an episodic pluralism of times, tending to include both diachronic and apocalyptic elements.

speak of the boundaries of its relevance in terms of other actually constituted phenomena.

In chapter 2, I describe the process of communal group formation. Subsequent chapters deal in phenomenological terms with time and the enactment of social reality, and in interpretive terms with the satisfaction of wants and government. The analysis of communal groups from these facets permits the specification of ideal types of communal groups in both phenomenological and interpretive terms in the concluding chapter. These types are discussed in terms of their courses of diffusion in society-at-large, and some speculations on the contemporary situation are offered.

The conclusion may be briefly stated here. Quite simply, the revolutions of utopian communalists are revolutions of time. In any of diverse ways, participants in communal groups modify the diachronic subjective experience and social construction of time which prevails in the established order. The utopian communal reconstructions of time are contextualized by other cognitive assumptions about social enactment, namely, whether the world is to be 'taken-for-granted' as involving 'multiple realities,' ethically and exemplarily produced via one or another kind of socially shared value rationality, or mystically transcended via ecstasy and contemplation.

Mysticism, as Max Weber (1968:547) has observed, typically involves an 'aristocratic' abandonment of the world of mundane affairs; its effect on conduct in the world is at best spasmodic. Similarly, the ethic of ultimate ends which arises in an apocalyptic orientation toward time does not typically offer an attempt to ethically remake the secular world; instead, the course of development is toward one or another specialized sectarian mission of an elect group. It is those I call the 'worldly utopians' who seek to remake the world of mundane affairs. Their approaches are particularly discernible in the nexus between the organization of time and of work. In the produced diachronic (or clock-based) worldly utopia, adherents expect to liberate people from the alienation of production - which seems endemic to any industrial division of labor - by a more complete rationalization of time-based productive activity. The proclaimed result is greater equity in individuals' access to diverse work roles and increased personal free time. On the other hand, in the episodic and event-centered world of the synchronic utopia, the attempt is to deal with the problem of alienation on a spiritual basis, by establishing work as one aspect of communion within an intersubjective community.

To a degree, the technical processes of production available to worldly utopian communal groups are similar. The attempts at reconstituting the time-based human relationships surrounding production may thus be construed as explorations in reorganizing modes of production and developing situationally adequate ethics of conduct for participation in those new modes of production. The worldly utopian communalists, in other words, stand in relation to collectivism in much the same posture as the early Protestants stood in relation to individualism. They would claim to be the avatars of the new age.

In the literary utopia, time is employed 'not as real time, or even as literary time, but as a convention of its own for articulating conditional possibilities. It is time marked off from clock time just as surely as the time of a chess game' (Holquist, 1968:112). So it may be with the utopian mentality; the daydream does not have to be lived to be experienced. But in communal groups, whatever the ideas entertained or embraced, the mentality moves beyond the fantasy or wish which Mannheim described to the development of an alternative world. Social change is embodied as a change of the immediate social world itself. Consciousness of those who seek a way out is altered not in a purely illusory or 'play' setting, but in everyday worlds where attempts at resolution of the often ambiguous relations of ideas and actions, of ethics and material interests may come to yield up historically new ways of life. It is to the origins and developments of such new worlds that I now turn.

2 Beginnings

> They come here to live normal lives, away from the maddening crowd's ignoble strife....
> Diary of an anarchist at Home colony, Washington state, 1903.
>
> (LeWarne, 1975:192)

Communal living groups are begun as value-based alternatives to habitual and conformist participation in institutions of the established order. During the 1960s and early 1970s, large numbers of people, especially the young, went 'on the road,' seeking their fortunes away from any supportive web of previous family and community ties. But to 'drop out' does not ensure that one can drop into a more satisfactory world.

In this chapter, I trace the formation of communal groups. The emergence of an operational communal group is found to be predicated on the mobilization of people who invoke one or another myth of 'who we are as a group.' Such a myth is elaborated both as a turning away from the old order and a turning toward a new way of life. The successful development of a group way of life hinges on the resolution of tensions between a myth and the diverse problematic concerns of initial collective life.

PEOPLE

Formation of a communal group initially depends on the gathering together of a group of people committed to that enterprise. Conditions in the larger society are conducive to communal group formation only in so far as potential participants invoke such conditions in their own biographies. Many persons who are alienated from themselves (as evidenced by neuroses, alcoholism and the like) still strongly identify with the established order of society. And many young people who feel alienated from society still come to make the compromises necessary for coming to terms with it. Thus, sentiments of opposition to the status quo are more widespread than the seeking out of communal association. A young career woman may 'see the eventual need to live in communes, as things disintegrate,' but choose not to change patterns of association because, 'they really make you feel the need to be an individual, and that is hard to overcome.' No matter how pessimistic a view of civilization people hold, both personal values and the web of already constructed social life (job, friends, family, consumption style) provide a security not readily abandoned for utopian dreams.

Among the alienated, however, certain individuals entertain the utopian wish - of living in a new and meaningful world with others who share their dream. For them, neither previous class nor status identifications seem particularly compelling; nor do individual deviance and perfunctory participation in ongoing institutions satisfy the urge toward a change of life. Especially in the era of modernist rebellion against norms, widespread individual deviance remains an essential feature of the old regime itself. This very normlessness of modernist life can be disconcerting to those who search for meaningful existence. For them, the move is toward collective deviance - a shared charismatic rejection of the old ways (cf. Berger and Luckmann, 1966:106). Thus, those who want to move beyond alienated existence tend to seek out others with whom they can share a deviant perspective. For some, it is a matter of discovering a new, prophetically revealed way of life; for others, the impetus is simply the possibility of salvation from bleak possibilities in a world experienced as gone awry.

Communal groups are formed by people who have not yet settled down, as well as by those who simply want to change their lives. The search for a new basis of association may be more or less ideologically grounded and it may be more or less self-interested. One individual may see civilization crumbling and dedicate his life to providing an ark of survival, while another, living alone for some time, may only fear an 'autism' in herself, and want 'to be more open with other people.' Still another person living alone cries, 'I can't stand it any longer; I want to be with people and I see a commune as the best way of doing it.' The perceived potential of communal groups for solving personal problems is not restricted to individuals. Couples, who have played out boundaries of intimacy to a point of no exit, may seek out communal life in an attempt to save a crumbling relation. Others have neither strong ideological persuasions nor the desire to reshape their lifestyles, but only motives of simple expediency - getting off the street scene, finding a way of cutting expenses in a time of slow money, and so on. Finally, there are those circles of friends who simply want to live together, having rejected the 'private lives' formula.

Whatever the motivations (and in any group they are diverse), forming or joining a communal group requires for each participant the termination of one set of life circumstances and the beginning of another. Such a transition may occur in a single and direct move, or it may be accomplished through an interlude, after 'things have fallen apart.' Social mobility in either case involves not the upward or downward movement in some prescribed hierarchy of statuses, but the abandonment of one household circumstance in favor of a newly created one. Social change encompasses not broad structural features of society, but a change of living sites, social arenas, patterns of association, and modes of satisfying needs. While belief and worldview may influence the direction of such mobility, people who engage in ad hoc status passage (Glazer and Strauss, 1971) do so when a previous construction of life is no longer seen as rewarding, viable, or important.

Some groups begin with a preexisting household whose members open their doors to other individuals. Usually, however, the group comes into existence before a site is acquired. Through any of a variety of circumstances, people come into a circle of association and begin talking of the possibility of living together. Such a pre-formation circle may represent an already existing web of friendship and acquaintance, or it may come together through mediated association, as with a magazine advertisement, 'lifestyle conference' or the like. In any event, an individual or core group takes on the entrepreneurial mission of attracting others to the idea of a communal venture. The number of people in the circle grows as word spreads of the possible venture, and while people come to be sounded out as to their interest, an ongoing discussion of the group's projected ethos takes place. In this process, some people come to be identified as 'definitely interested,' others as 'wavering,' or 'on the fringe.' Paralleling these discussions, various members of the circle seek out potential sites. The move toward communal life becomes concrete when a site is located. At this point, members of the circle face an initial moment of truth. As Ken Kesey once remarked:

'You're either on the bus or off the bus' (quoted in Wolfe, 1968:83). Both individually and, upon assessment of individual commitment, collectively, members of the circle either embark on a communal enterprise, decide to await a new concrete opportunity, or disband the enterprise of commune formation.

THE GROUP MYTH

For a new association of people to come together in a communal arrangement of any scope beyond the simple cooperative sharing of living facilities, a previously non-existent entity, the group, must be invoked as real. In the strictly cooperative household, participants feel no need for conception of a reality beyond the summative relations of individuals involved. But in the communal organization, motivations for association are felt to go beyond purely utilitarian ones. Each new participant must acknowledge an interest in more intimate interchange than that of a cooperative. The individual and the group are to have reciprocal obligations to one another. For such an exchange relation to occur, the group must first obtain a mythical existence in the minds of would-be participants (member of 'URON'):*

> 'We started with the myth and everybody we met believed it, so then we started believing that maybe it wasn't a shuck, and actually began believing it ourselves.'

The function of the myth remains the same in all cases: to transform the scheme of interpretation from an intersection of individuals to invocation of a group with autonomous existence. It serves to provide an account of 'who we are.' In this respect, as Simmel (1950:36-9) has noted, the basis of the group must be something that is available to all members and recruits, for the group can be constituted only as the 'lowest common denominator' of individual orientations.

The structures and sources of myths, the ways members evolve for invoking them, and the consequences for group life are all closely linked. The myth may range from the

---

* Here and throughout, I acknowledge quotations gathered through participant-observation and interviewing by referring either to an interviewee or to a communal group. The reference is eliminated only in instances where protracted analysis deals with a group clearly identified in the text. Brief descriptions of the groups on which field research was conducted are contained in appendix 1.

loosely specified utopian imagery which Sorel (1961) recommended for revolutionaries to a highly developed specification of belief which justifies a plan of utopian action. The myth may be derived from a previously existing program, from the revelations of a visionary prophet, or from subjective assertion of 'brotherhood' and 'sisterhood' by members. Whatever its structure and source, the myth comes to be invoked in social situations, in full view of all participants, so that it may serve as a vehicle for further action. Several kinds of myth configurations may occur.

The best known kind of contemporary commune is the loosely structured 'hippie-anarchist trip' (Yablonsky, 1968; Houriet, 1971), hallmarks of which include a 'do your own thing' ethic and close attention to the 'vibes' of the vivid present situation. This kind of communal group was especially prevalent in the initial wave of new communal formations during the latter half of the 1960s. At that time, when geographical mobility was at a peak, hundreds of thousands of youth abandoned (many only temporarily) their previous lives to seek the ecstasy of 'getting off' on drugs and a group scene in transitory association with other similarly situated 'hippies.' In some cases, what were called communes amounted to little more than crash pads (Speck, 1972); other groups which came out of the 'hippie' scenes, such as the Bear Tribe and the Rainbow Family, came to have more permanent existences. The generalized myth for all such groups was derived in part from the Haight-Ashbury latter-day beatnik scene of San Francisco, especially as promulgated in national media such as 'Time' magazine, without which many 'flower children' would have missed the boat entirely. For a given group the sources of myth were seen as largely self-evident, unproblematic and irrelevant. Invocation of peace, love, freedom, and sharing of drugs and food in incense-filled rooms and around summer campfires represents myth as contained in the event itself (participant in the Los Angeles street scene):

> 'Most people came around because of drugs, so they could all get high together, so they all lived together. The social life was all they had and that always died out. They were just people who rolled in off the streets. This was when Sunset Boulevard was just a - there were kids from, you name it, all over the US, and they were all jampacked all over Sunset, hitching back up and down the strip; it was just crazy. If you wound up in a real crash pad, you'd walk in and there'd be mattresses all over the floor, and people crashing and people balling, all over the place

different activities happening: a dealer hanging around the door.'

Rent and food, at least in some such scenes, was financed solely from 'dealing dope' (marijuana, LSD, amphetamines, etc.). 'Slug Bottom' 'was like that; all people would do is sit around and smoke grass and wait for people to come around and buy lids.' The myth and the basis for support attained some sort of symbiosis. The myth of the hippie trip exists in the ecstasy of the given moment, and where people come from or where they will be tomorrow bears little relevance to the shared immediate experience. Commitment to the immediate moment and little beyond derives from an understanding that each individual has a path to follow, that to interfere with the flux of social intercourse in the magical 'now' would only 'bring down bad karma, 'cause you can't fight the changes.'

Kanter (1972:165ff) has written that such communal association is based on 'negative integration,' on a turning away from what others have called the 'easy off/easy on plastic drive-in society.' She argues that association derived from a 'moving away from' rather than a 'coming to' does not embody sufficient commitment for survival. It is true that persons who 'drop out' of the 'straight world' have often engaged in a series of transitory communal associations. But to suggest that such associations are based solely on negative integration is to treat positive integration in a value-based fashion as restricted to the realm of commitment to a stable and enduring communal association. As Ogilvy and Ogilvy (1972) have observed, pluralistic communes may better serve purposes of personal development than those of institutional persistence. Clearly invocation of the transitory 'now' may be a consciously held value in itself. In a way, hippie nomadism parallels the charismatic monasticism of 'freely formed herds' whose participants have 'no abode in the world' (Weber, 1968:1168).

The derivation of a collective myth may take other channels than invocation of the 'now.' For circles of people involved in anti-war actions during the latter half of the 1960s and the early 1970s, formation of communal groups often seemed the natural outgrowth of friendships developed in 'The Movement.' In many cases, networks of political association served as the community out of which both demonstrations were produced and communes begun. The myth of revolution was promulgated by communal political action groups, through demonstrations and urban guerrilla actions. The general myth of revolution found its parallel in the myth of communal groups forming a revolutionary society within the bowels of the monster. In some circles, immediate and total transformation of existing society came to be seen as unlikely, and the myth of 'living the revolution' came to serve as the basis for building an everyday life in a model of post-revolutionary society.

In radical groups, and especially among more militant ones like the Symbionese Liberation Army, the myth is purposely unspecific and inspirational (Symbionese Liberation Army, 1974:A16):

> we of the Symbionese Federation and the S.L.A. [Symbionese Liberation Army] do not under the rights of human beings submit to the murder, oppression and exploitation of our children and people and do under the rights granted to the people under the Declaration of Independence of the United States, do [sic] now by the rights of our children and people and by force of arms and with every drop of blood, declare revolutionary war against the fascist capitalist class, and their agents of murder, oppression and exploitation.

For such efforts at bringing about revolution, a potpourri of Marxist, anarchist and critical theorists may be heralded as forebearers and influentials. But in keeping with the advice of Lenin (1947), the concrete nature of the revolution being built is seldom spelled out. The focus is on the enterprise of praxis; myth initially serves as an account of justification. Behind the inspirational myth lies some overall strategy. People in the Symbionese Liberation Army, for example, were not willing to wait for a vanguard party. Participants seem to have been ambivalent about the 'vanguard' nature of the SLA itself: engaging in self-criticism after their capture, several persons disdained as paternalistic the mentality (inherent in their first 'propaganda of the deed,' a political assassination) which takes action for other people. The SLA was not held to be 'the vanguard of revolutionary struggle,' but still participants, according to William Harris, 'wanted to project what a relatively small group of people can do - that we are not as powerless as we are led to believe' (Harris et al., 1976). In a direct way, their vision parallels that of the nineteenth century Russian anarchist Michael Bakunin, who sought to organize an underground federation of terrorist groups. Just as Bakunin had parted ways with Marx's vanguard party, so the SLA abandoned above-ground radical politics to try to demonstrate the feasibility of, and act as a catalyst for, terrorist insurrection among the masses. Particularly because of their outlaw practices, such groups usually unfold as secret societies, for which association is not dependent on, and sometimes antithetical to, coterminous living at a shared site (cf. Simmel, 1950:345ff). Still, the terrorist orientation toward action is both utopian and communal.

Less radical communal groups typically invoke specific historical or at least distant figures as patrons of their utopian societies. The example of the 'Jesus freaks' (cf. Ellwood, 1973) is well known. Other cases include the International Society for Krishna Consciousness, Inc. (ISKCON), a contemporary revival of allegiance to Krishna, the manifestation of the Hindu godhead who appeared in the fifth century, A.D. and gave the world the 'Bhagavad Gita.' A.C. Bhaktivedanta, spiritual master and director of the contemporary ISKCON, has provided a new translation of the 'Bhagavad Gita' (1972) which is at considerable variance with scholarly translations (cf. Edgerton, 1972) of the work. Bhaktivedanta claims to provide in 'purports' an extension of the 'Bhagavad Gita's' wisdom 'for our age.' Derivation of myth, no matter how traditional its sources, may thus involve an interpretive modulation to suit a contemporary situation.

A less distant relation is that of the intentional community Twin Oaks to the behavioral psychologist B.F. Skinner. Skinner, a professor of psychology at Harvard University, wrote 'Walden Two' (1948), a utopia based on management of society through use of positive behavioral conditioning principles. Skinner gives his blessing to the utopian experiment at Twin Oaks in a foreword to a history of the community (Kinkade, 1973:x). He recognizes that the participants 'muddled through' on their own, but nevertheless claims that the group survived its first five years because 'certain principles have stood the test.'

For other groups, the myth may be derived not from the sharing of an immediate life association or the harking back to a previously delineated utopian ideal, but from the direct experience of a 'higher truth' by a visionary leader. For example, the man who calls himself Love Israel, founder of a religious community of over a hundred people in Washington State, Alaska and Hawaii, was reportedly a well-to-do car salesman. He had the resources to do what he wanted, and began traveling around practicing yoga and vegetarianism, while reading books of spiritual knowledge. On a bus in Texas, says an associate of the Love Family

> 'He had a vision, a revelation of heaven on earth, and that he was supposed to head it up. He saw himself as the person in Revelations who receives a white stone with his name written on it. On the stone is written "Love"; and "Israel" is the surname of the children of the Resurrection, so he took on the name, "Love Israel."'

Such visions provide a pipeline to truth available to the seer, but followers must take the revelations on faith.

Other charismatic legacies are not so specifically bound up in the lone visionary. Stephen Gaskin, for example, is teacher and spiritual leader of The Farm, a religious community of over eight hundred people (in 1973) living on 1700 acres of farmland in Tennessee. Gaskin has never claimed a monopoly on revelation. Instead, Stephen (1970:2), as he is called by his followers, begins from the Buddhist idea of 'Mahayana' (the Great Boat), 'the one that includes everybody,' and leads conversations of 'truth speaking' in groups ranging past the thousand mark. The myth and the belief is that people who commit themselves to speaking the truth together can tap the energy to accomplish anything they set out to do. It is this enterprise, available to any people who engage in it - not any arcane knowledge held by Stephen - that is seen as providing the sustaining basis for group action.

Originative group myths - derived from participants, previously existing utopias and belief systems, or a 'new' revelation by a founding member - have important consequences for the subsequent nature of group life. At a minimum, the myth provides a basis for invoking 'groupness' where none existed before. A given myth may also provide a boundary of relevance for the subsequent playing out of group life. Thus, Love Israel and A.C. Bhaktivedanta receive charters of ultimate authority in the beginning, while other groups take on revolutionary and spiritual mandates for enactment of utopian possibilities, and still other groups find the boundaries of authority defined by a 'do your own thing' ethic. But the initial myth does not totally preordain the character of group life, much less insure that a viable group life will emerge. Generalized myths of the type recommended by Sorel and Lenin leave a wide latitude for action, while highly specified utopias such as the nineteenth-century American Fourierist phalanxes often prove irrelevant to the everyday problems of initiating group life. Group myths only provide a grounding for action so long as they are invoked as group life continues.

INITIAL COLLECTIVE LIFE

Starting a communal group involves a number of situational living problems that are seldom again encountered on the same scale. A lot happens all at once. What happens is taken to be of critical importance by group members, both for personal reasons and because the future character of group life is seen to be at issue. Even when a group myth is both highly specific and relevant to the immediate tasks of group life, the application of myth to situation is seldom straightforward. When a myth is less specific, the members of a group are faced with a situation that is problematic in almost all respects. It is in the attempt at solving the early problems of group life that many groups fail, and it is in the broad solutions to such early problems that group ways of dealing with situations - whether through play, custom, policy or authority - are set in their general form.

While solutions are diverse and often linked to the specific character of an evolving group myth, the form of creating a new world remains generally the same for all groups. This form - an interaction between substantive issues and potential 'ways of doing it' - may be interpreted in terms of Alfred Schutz's theory of relevance. A substantive issue or 'topical relevance' (Schutz and Luckmann, 1973:182-229) is any situational concern that becomes thematic, such as when to cook a meal, what kinds of fertilizers to use in a garden, how to allocate and co-ordinate work, and the like. These topical relevances come to the fore of intersubjective consciousness as themes through the imposition of circumstances or by voluntary choice. Once they have become thematic, their resolution hinges on the playing out of other, non-topical factors of relevance, both 'interpretational' and 'motivational,' which people hold to be important. In Schutz's terms, interpretational relevances are those elements of consciousness available in the intersubjective 'stock of knowledge' with which a current topical relevance can be compared, while motivational relevances represent those elements which provide an account of the genesis of action ('because' motivations) or prescribe a basis for action ('in order to' motivations).

It is in the development of patterned modes of resolution for thematic concerns that a communal group increases the field of the 'world-taken-for-granted.' More and more, over the passage of group time, a residue of procedural devices and understandings comes to be shared, and it is this residue, at later stages of group life, which streamlines the kinds of issues that would become topically relevant in the first place, the ways they may come up for consideration, the nature of the vivid present flow of interaction into which topical relevances must be interjected, and the interpretive and motivational relevances which come into play in their resolution.

The substantive issues which may become topically relevant as a group of people embark on communal life include all the possible material considerations of group life, as well as concerns of social relations. Material concerns are but a subset of social concerns - those which are not purely social, but instead involve objects of culture and their relationship to various actors within the social situation. Such concerns include the acquisition of a site, construction of living spaces or modification of existing structures, use of available space, methods of acquiring food and development of a diet, development of systems of resource supply (water, heat, refrigeration, cooking and bathing facilities), ways of handling waste materials, means of obtaining supplies not readily developed by the group, and ways of storing, accessing and using personal and collective cultural items - this is a partial list of the immediately pressing concerns of initial communal life.

The ways of dealing with such material concerns, as the thrust of ethnography has shown, are not straightforward or purely functional. While 'necessity' may seem to dictate some solutions, even in societies based on marginal self-sufficiency, patterns of culture transcend simple necessity. This is similarly the case with communal groups, especially those of a utopian bent, in which the attempt to achieve some concept of the good leads far beyond the dictates of circumstance. The nature of the good, whatever its conceptual basis, is still generally problematic in the playing out of group life. Architecture, for example, may maximize utility, technology of support systems, space allocation and use, aesthetics of design and location, and so forth. But rarely do people feel they have maximized all values in a single structure. Similarly, the desire for a good and wholesome diet may lead to more and more extensive dictates of agricultural methods and food preparation; but the schools of nutrition and of organic farming do not always agree about effects of various diets and cultivation techniques. And while, for some people, diet may be crucial, others will see it as an unimportant detail of mundane life. Initial periods of group life are thus typically marked by confusion and disarray. In this state of affairs, various individuals propose ways of making sense out of the material chaos.

The field of social relations is similarly undifferentiated at the onset of communal life. People come to a communal group from other places. Joining a group represents for many a turning away from previous patterns and associations of life, as well as a rejection of the larger social institutions which supported such life. Nevertheless, people do not shed their habits and customs easily, and their images of communal life are often at variance with one another. Everyone is someone else's deviant. What is taken for granted in a private world may be called a 'hangup' in collective life.

People have different ways of invoking the social in a vivid present situation, and of fitting personal concerns into the flux of collective life. Some individuals may see the group situation as the 'place' that all participants should be 'coming from,' while others may see it as an arena for resolution only of matters that cannot be dealt with through fiat. Some people may desire transcendence through group communion and ritual while others see the group arena as the place for display of a particular aesthetic of sociability. What is to happen when group members are together, as well as the weaving together of individual lives, intimate relationships and group life within an emerging and interdependent set of episodes - these various aspects of social life may all be problematic.

There may be parallel differences in individuals' constructions of symbolic group life. One person may be concerned with a right to privacy, while another seeks to eliminate privacy as an operating concept. One person may seek to create a new utopian order of social relations while another sees that enterprise as 'just laying another trip on people.' One will seek some system of authority, while another denies the legitimacy of any authority whatsoever. One may be concerned with a right to be tolerated as 'different,' while another seeks conformity of group members along certain lines. Yet another person may see all these differences as based on 'the constructions you carry around in your head' and seek for the group to abandon all such symbolic notions and 'live the vibes.'

None of the concerns about material culture or social relations exist as themes of social negotiation unless they 'come up' through participants' invocations. A topical relevance may come into play through any of a variety of occurrences. One member of a communal group may find another's actions at variance with his or her own expectations and talk about it at the time or bring it up elsewhere. A member may notice a material state of events (e.g. that tools were mistreated) and begin tracking down the source of the condition. More general topical relevances such as those relating to diet or allocation of work tasks may be discussed among various individuals prior to a general meeting in which resolution is sought. And actions of visitors may draw into the realm of the problematic issues which no members had ever considered (participants in 'Free Union'):

P: (visitor to new household on open land) 'Brother, it's good to have you here. I hope you get the trip together, 'cause if there's one thing we've got to be, brother, it's together. 'Cause those motherfucking rednecks are gonna come up here some night and we're gonna have to kick their asses in. But we can have a good trip. The Holy Spirit is coming to me and telling me that this is gonna be a place of spiritual growth.'

T: (in front of other group members) 'Listen brother; I'll tell you something. I've got my gun and I'm ready for any one of those motherfuckers who wants to get on the wrong side of me; I'll deal them all they can take and more, I'll guaran-damn-tee you that, but I don't want to hear any more of this Jesus talk around here, 'cause I don't believe it and I don't want to hear any of it.'

Invocation of topical relevance may serve both as a way of resolving the ambiguity of a situation for a communal group, and as an attempt at influence by an individual who has a special axe to grind. The difference between such cases is indicated neither by the nature of the concern nor by the process by which the concern comes up, but rather by the credence a concern gains among others when it is aired. Individuals may come to be labeled as obstructionists or 'weirdos' if the concerns they voice consistently escape the sensibilities of others. But short of this extreme, a participant may force resolution of a concern by airing it. And those who consistently focus on topics which others deem relevant come into the esteem of others and may come to cast as leaders. Thus, initial encounters over topics of group concern serve not only as the means of dealing with the substance of such concerns, but also - unless roles are preordained through myth - as arenas in which the political roles of participants in the group become manifest.

In the incipient communal situation, things which become topically relevant typically cannot be resolved through reference to an already established set of interpretational and motivational relevances. Instead, the surfacing of topical relevances brings to the fore the problematic character of interpretation and motivation. Resolution, or even failure at resolution, of topical relevances begins to set the boundaries of a relevance structure of the group. What is involved, then, is what Jay and Heather Ogilvy (1972) have termed 'a reconstruction of reality.'

The nature of the group myth may of course provide initial boundaries of relevance. In the incipient revolutionary terrorist organization, for example, development of mutual trust is a decisive precondition for collective action, and people must 'feel each other out' about their respective orientations toward direct political action (Harris et al., 1976:28). The myth thus sets a basis of association (revolution) in which mutual security is a primary concern.

In other kinds of groups, the mythic basis of integration may involve belief in the absolute charisma of an individual: so long as charismatic acts continue to attract a following, it only remains for the person of knowledge to reveal to followers the nature of their mission, the items of topical relevance that must be attended to, and the interpretations and motivations necessary for proper resolution of topical relevances. Thus, after Love Israel received his initial revelation about beginning a kingdom of heaven on Queen Anne Hill in Seattle, he began by attracting street people to a crash pad scene. It was only gradually that he and his close associates developed the forms of the 'Love Family,' its superstructure, the 'Church of Armageddon,' and other practices and institutions of group life. What began as a personal vision flowered only as the man convinced others of his mission and drew them into rounds of action.

Love Israel's vision was a personal one that he came to share with others. Stephen Gaskin, on the other hand, provided the basis for a broader, shared charisma by developing the revelations in a large group situation. In revealing the form of charisma for those who came to follow him, Gaskin thus indicated the boundaries of motives and the dynamics of interpretation, while topical content was to be resolved in the course of events. In both of these charismatic cases, however, the system of relevances became taken-for-granted through the continued revelations of an individual.

The leader of the contemporary American Krishna movement, A.C. Bhaktivedanta, also provided a personal revelation, especially in his 'Bhagavad Gita; As It Is' (1972). Whether one considers the teachings themselves to be traditional or merely a convenient rewrite of the wisdom is not the point: in either event, according to myth, Bhaktivedanta serves as the best living authority on practice of Krishna consciousness, and thus acts as arbiter, both in his writings and in consultations, for any disputes that might arise concerning a highly elaborated system of relevances. Ignoring alternative disciplic lines of succession, such as the International Theosophical Society founded by Madame Blavatsky, Bhaktivedanta claims to be the last in a direct disciplic succession from the most recent incarnation of Krishna on Earth. On the basis of his 'authoritative' rendering of the 'Bhagavad Gita,' he has directed the establishment of religious communities around the USA and the world.

Whether authority is based on tradition or charisma, and whether the focus of revelations concerns the substance of group life or the forms of being in social intercourse, its invocation in a collective myth provides a formula for resolution of the problematic character of group life.

Other myths of a utopian bent, even when they do not invoke the legitimacy of a leader, similarly serve to set out broad boundaries of relevance. The people who started Twin Oaks, for example, were interested in living in a community based on Skinner's utopian novel 'Walden Two.' They simply adopted many of the institutions and aesthetics of the novel, including a labor credit system for allocating work according to maximization of personal preferences, a board of planners, a procedure for setting policy, a set of managers, and so on. Whatever issues became relevant in this frame were either those pragmatic ones of survival or interpretational ones based on a relevance system for which certain themes had been established. Thus, a chronicler of Twin Oaks's early years states: 'Simon kept the board of planners busy all spring and summer with questions of equality versus special privilege' (Kinkade, 1973:33). It is assumed that such issues are within bounds. If an individual invokes them as topically relevant, other members of the community must bring energies to bear on the resolution of policy ambiguities, no matter how much they see it as a waste of time.

But at many communal groups in formation, people can turn neither to a preordained leader nor to a specified utopia for resolution of ambiguities. In such groups, formed on the basis of friendship, general myth, and perhaps some economic enterprise, things which become topically relevant cannot be resolved through an already outlined and taken-for-granted set of relevances. Often an early challenge to the validity of a myth, through failure of charisma, by inclusion of participants who do not subscribe to the myth, or by other occurrences, renders problematic any relevance structure derived solely from myth: 'I didn't come here with any understanding about revolutionary action, and I don't want any part of any revolutionary action' (member of 'URON'). When myth is called into question (even though it may have broad support), or otherwise fails to provide a basis for reduction of the problematic, interpersonal difficulties are most likely resolved by a drift toward pluralism - the maintenance of multiple viewpoints. Under these conditions, the communal relationship is maintained, as Weber (1968:40) says, 'if and insofar as the orientation of social action ... is based on a subjective feeling of the parties that they belong together.' Thus, when a pluralist ethic obtains, group life is not necessarily concerned with building an ideal social order; it may tend to simply be directed to the everyday concerns of people in the collectivity.

While fully operational communal groups often seek to give the appearance of unity, both for themselves and especially to outsiders, such unity is of a mythical nature: even in the most ideological of groups, individuals may covertly maintain substantially different world views from one another. What emerges from initial communal life is not necessarily total agreement, but rather a holistic conception of field and ground, of public essentials for which all members may be held accountable, and non-essentials, in which differences in conception and behavior may be tolerated. Where a leader dictates the system of relevances, the minimum requirement for participation will be presentation of behavior which shows commitment to the leader. In the utopia, all that may be required is participation in the utopian institutions of communal life. And in the pluralist case, the communal relation can be based on the subjective feeling of 'belonging together.'

EARLY FAILURE

The problems encountered in forming a communal group are formidable. Participants must effectively deal not only with their own social and material situations, but also with constraints of the encompassing society from which they hope to withdraw. Unsympathetic neighbors, zoning and health regulations, police harassment and similar difficulties can severely test the determination of people who want to live communally. Some groups have succumbed to these pressures, but others have gained unity through dealing with potential external adversaries. Typically, internal difficulties - rather than relations with the outside world - pose the greatest problems for would-be communalists.

Many groups of people that come to live in communal association never 'get off the ground.' Instead, during an initial period of collective efforts at 'getting it together,' things begin to fall apart, usually in a number of ways at once. The feeling of belonging together is never achieved, or becomes problematic. Most participants can readily provide accounts of why things are going badly and how they have responded to the specter of failure.

Seldom are the causes of early failure to be found solely in economic difficulties. It is true that the interdependent character of contemporary production of material necessities makes self-sufficient satisfaction of wants practically impossible; many groups are therefore plagued with ill-defined boundaries stemming from a need to obtain income outside the communal nexus. Still, almost all communal groups provide a less expensive style of life than more conventional alternatives, so economic burdens need not require full-time jobs for all members. If, however, individual sources of income dry up all at once, or if the participants engage in a collective economic enterprise that fails, members individually or in small numbers may seek out other living 'gigs.'

Such was the case with a group of musicians from Louisiana who came to pass the summer in the mountains of Colorado while seeking their stardom. When personal resources had been stretched to the limit and jobs for the group were still not coming in sufficient numbers, one of the guitar players convinced two of the other musicians to come with him to Wisconsin, where he thought they could 'get something going.' The departure of these members of the group left the remaining people without a marketable service, and they returned to Louisiana. Similarly, a group committed to making radical documentary films in Maine was largely dependent on a parent urban group for funds. The urban group withdrew support because they felt the work of the Maine group 'wasn't radical enough.' ('It made no sense in Maine to call the police "pigs".') The group continued political work in Maine, concentrating on Indian and ecological issues (a Boston resident):

> 'But our biggest problem was money, and we couldn't make it. Finally the guy that owns the farm went to Arizona and people went in various directions. We're still friends; we still write.'

Such economic failure is rarely the only reason for the passing of a communal enterprise; it is usually part of a broader complex of problems.

Absence of any collective purpose, interpersonal conflict and personal mobility - all clearly linked - are the typical reasons given by members for group failures. Such accounts are all tied to failure of a group myth and intersubjective understandings. A great deal of energy may have been devoted to development of such a myth with dismal results: members of 'Leaping Star Ranch,' a

Colorado group of dropouts from the university scene, spent long hours sharing their fantasies of communal life with each other. In these conversations, each party strived to give at least the appearance of agreement with the other. One person would make general statements using words such as 'energy,' 'flow,' and 'karma.' He would receive responses of the form, 'I can really dig what you're saying, but I think it's equally important that ...,' or, 'What I'm saying is like that but in another respect.' While the participants agreed that 'music is the most important thing - what it's all for,' only one person was a reasonably competent musician, and he set about teaching the others how to play. Over the summer, one person became fascinated with a theory of the 'cosmic clock' while another saw their world to be 'like The Beatles' Pepperland.' And while the participants tried to develop a shared imagery from such diverse and fantastic sources, plans for a winter structure were constantly revised until it was too late to implement any of them. As the bitter cold of winter came to the mountains, people began to drift to other living situations. The group basis for life had been realized neither in a generally accepted myth nor in an organization of effort to accomplish tasks necessary for survival.

Absence of a shared myth seems to spell certain doom, but a highly developed myth may also prove inadequate for marshalling of commitment. One group, the 'Salt of the Earth Cooperative,' began on the basis of a carefully thought out ideology concerned with the economics of socialism, work equity, non-alienating work situations and communal property. Businesses were to be collectively owned by workers who lived together in a large house in an urban location. But a series of interpersonal conflicts ensued. One recruit left in anger, saying he could not stand the way a woman treated her children. A member regarded interpersonal relations as beyond the scope of their utopian vision, saying, 'It's not ideology or anything; it's just how the personalities mix.' The group decided to split into households of people who felt they could get along together, while continuing to develop the collective businesses. Gradually, even these households broke up, but still the businesses continued. The ideology and collective energies had proven sufficient for developing an economic but not a communal basis of life, and those people committed to radical economics continued to develop the businesses independent of any structured communal base.

In these and other early failures at communal life, the forms of social disintegration bear marked similarities.

As in all groups in formation, the initial approaches to material concerns and social relations are problematic. But no basis for resolution of the problematic emerges. Differences are seen as irresolvable by individuals committed to their own visions of things, and conflict leads to a withdrawal from the social arena by one or more parties (participant in a failed rural group):

> 'It's true I don't talk about this stuff with him anymore. He says the whole country is fucked up because of too much planning. I just see it differently, that's all. Planning isn't bad itself; it's just bad when it happens only with economic criteria.'

Through distrust and an inability to come together to resolve the problematic, more and more issues come to be placed on the 'backburner.' An attempt at resolution of an issue by one faction or an individual is countered with charges of 'laying a trip' or 'ego tripping' by others. People spend less and less time with each other (Gardner, 1970:32):

> By this time [when winter was coming on], Tritam and Sue Ellen, Don and Heidi, and Caroline had moved out of the big house entirely, to their own shelters, where they cooked and lived completely separately.

Some people 'cover their bets' by pursuing outside careers or cultivating friends in other households, and eventually withdraw. Inability to act 'for the group' and a decline in the labor force leave collective projects in greater and greater disarray. Those who remain may begin to talk of their personal futures and dream of future communal enterprises.

Such declines may take place over a long time. It is difficult, even for participants, to pinpoint when they began, but once started, the withdrawal of commitment feeds further decline until the remaining people can only pause and reflect on the passing of their group life (Gardner, 1970:48):

> We were completely out of the context of a larger clan or tribe or group of any kind. But we were never even conscious of the need for a clan or tribe - a mythology and ceremonial duties, a social framework which could include warriors and chiefs. We had rejected the American answer of Church and State, but we had put nothing in their place. And so, we soon discovered that our lives seemed empty and unfulfilled, that there was division amongst us, that we were unable to work in peace together to meet our needs. We had been so anxious to work together, but we never learned and seldom had time to relax and play and grow together.

In groups where there is a failure to develop a myth-based

way of invoking 'being together,' the daily life is one of recurrent problematic encounters. People disagree about what is important and how to deal with what is important, and there is moreover, no agreement about how to resolve such disagreements.

If participants are unable to invoke a shared myth and develop 'ways of doing it' that prove satisfactory to those involved, the continuing problematic character of group life comes to be regarded as a sign of failure by those who depart. Such departures may lead to a situation that is no longer considered problematic; the people who remain then label those who departed as the cause of difficulties. If no such thematic resolution transpires, attrition takes its toll until revival is no longer possible.

Other groups manage to create and maintain ways of life that make sense to participants. People - drawn together on the basis of a shared myth - construct a new basis for going through life together. They reduce the array of problematic issues by forging a new ethic of association, and by creating a calculus of relevance for resolving subsequent problems. While such groups continue to go through changes, the changes take place in a world that is, on the whole, taken for granted, or as Schutz and Luckmann (1973:9) have explained it, 'capable of explication.' The world comes to be embraced as 'the way,' not only by utopian visionaries, but also by those who simply wanted to begin a new life outside the boundaries of the larger society.

3 Time and communal life

> Keep in mind that Time's a rabid gambler
> Who always wins without cheating - it's the law!
>
> Baudelaire

> Or say the end precedes the beginning,
> And the end and the beginning were always there
> Before the beginning and after the end.
> And all is always now.
>
> T.S. Eliot

New communal worlds, like the one-dimensional realities of a society left behind, involve a weaving together of individuals' lives through a series of episodes which comprise both subjectively experienced time and a pattern of sociation for the enactment of group life. Alfred Schutz (1967) found the structure of the lifeworld to be predicated on the temporal constitution of events in consciousness. And Karl Mannheim (1936) suggested that time can be experienced as a fundamentally different phenomenon through alternative utopian mentalities. The character of ongoing communal life may thus be understood by considering the social construction and personal experience of time. In this chapter, I describe a phenomenology of time possibilities and go on to examine various ways in which time is constituted in communal living groups. Since communal groups are spawned in 'old times' of the prevailing order, it will be useful first to briefly consider the genesis of objectified, linear time as an organizing principle in contemporary American society.

TIME IN THE ESTABLISHED ORDER

Given cultural variety, the extra-personal realities of time are not the same for all of us. The twentieth century atomic clock notes the beats of passing seconds the world over. But aborigines who have been taught to read clock time still fail to understand what it means (Whitrow, 1961). Certain African tribes are reported to have no word for time, and the Hopi construction of time is said to be a cyclical one (Goody, 1966:30). In Mircea Eliade's view, archaic social life involves the recurrence of archetypical actions, so that the present always springs from an 'eternal return' (Eliade, 1959). The mythic rather than the historic past dominates the present in such societies, so that in theory an unknown future can never bring about unsettling anxieties.

Significantly, though other civilizations, such as that of China, had the ability to measure linear (or diachronic) time in refined ways, it was especially in the Judaeo-Christian crucible that the objectified time of rationalized segments became important in economic activity. Murray Wax (1960) has suggested that the genesis of Western linear time can be traced to ancient Judaism. The Hebrew people are said to have abandoned magical and cyclical time, and adopted linear time both as the historic movement of a people and as the social scheduling of activity. Time as schedule recurred as a theme in early heretical and apocalyptic Jewish sects such as the Essenes (cf. Dupont-Sommer, 1954:136ff). The Essenes lived out a scheduled life in which God was regarded as the sovereign Master of Time. And in the sixth century, the 'Rule' of St Benedict specified the organization of a monk's day (especially his prayer rounds), according to the ringing of bells. The monk was expected to be punctual in all his activities. The obedient monk could rest easy in his God-directed activity, 'give no thought for the morrow,' and never face that awesome question, 'What shall I do next?'

By the eleventh century, as ecclesiastic domains prospered through donations of nobility, some monasteries became rationally organized in work as well as in scheduling of time (Duby, 1968:175-81). Under secular feudal arrangements, by way of contrast, administrative power turned on taxation and protection services. Feudalism provided neither the daily authority over vassals and peasants nor the calculability of production that became possible on the monastic side, where work could be directed under the shield of God's overarching authority. In the monasteries, ascetic work was held to be a selfless act of devotion to God's will.

It is in the context of this other-worldly monastic development of both a diachronic work organization and an ethic of asceticism that Max Weber's famous thesis concerning the Protestant ethic becomes salient. Other-worldly monasticism comprised a nascent capitalist form of work organization. The bureaucratic administration and diachronic scheduling of activity were slowly adopted as the forms of organization in secular industrial companies. Paralleling these developments, the ethic of work asceticism which had been maintained through external authority in monastic life was transmuted to an inner-worldly ethic. Secular Protestant 'monks' took on inwardly-held ethics and discipline of conduct. Monasticism had not been devoid of inner-worldly aspects: mendicant friars, for example, took spiritual sustenance from their inner visions of God while they were adrift in the turmoil of secular life. But among the Protestants, inner-worldly ethics came to be applied to secular economic activity. In this transformation, the monastic ethic of devotional work under the authority of God gave way to both religious certification of economic integrity and successful economic activity as a sought-after demonstration of predestined grace (Weber, 1946). While even the monks had lived only under an exterior authority of scheduled social time, the secular Protestant 'monk' accepted an inner discipline which had as a main feature the rational and efficient use of time (Weber, 1958).

Linear time had existed in other societies. For instance, Joseph Needham (1965) has shown that Chinese dynastic bureaucracies, especially under Confucian influence, held to a sense of history. And measured time was available in China by means of the escapement-controlled water clock. Since linear time was available in China in both of these respects, Needham has dismissed existence of rationalized time as a necessary condition for the rise of capitalism. But he added an important disclaimer: 'Linear time could not of course have been one of the fundamental economic conditions which made this [rise of capitalism] possible, but it may have been one of the psychological functions which assisted the process' (1965:49).

The production of an ethic concerning the use of linear time in worldly affairs was, I suggest, a necessary condition for the emergence of the spirit of capitalism. If, following Marx and Engels (1967:409), we take the materialist position to be concerned with the forms of interaction of people engaged in production, then capitalism, like any other mode of production, is sociologically meaningless independent of its staffing with people who engage in particular kinds of activity. In Marx's conception, a mode of production is comprised of a confluence between a material process of production and people with particular situationally adequate ways of relating to one another. It is thus highly significant that, as E.P. Thompson has shown, the rationalization of time in industrial capitalism did not transpire without resistance among workers. The early sermons of Protestant ministers are filled with admonitions on the use of time. Congregations were warned, for example, to 'use every minute of it as a precious thing, and spend it wholly in the way of duty' (R. Baxter, quoted in Thompson, 1967:87). The rise of industrial capitalism was promoted through the internalization of a diachronic ethic whereby time came to be construed as an abstract commodity to be used, saved and morally spent. An isomorphism came to obtain between a repetitive process of production and the diachronic sense of time held both by those who set up the process of production and by those who came to interact with the process of production.

Linear time provides the possibility of history and progress. Its inward adoption by people stimulates efficient production. Yet the ultimate rationalization of time into arbitrary and abstract units introduces a timelessness of repetition. The epitome of such objective time comes in the assembly line, at which events are reproduced over and over again in a preordained sequence of production. Conceptions of 'newness' may be reaffirmed through cyclical introduction of borrowed aesthetics, stamped into the forms of mass production. Progress may still be heralded via the introduction of one or another technical innovation. But to the degree that bureaucratic industrialization predominates in both material and cultural production, history ceases and only its illusion persists.* The diachronically structured mode of production dominates the themes of consciousness and action independently of any immediate and personal exercise of authority.

If the ordering of time and the experience of change are crucial avenues through which a mode of production predominates, the abolition of that time-ordered

---

* Cf. the similar formulation of 'post-histoire' by Arnold Gehlen. In Gehlen's conception, the history of ideas comes to an end with the rise of scientific civilization; the world is 'without surprise' as 'the alternatives are known.' See Gehlen (1963:323), cited by Schluchter (1972:213).

domination becomes important for those individuals who maintain alternative interests and values. The clocks are to be shot down in revolution (Walter Benjamin, quoted in Marcuse, 1962:213), and the defeat of an old order is typically marked by abolition of an old calendar and introduction of a new one. The victorious revolutionaries are faced with the need to take time into their control. Thus the Soviets established 'Time Leagues' whose members were to inform against those who wasted time. Frederick W. Taylor came to be almost worshiped in the Soviet introduction of scientific management reforms (Bendix, 1970: 216-17). Whatever else the dictatorship of the proletariat accomplished in the Soviet Union, it did not revolutionize, but only sought to internalize, the discipline of linear work time.

For people in communal groups, the revolution, whatever its nature, is carried out in everyday life. What has been taken for granted in the constructions of time in the dominant order becomes problematic, for status passage (Glazer and Strauss, 1971) from old times does not prescribe what new times are to be. Alternative communal groups thus give new accounts of the times - both of the old world of the established order and of the new communal world.

In the present chapter, I consider how people in communal groups constitute time through accentuation of one or another a priori aspect of time. Alternative social time constructions are treated as providing phenomenal contexts of group life and action.

Such an inquiry first requires a vocabulary in terms of which various constructions of time may be understood. In the following section, I discuss only personal and social dimensions of time, and do not dwell on the fixed character of day and night, the seasons, biological aging, and the like. Nor do I provide an exposition of the innumerable philosophies, psychologies and sociologies of time. Since Alfred Schutz and Thomas Luckmann have elaborated the phenomenal constitution of time in the world of everyday life, I draw on their ideas and those of persons who have influenced them directly, namely Henri Bergson and Edmund Husserl.

ON THE PHENOMENOLOGY OF TIME

For some of us, the moment is all; for others, it is hardly significant enough to bear notice. Yet all unique experiences of time are but special accentuations of a range of temporal possibilities which seems to have limits. We are all born, grow older and die. The vast majority of us live in worlds where day fades to night and darkness gives way to dawn, where seasons pass in a yearly cycle, where weather can impose situational time. Our biological nature requires repetitive acts of sleep and sustenance. Each of us has available what William James (1890) termed a stream of consciousness. We may reflect upon ideas and on previous, future or contemporaneous though distant events; or we may attend to the moment at hand. We each have available as our 'preeminent reality' what Schutz and Luckmann (1973:1-4) have called an 'everyday lifeworld,' where we operate by means of our 'animate organisms.' For each of us, a part of that lifeworld involves social arenas where we and others may experience each other simultaneously. Beyond the field of our immediate personal and social experiences, we expect to find a social time consisting of other streams of events. Just as in music, where many tunes and rhythms may be played on the same instrument, so in social life, the varieties of organizing time constructions occur in lifeworlds which have basic characteristics and limits in common.

Subjective time

The individual, prior to any reflection or analysis, experiences a flow of events. Inner duration, as Bergson (1960) has called it, or an event of consciousness, is a 'now' that proceeds from just past experience into the future in a stream of consciousness. Each event of consciousness in the flow occurs not as a discrete unit with beginning and end, but as Bergson says, as a phase which comes to the fore of awareness and again slips away as it is replaced by a succeeding, similarly phased event (1960: 227, 237). The experience, when one attends to it without imposing interruptions, is not of a series of discrete ideas or thoughts, but rather of the 'running off' of now into the past, as ever new events of consciousness come to the fore (Husserl, 1964:45-50).

Nor does the flow of experience have any necessary grounding in an objective structure of time. The passage of objectively measured time is unavailable as an experience to the person totally immersed in the flow of consciousness. The successional phased nature of inner duration provides no benchmarks with which the passage of time can be noted. Only if one subjects oneself to repetitive and equalized events of motion - a beat, for example - does one gain a standard by which to mark the passage of objective time. Non-standardized activity in the lifeworld provides only a sense of the passage of time, of a before and after, which is equally available in the sequenced character of events of inner duration.

Independent of homogeneous, repetitive motion, a 'now' recedes into a 'just past now' and further into a 'past now.' What seems like hours of experience may take only minutes, depending on the objective density of inner durations and the individual's alertness (or, as Bergson calls it, 'attention à la vie') (quoted in Schutz and Luckmann, 1973:25). Whatever the immediate experience of time passage may be, the events of inner duration or, as Husserl calls them, 'primal impressions,' provide the material of memory. The running off of the now involves a 'retention' or 'primary remembrance' which Husserl likens to a tail of the comet of the now (1964:50-2). In some future flow of inner duration the individual may come to reference events experienced previously, and call up such experience through what Husserl terms 'reproduction' or 'secondary remembrance' (1964:57-9). Such remembrance is of primal impressions - the events of consciousness - and not of objective events; thus memory cannot be isomorphic with 'what happened,' but only with those aspects of 'what happened' which were previously constituted in consciousness, however peripherally. Further, reproduction may be of an event of consciousness which has no spatial existence, i.e. of an idea (1964:55-7).

It is through acts of retention and reproduction that the primal impressions of undifferentiated experience come to be 'thrown in relief' and are given forth as grounds for meaningful reflection concerning typicality or uniqueness. Initial retention involves grasping the totality of an experience; on the other hand, reproduction initially references an event as a unity, and only then can it involve a reconstruction of the diversity of elements which made up the original experience. Recollection of music provides a typical example. Though a retained tune is referenced as a unity, to be meaningful in reproduction, it must be 'played back' as a sequence of diversely toned and rhythmed vibrations. In the realm of action, the sense is of an ability to 'do the same thing' again in all its complexity.

Retention and reproduction open the way to a third capacity of the individual beyond simple experience of the stream of consciousness - that of 'anticipation.' If the individual has experienced events as meaningful and typical, and can provide an account as to whether currently experienced events fit a certain model, then anticipation presupposes completion in a certain form. When someone begins a sentence, we expect an end to it; when we hear the beginning of a familiar tune, we may anticipate the resolution according to some already held and remembered general model of the tune (Schutz and Luckmann, 1973: 55-6).

The individual is always immersed in a stream of consciousness. Either through a relaxation of attention to life, one engages in direct consciousness of the internal flow of experience, or, through various tensions of consciousness, one engages in life activity, as well as retaining, remembering, reflecting upon and anticipating experience. Throughout a biographical history of lived experience, the individual develops a stock of retained experience and recipes of reproduction which more and more comprise a style of attending to life, a way of being interested. As Schutz and Luckmann (1973:25-6) suggest,

> This interest is the fundamental regulative principle of our conscious life. It defines the province of the world that is relevant for us. It motivates us so that we merge into our present lived experiences and are directed immediately to their objects. Or it motivates us to turn our attention to our past (perhaps also our just-past) lived experiences and interrogate them concerning their meaning, or rather to devote ourselves, in a corresponding attitude, to the project of future acts.

The individual's general mode of attention shifts somewhat in the course of engagement in various activities in the spatio-temporal world which dictate or permit particular rhythms of relation between the various acts of consciousness. Thus, baking bread involves: reproduction of a recipe at key points in the project, a particular sequence of mixing ingredients, modifications of action according to unanticipated outcomes (too doughy? add milk), as well as physical manipulations during which the tension of consciousness may yield to the flux of undifferentiated inner experience or to other provinces of reality such as sociability. Interludes come about when the bread is taking care of itself (while rising or baking), and the individual may 'wait' or take on other activities.

The degree of attention to life, together with the experiences and acts taking place in the vivid present, provides a subjective experience of lived time (Schutz and Luckmann, 1973:56). Various possible relations may obtain between the internal stream of consciousness, various acts of consciousness involving memory and anticipation, and the actions of the individual in relation to the world. Further, styles of attention to life involve particular rhythms and speeds of event constitution. Subjective time consciousness transpires both as a pattern and a tempo of event constitution.

The social vivid present

The vivid present, or 'now' of the individual's stream of consciousness, occurs in a spatial setting. If the individual orients action toward contemporaries who are not present, or if the vivid present contains other persons, it may be said to be socially constituted.* A social situation ensues even at the extremes of what has been called catatonic schizophrenia, or in the relatively neutral case of walking 'alone' down a busy street. In both such cases, action is social, in the first case as a 'deviant' withdrawal from social life, and in the second case, through the maintenance of boundaries (the person walking hurriedly in the opposite direction does not stop to chat). While different actors are simultaneously present in a social setting, they may maintain personal space and avoid interaction. Though the situations are social in that action takes account of other persons, the action is that of exclusion or alienation.

At the other extreme, the social construction of the vivid present involves engagement or interaction. In such a vivid present, persons recognize one another as they consider themselves to be - as 'psychophysical unities.' For the parties to the social vivid present, the mutual recognition of others and engagement in interaction with them involves a we-relationship, as Schutz terms it, or, as Bergson has described it, a simultaneity.

In a face-to-face situation, the inner durations of two or more persons may be made partially available to each other through an assumption by each that the other has a consciousness similar to his own, capable of attention to themes of experience that are invoked. With this assumption at hand, and with mutual commitment to sharing themes of attention, what Schutz calls 'intersubjective understanding' becomes possible. In other than a face-to-face situation, the 'observer' has available for understanding only a produced artifact of action, a fait accompli, the genesis of which can only be surmised. But (Schutz, 1967: 115),

> When an observer is directly watching someone else to whom he is attuned in simultaneity, the situation is different. Then the observer's living intentionality carries him along without having to make constant playbacks of his own or imaginary experiences. The other

---

* See Max Weber (1968:22-4). Action without persons present may be social under Weber's definition, so long as there is subjective orientation toward others.

> person's action unfolds step by step before his eyes. In such a situation, the identification of the observer with the observed person is not carried out by starting with the goal of the act as already given and then proceeding to reconstruct the lived experiences which must have accompanied it. Instead, the observer keeps pace, as it were, with each step of the observed person's action, identifying himself with the latter's experiences within a common 'we-relationship.'

Certainly the fact of simultaneous streams of consciousness does not mean that we experience the same things in the social vivid present. Each of us has available diverse sources of totally private thought and a personal tension of consciousness. Our rhythms, tempos and topics of subjective experience can thus be quite different. Schutz (1967:106) observes, 'If I could be aware of your whole experience, we would be the same person.' Nevertheless, in a vivid present situation, occurrences that can be sensed and especially those which involve overt acts by individuals (voice, inflection, words, eye contact, and physical actions) are immediately available to both of us as objects of experience to which meaning may be assigned. To the degree that we, at some points, experience the same things, we have intersubjective streams of consciousness (simultaneity); to the degree that we place similar subjective meanings on events, we have intersubjective understanding. In that situation, prior to any retention, reproduction of memory or anticipation, we grow older together, not in any objective time sense, but in the sense of 'passing time' together (Schutz, 1967:167-72).

The social episode involves a complexity far greater than the purely personal one. While the subjective stream of inner durations is a given of conscious life, the simultaneity of social time passage is problematic for at least two reasons. In the first place, to any social vivid present, we bring personal tensions of consciousness which permit more or less simultaneity or estrangement. While we experience the passage of time together, we may share more or less intersubjective understanding, depending on whether we share rhythm, tempo and ways of shifting among the various acts of consciousness such as retention, reproduction and anticipation. Secondly, even if we share a rapport of time experience in the episode, we may 'see things differently.'

In addition, each individual brings to the social vivid present an agenda which may pertain not only to immediate affairs, but also to personal, biographical or career concerns. Situation is defined not only in terms of simultaneous experience, but also through 'backburner' concerns which may be held temporarily in abeyance or included in the intersubjective stream of events - according to our intentions and perceptions of relevance. It is through negotiation and explication that situations are defined and concerns dealt with or left unresolved. The 'play' of the situation provides an opening for interjections, repartees, and other ploys of interaction. However the situation may be construed at one moment, the 'running off' of the moment provides the basis for a continual shifting of focus and reconstitution of the situation. The individual comes away from the social vivid present having experienced not only the simultaneity of consciousnesses, but also 'changes' based on the outcomes of interactions and actions engaged in within the situation.

The social vivid present does not occur as an indistinguishable series of experiences. Rather, onsets and completions of intersubjective streams of events can be discerned. Such beginnings and endings mark episodes roughly equivalent to musical fugues. For any such episode, certain persons are present, and certain events occur, both intersubjectively and in personal consciousness.

Each individual passes from one social episode to another, and through interludes of purely personal experience. Episodes may be either autonomous (as in the case of pure sociability) or interrelated through the resolve of individuals in the episode to take care of certain matters 'elsewhere' - beyond the boundaries of the episode. While each individual participates in a sequence of episodes and interludes, intersecting with various other individuals in the course of this stream, the flow of events is not inherently mythic, cyclical, simultaneous, linear or progressive. Though what comes to the fore in one episode may prescribe later actions, such other actions typically do not fall immediately after the episode. Instead, it may be that they are taken care of only when a particular site is available, when particular individuals are present, or when they 'come up' again. Past episodes become relevant to new episodes only to the degree that meaning in the form of future intent and past remembrance is invoked.

World social time

Provinces of reality exist beyond the vivid present. These other realities would exist for us only if we as individuals constituted them at some future moment. Some of these realities occur in the nexus of other individuals' actions. Such other events, as well as the passage of days and seasons, are objective to us in the sense that they represent external, time-based conditions which transcend the times of subjective and social vivid present experience (Schutz and Luckmann, 1973:46-7). Some such events are not scheduled, while others constitute a frame of social time in which we may participate if we so choose. Participation in any realm beyond the episodic running off of the moment may involve such scheduling, for interaction within organizations is 'mapped' in terms of diverse agendas of persons, collective activities, times of day, days, weeks, accounting periods, seasons, and so on. While some potential episodes may be handled on demand, when a need for them is invoked, others - such as eating, working, and sleeping - typically happen within the framework of a broadly organized social schedule.

For a given social arena, group or organization, subjectively transcendent ways of scheduling events and activities comprise what I shall term world social time. An individual who acts in relation to more than one group moves between different world social times. To the degree that some individuals produce a schedule in terms of which others act, domination may be said to take place. The character of any given world social time is subject to both collective concerns and activities, and spatial and social arrangements through which such activities occur. Beyond enterprise and ecology, however, there exists considerable room for play.

We can order the nexus between our temporal streams of experience and the world in various ways. We may attend wholly to the internal flow of consciousness; we may fantasize, daydream of the past and of contemporary but not immediate experience, or we may anticipate future events; we may attend to the vivid present, either as reproduction of previously retained experience, or in a generation of wholly new phenomena. In experiencing these various aspects of subjective time, we may have more or less tension of consciousness and feel that 'time is passing very slowly,' or report that 'the whole thing happened in a flash.'

The social vivid present in which we act may involve various degrees of boundaried personal time or intersubjective simultaneity of experience, and the weaving of episodes and interludes may similarly comprise a world social time of either interpersonal intersections of autonomous individuals or a general social simultaneity. World social time as a device of organization may take many different forms - people may coordinate through use of clocks and watches, by other signals such as chimes, gongs and bells, by word of mouth, or through episodic negotiation. The invocation of these various orientations in concert with the events of life constitute different worlds of time.

TIME ORIENTATIONS IN COMMUNAL GROUPS

People who have 'dropped out' of established arenas of American life often speak of the importance of getting out from under the 'rat race.' When the old world is left behind, ecstasy may replace the previously experienced boundaries of time. One young woman, who had lived in a communal group of transients before joining a more stable group, recalled her initial months of communal life: 'That was the first time I ever lost track of what day it was.' The broad concern of American youth with the 'here-and-now' may be seen as a revulsion from the work shift - weekend construction of American life. This revulsion indicates the failure of an ethic for such young people: neither inner-worldly self-discipline of the Protestant ethic nor the rationalized rewards of managed work provide sufficient grace or freedom. The sources of such a view are both hedonistic and utopian. The young person who has never worked may 'want the world and want it now,' as rock lyricist Jim Morrison put it. The relatively carefree leisure of youth coming to grips with 'realistic' demands of working life yields the well known phenomenon of the 'identity crisis.' Still, abhorrence of the 'rat race' involves, for many, a value-based rejection of contemporary conditions of work and social life.

Personal quests for transcendence are heightened in the event of perceived collapse of the established social world. When national events lead to a collective sense of crisis or panic, when things are seen as 'worse than they used to be,' the ideology of progress becomes open to question. A discontinuity occurs in the myth of collective experience of the social. In a period of uncertainty, people move to reorient themselves, to provide a new account of what is going on. The conservers of ideology attempt to persuade others that things 'are going along as usual.' The action of courts in dealing with crime, for example, is touted as proof that 'the judicial system is still working.' But long before crisis drives ideologists to statements proclaiming the orderly processes of institutionalized society, others have come to withdraw allegiance from the established order. The lonely street signboard carrier who perennially hawks doomsday is generally ignored, but at certain points, substantial numbers of people come to perceive an extraordinary situation encompassing the whole character of established social integrations. Such people come to search for an alternative account of 'what time it is.'

Conservers of ideology may attempt to incite longings for a more glorious or simpler past, or they may stage nostalgic revivals of various heydays: old movies, fashions of another era, dances and fads come to be publicized, and those who participate in the revival live vicariously in another age, rather than perceiving the contemporary historical situation as extraordinary. Even if the times are experienced in a current fashion, a sense of imminent doom may preclude any but a decadent experience: 'eat, drink and be merry, for tomorrow we die.'

Those who do not subscribe to ideological accounts of the times and still search for hope beyond doomsday - these people are susceptible to what Karl Mannheim (1936) called the utopian mentality, in which an alternative and 'situationally transcendent' account of the times is provided. Coming to embrace a utopian mentality need not produce change in one's patterns of social life. One may simply wish for another situation, and the social implications of such an approach are then bound up in how one relates to the existing institutions of an established order.

Communal living groups, however, inevitably involve alteration of lifestyles by the mere fact of entry into new living situations. The utopia (or anti-utopia) provides the possibility of a boundaried site for the enactment (in the dramaturgical sense) of a new world.

As Mannheim has argued, it is in the 'conception of time, in the light of its hopes, yearnings and purposes that utopia becomes comprehensible' (1936:209). If the implications of rationalization are seen as irreversible, the utopian mentality can only seek to progressively improve the quality of life under a regime of objectified time. But if the end of one's own time in the diachronic world is found in personal apocalypse, the millennium, ecstasy or world-historical revolution, then other forms of communal organization emerge. An alternative account of time provides a rationale of communal organization, and an organizing social time parallels that account as a way, model or mission.

At all communal groups with which I had contact, people invoked apocalyptic or millenarian imagery. Whether the group was pluralist, socialist-revolutionary, progressively technocratic, Buddhist, Hindu, primitive Christian, eclectically religious, or based on personal friendship, the imminent or already transpired collapse of an immoral and decadent established order was a key consideration in the formation and unfolding of group life. News from the outside could always be taken as confirming one's most dire predictions, and a satisfaction could be felt from having chosen an alternative path. Thus, a 1973 discussion of the energy crisis and the Watergate caper at a rural commune in the eastern USA could conclude with the comment: 'It'll be the people with the land who will have it together when the rest of it falls apart.' Each true believer jumps at the opportunity to account for continuing decline in terms of a particular world view. The apocalypse may be viewed as having already transpired. At one Rocky Mountain group, talk of outside politics was dismissed with the comment, 'It's all over, finished - so why do we harp on it?,' while a member of a rural Washington State group felt, 'There's no point in dealing with anyone who doesn't cop to the apocalypse as real.' Not everyone would subscribe to the radical view expressed by a member of a rural Washington State Christian group:

> 'Jesus was sent here before and they weren't ready for him, but the Bible says he's coming again, and I believe that, 'cause the world that's going now is falling apart, and the people who are clinging to it will go down with it, 'cause they're all out for themselves and their personal egos are directing them, and it's not the way of the Lord. And the good souls who have gotten away from that will find themselves transported to a new world, where they will live in heavenly grace.'

Whether the apocalypse is perceived as already having transpired, as imminent, or ongoing, the communal group exists beyond the definitions and boundaries of the old order. It is in 'new times' that new ways are provided.

In all communal groups, regardless of their idealizations of time, day-to-day life occurs in the passage of experiences. To the degree that groups are utopian, they try to produce their worlds in dramaturgical enactment of idealizations and beliefs. Time, if it is important in the lives of communal participants, must be apparent in its lifeworldly manifestation.

Three broad alternatives of time constructions exist as analytic possibilities. A diachronic or linear time of rationalized physical duration may be imposed as a scheme for the coordination of group life. A purely synchronic formation may emphasize the vivid present as the arena for coordination of group and individual concerns. Finally, time may be construed in an apocalyptic fashion. In this case, the last days of the diachronic world of the established order are seen as giving way to a new world with a new time. The constitution of time in communal life under each of these ideal-typical orientations can best be understood by considering various groups which approximate such orientations.

THE DIACHRONIC WORLDLY UTOPIA

A diachronic structure of world time provides an objective standard of physical duration in terms of which the work and life of group members may be coordinated. Twin Oaks, the behavioral community in Virginia, provides the most developed contemporary example of such an approach.

At Twin Oaks, irrationalities in established diachronic schemes of time are eliminated. Above all else, time is labor; all individuals must earn an equitable quota of 'labor credits' each week. Sunday is not a holiday, nor is there any demarcation of 'sacred time.' At many jobs, a person can work any time of the day or night, and the minutes, hours and days roll by at a steady pace whether one is working or enjoying leisure time.* Rationalization of time is seen as the premise of efficiency: it is held that through a managerial system and planning of productive processes, the community derives the maximum possible benefit for a given unit of labor input. People at Twin Oaks do not stop at simple efficiency to maintain a steady state system; collectively, participants hold to a strong sense of progress - of taking on a higher labor credit quota now in order to build for a happier and more leisurely life to be enjoyed at some future point. But the progressive orientation of Twin Oaks includes, ironically, the 'here-and-now': at a planners' meeting, members listed as one goal, 'living more in the here-and-now.'

Ultimately, however, Twin Oaks does not abandon the prevailing time orientation of the established order. Instead, it proclaims an advancement along the same lines. Such an approach to communal life is of a worldly utopian nature: the suggestion is that the prevailing order, though diachronic in nature, still contains non-rational elements which should be eliminated. The old order suffers, not from too much rationalization but from too little. Increased rationality in the coordination of activity is seen as a basic key to a better life for all. For through total rationalization of time and other elements of group life, inefficiencies and inequities can be

---

* This total homogenization of time parallels early Soviet attempts to eliminate the sacred week and calendar. See Wilbert Moore (1963:122).

eliminated and individual preferences about expenditure of time can be maximized.

The heightened rationalization of world time is provided according to the clock. Twin Oaks Time (TOT) is synchronized with the outside world, but set one hour ahead of 'outside' time: the departure to the nearest city may occur at the same time as the desired arrival time. Each individual has a schedule of work slots at various activities, as well as hours of work assigned that may be 'self-scheduled.' Meals are available at certain scheduled hours, served by community members working for labor credits. During the course of the day, people move from one activity to another according to their personal schedules. The scene is thus one of individuals coming to a site, working alone or with other people for a specified period, then leaving to go to another site, fitting lunch in at some point, and the like.

Life is not unlike that of a college campus where classes are scheduled with gaps of free time. Just as at colleges, coordination is accomplished through bureaucratic scheduling. The difference is one of degree: at Twin Oaks the schedule changes weekly. There are no weekends except as people choose to create them. Time is rationalized almost to the point of abstraction where any event-moment is interchangeable with any other, largely according to individual preferences. At Twin Oaks, the pattern of scheduled time changes frequently and at the preference of individuals, while at most colleges, schedules are altered less frequently, but students may ignore them altogether if they are willing to face the (largely symbolic) consequences.

At Twin Oaks, clock time serves both as a commodity and a standard of efficiency. People talk of time as an investment. Since time is routinized, a change in policy concerning its use has consequences for future, similarly demarcated units of time.

B: 'I'm thinking of changing around the apprenticeship, 'cause I waste a lot of time now sitting around while others are milking, and when we get six new cows, we could really save some labor credits.'

(later)

W: 'Well, it's time to milk. Do you want to come out to the barn?'

B: 'No. I'm changing it around; I'll be out in a bit.'

N: 'What's the matter? Don't you like our company?'

B: 'Of course I do, but this'll save some labor credits.'

The sense of time as something with a use value can involve people as well as work.

> 'People only have so much time in a given day, and they can either get to know visitors or get to know members they are going to be with. And a lot of people would just rather not waste time with visitors.'

Though a person is free to spend time according to personal wishes (so long as the labor quota is met), the pressures of the quota and personal desires leave little time for wasting time - it is too precious a thing.

World social time, by the agreement of people at Twin Oaks, dictates the individual's presence at certain sites at specific times and for specific durations, on the basis of maximizing individual preferences. Almost predictably, Twin Oaks endures occasional synchronic backlash; the clamor by some is for a reduced labor credit quota and more free time now. Steps have been taken in the direction of more synchronic forms of work coordination (e.g. through institution of self-directed work crews). But such changes do not alter the ultimately diachronic ethic; indeed they have been justified by some people under a rhetoric of progress, of making the system more efficient through creation of more palatable working conditions. Such new developments notwithstanding, the vivid present work situation is in general one of a simultaneity of people who have been scheduled to appear at a site from diverse locations.

It is individuals who have responsibility for meeting demands on their time. Each person must remember each scheduled appointment, anticipate the reaching of that point on clock time, and appear at the designated time and place. Particularly in the realm of work, remembrances and anticipations can interrupt ongoing socializing. There is always another place where one has to go.

> D: 'Well, I missed my shift on typing this morning. I'm gonna see if anyone else is on the machine right now. Maybe I can make it up.'
>
> M: 'O.K. Catch you later.'

Thus, a person's schedule is only an idealized framework, subject to situational modification. On occasion, people fail to act in terms of their schedules. In the above example, the person merely requires access to a machine which has been scheduled for maximum use. In other cases, however, scheduling involves coordination among two or more people. When appointments are not kept, adjustments of world time can be made by individuals who are parties to the confusion.

> M: (passing another person at work on a project at 3 p.m.) 'Wasn't I supposed to do that with you?'

K: 'Yeah, it's on our labor assignment sheets for 2 p.m.'

M: 'Oh. Well, I got into this heavy rap with Alice and had no idea what time it was.'

K: 'That's cool. I just started 'cause I had the time and was tired of doing book work inside.'

M: 'Good. You want to switch off on something then?'

K: 'Sure. Let's see.' (looks at labor assignment sheet) 'I have stretcher drilling at 4 to 5 p.m. You could take that if you want.'

M: 'O.K. That works out well, 'cause I already have it from 3 to 4, and I'll just truck on through.'

Persons who 'fall behind' the labor credit quota may come to feel pressured by anticipated work loads, and either knuckle down to working themselves 'out of the hole,' or eventually leave the community with labor credit deficits. Others build up surplus labor credits and feel no qualms about taking a vacation. So long as a person obeys the rules of the community, obligations to it are met through the labor quota.

Beyond the realm of scheduled work and obligations to the accumulation of labor credits, one's time is one's own. Within the diachronic framework of world time (and beyond its interruptions), a person can constitute time subjectively and in the social vivid present in a number of ways. It is possible to live at Twin Oaks in near isolation, working and eating, but keeping apart from other people. Few choose to do this. Instead, various episodes of intimacy and sociability occur. People who pass the time by encountering, playing music, talking and partying, often do so in semi-public arenas:

L: 'You still want to play music tonight?'

B: 'Yeah, after I go to Charlottesville.'

L: 'How about 8.30 in the living room of Tai Chai?'

B: 'O.K. See you then.'

Beyond isolation, intimacy and various aesthetics of sociability, a vivid present social life open to all transpires. It is in this public sociability, both at work and elsewhere, that people get to know one another, and talk about recent and upcoming events, as well as current community issues.

The ultimate diachronic framework of world social time provides a means by which individuals may contribute to the collective needs of the community in a rational nexus of social commerce. Each person must participate in a schedule directed in part from beyond face-to-face interaction of the vivid present, and in so doing, comes to allocate time for both work and leisure. Paralleling a diachronic world time, members of Twin Oaks experience subjective time constituted in part by memory and anticipation. The diachronic framework assures the satisfaction of material wants, so long as people act in terms of it. Available time beyond work is thus similar to those pluralist patterns of sociability found in natural synchronic groups (discussed below): individuals and circles of individuals may invoke the vivid present in any way they choose, for they are beyond the bounds of community demands on time. In the diachronic worldly utopia, a liberal ethic of freedom finds realization in part in the availability of free time for everyone.

SYNCHRONIC TIME IN COMMUNAL GROUPS

The synchronic approach to time is diametrically opposed to the imposition of a rationalized world time schedule for the coordination of work and group life. Group life is held to exist solely in intersubjective vivid present episodes. But the constitution of the 'now' may be accomplished in several ways. In the natural approach to enactment of a communal way of life, no special effort is made to constitute the social vivid present in a particular way. In the produced ethical enactment of a worldly utopia, on the other hand, the 'now' is heralded as the solution to problems of alienation in the established order. Ethical procedures are invoked for the processing of the moment. Finally, in the transcendental approach, the vivid present exists prior to symbolization, and it is to the phenomena of absolute presentness that attention is directed.

Natural synchronism

In natural communes variously characterized as 'hippie,' anarchist, or pluralist - those in which group life is constituted through a dialectic and synthesis of individual viewpoints - in such groups, people do not embrace a unified collective concept of social world time. Various approaches to the conceptualization of time, as well as the lived experience of time, remain 'in play' with one another. If these approaches are subsumed under any group conception of time, it is of the 'here-and-now.'

Any dimension of time may be invoked in a particular situation, depending on perceived needs, interests and goals of both individuals and the collectivity. An opportune call to 'seize the time' for revolutionary change may be sounded at various junctures of historical time of the society-at-large, and at other times people may talk of 'stopping time,' transcending time, living in the here-and-now, or 'spending time together as a family.' At any point, a person's conception of time may be called into question (members of 'URON'):

K: 'Do you think your attitude will change with time?'
T: 'Time!? There is no time. It's either happening now or it isn't.'
L: 'But we began here knowing we weren't where we wanted to be, and we keep working towards it, and I think we are making progress.'
C: 'Becoming. We are in a state of becoming.'
T: 'Yeah, I can dig that, as long as the becoming is now.'

In this example, T appears to challenge K's structured and historical conception of time, opposing it with a totally episodic time sense. L retorts with an extension of the historical conception as embodying the possibility of progress, and C seeks to reconcile the differences with the idea of becoming. Time, it seems, is in the eye of the beholder.

Each individual may hold a conception of time and express it in various ways. At 'URON,' various people speak of 'time as energy,' the moment as having no particular dimension, ritual as a means of transcending time, and moving backwards in time 'to the original perfection from which we all unfolded.' In this group, the general myth of the now does not provide a highly specified utopian alternative which totally excludes the past (members of 'URON'):

J: 'Why'd you do it that way?'
E: 'Gee, that's the way I've always done it.'
L: 'Wow, I never thought I'd hear those words around here.'

Still, a myth of 'provisional revolution' permits the sporadic and ad hoc wiping out of the past as a legitimate basis for life. The 'revolution' is redefined continuously (when it comes up): 'It's whatever we come together on whenever we come together on it.'

Communes of a pluralist nature, especially in urban areas, often include participants with diverse interests and outside activities. The group thus serves as a locus of household life, and not necessarily as a collective basis for want satisfaction. So long as the household commune simply bridges individuals' worlds of autonomous activity, the pluralist now allows different personal streams of life to be subsumed under a broad ethic of sharing and toleration. As with other elements of myth in the natural commune, the conception of time is eclectic:

though it is synchronic in emphasizing a 'nowness' of group life, the organization of time does not include schedules or norms of participation, and thus allows for broad freedom of individual agendas. It effectively allows for both privacy within the household and partici-pation in outside world times which may themselves be dia-chronically scheduled. The idealization of the now as happening 'only when people make it happen' leaves little room for domination of time beyond the moment, unless agreement is reached at the moment.

Such a pluralist 'do your own thing' ethic requires a world social time that individuals may participate in according to personally felt wishes or obligations. Some collective events such as chores and meals must be per-formed at particular times, or at least with regular fre-quency. A collectivized sense of the horizons of future time (Schutz and Luckmann, 1973:52) provides a way of in-suring that these various events are brought off. Beyond the fulfillment of a subjectively felt duty to the re-quirements of collective life, one's time is one's own. The now is thus invoked only at the interest of individual participants or through happenstance, and collective epi-sodes of the group ebb and flow according to personal sentiments.

Aside from the necessary activities of the day, a vivid present sociability is constituted in 'hanging out.' To a degree in urban groups, and especially in rural ones, the subjective experience of time unfolds as the running off of the moment among a collectivity of people. In these intersubjective episodes, the themes of conversation need not follow any rational course of association. Rather, the topic may shift among gossip, fantasy, future plans, the past, discourses on spheres of knowledge, intimate meanings, and music. At least in theory, the topic of conversation knows no bounds, for no collectively held rules of relevance exclude any concern, insight or dimen-sion of time from being invoked in intersubjective situa-tions. In natural groups, time is always broadly syn-chronic: what happens in the intersection of personal courses of life _is_ the now. But no basis for limiting the now exists. The constitution of the moment may shift among 'nows' that are not strictly synchronic - those of anticipation, remembrance and reproduction of conscious-ness. Similarly, degree of tension of consciousness linked to anticipation or remembrance may provide dif-ferent rhythms of life which border on the pace and trans-momentary focus of diachronic time. The synchronicity of time is maintained through collective attention to life that can shift from one rhythmic and time-dimensioned constitution of the vivid present to another without such changes being considered problematic. As the countercultural statement of the ethic would have it, people 'go with the flow.'

Worldly utopian synchronism

In groups which seek a great transformation of society by way of a worldly utopian example, the specification of time is of greater concern than in natural communes. The legitimacy of a utopian model, both for participants and in portrayal to the outside world, is in part tied to its eschatology of time at a time when the old order is perceived as collapsing. While the worldly utopian conception of time derives its inspiration from an apocalyptic wellspring, beyond that imagery lie more specific orientations.

At The Farm, the Tennessee community started by Stephen Gaskin and those who have accepted him as a teacher, we are told to learn the lessons of living in 'this world,' 'not in some fantastic time and space.' The present - the immediately available now - is viewed as the only arena in which humans really live. 'Future trips,' 'rear view mirrors' ('watching where you were instead of where you're going'), and personal fantasies are all held to be ego constructions which allow the individual to 'pass through' the vivid present 'without really being plugged in.'* The problems of the world are bound up in people who 'live in their heads,' and not 'where they are.' The solution to this state of affairs is said to involve something besides a gradualistic change.

> 'You aren't going to get salvation sometime in the future, and the people who think they are are really lost. This is it, now, so we might as well make it happen, because we are the creators of each new moment.'

The ideal is of attending to the vivid present, as an individual in a social situation rather than (as we will find with Krishna belief) as an individual in a personal relation with God. God, to people at The Farm, is 'not an authoritarian.' Instead, legitimacy for the now is derived from the social vivid present. 'What people agree on - that is truth.' The now, rather than being other-

---

* 'Plugged in' means, in the particular vocabulary of The Farm, to be related to, involved in, or a part of events which are thematic at a given moment, or projected to occur as part of a plan (my definition).

worldly and eternally the same, is unique, specific and subject to change. But entry into the world of the vivid present provides a key to the transcendence of the mundane.

> 'You have to get to the place where you're <u>totally</u> in the now. If you really do that, the now becomes infinite because the chronons [i.e. indivisible units of presentness equivalent to Bergson's inner durational events of consciousness] become smaller and smaller.'

While, as we shall see later, Krishna devotees experience a merger with transcendent and eternal time, participants at The Farm experience a synchronism grounded in immediate, vivid present experience, especially with other people. The shared moment in all its uniqueness constitutes a now of communion and salvation. In such a situation, there is little room for private thoughts. Group life is so structured that the individual is almost continually immersed in a collective social experience. It is during these moments that people certify to each other that each is 'plugged in' to the more encompassing collective experience of The Farm.

The emphasis on the here-and-now is derived quite clearly from belief. Stephen Gaskin has warned that American society and culture have rapidly become decadent: while the 'American way' no longer holds any mythic power, people go on living as before, only increasingly swallowed up by the decay around them. In such a situation, Gaskin is self-admittedly 'out to save the world.' He says that people should sort out what is worth saving, what is irrelevant, and what needs to be recreated. But this cannot be accomplished by transcending the here-and-now. Instead, Gaskin and his followers state emphatically that salvation comes not in the future nor in escape from 'the world,' but in establishing arenas where people can live and take care of business in the now.

The constitution of the 'now' at The Farm derives from individuals' sequential participation in various 'group heads' or loci of social interests, including household sites, work sites, and other recurrent associations of people. At the sex-segregated male and female households (for those who have not yet found a spouse), people sleep in a communal space, awaken together, take breakfast together, and then move to various work 'group heads.' At work group heads, the tasks of the day are outlined, and crew group heads are formed. Work crews then spend the morning together, sharing a break and returning to the kitchen for lunch, followed by more work. In the evening there will be time for a shower in the communal shower building, then dinner, followed by a group activity -

listening to tape recordings of Stephen Gaskin and the Farm Band on tour, shelling seeds for planting, and the like. Each individual (and especially the newcomer who does not have complete 'tripping' instructions yet) moves together with others in the interludes between various communal episodes. From waking to retiring to sleep, and even then, each individual spends the better part of the day in a procession with others through life.

The radical immersion into an almost constant inter-subjectivity can be somewhat of a shock to the newcomer. The recalcitrant person is drawn out, gently but firmly, into the social vivid present of simultaneous consciousness. Particularly visitors and potential members find themselves asked to be in the world where they exist.

H: (potential member) 'I feel like there is so much happening here that it's all I can do to take it in. I dig you people, but I don't know how to relate to it. You are so spiritually there, and I am trying to get there, but maybe it's just a long road for me.'

R: 'Hey, man, that's just a rap you want to give to us so we'll excuse you for sitting back. You say it's a long path, but what's really going on is you're sitting around sulking. You aren't really making any effort to come outside your head. And in your head, you're making up all kinds of fantasies about who you are and what's happening here.' (As R makes this statement, others in the room look around at each other; eyes meet; it seems that there is recognition that H's case is up, that he must be drawn out of his internal 'head tripping.')

H: 'Well, I really want to be more spiritual; I want to come outside my head, but I really don't know how.'

P: 'There's no secret about it. You just do it: pay attention to what's going on around you. This is the sudden school. This is Monday Night Class* right now.'

H: 'Now?! I can't change all of a sudden.'

R: 'That's the only time you can change, is now, 'cause that's the only time you have to work with. Don't think we're coming down on you because we're on your case right now. We just want you to loosen

* The speaker refers to a class held in San Francisco by Stephen Gaskin, before he and his followers moved to Tennessee. See Gaskin (1970).

up and get straight.'*

H: 'I want to do that; it's why I came here, but I just don't know how ...'

P: 'Just do it and stop doubting you can do it.'

In such a fashion, people at The Farm bring newcomers into the now of simultaneous consciousness. It is an initiation of sorts, one in which the initiate is engaged in direct conversation about his situation. He is told he has been 'laying back' and holding in his feelings. Through others' attention he is then given the opportunity to talk about 'where he's at' and receive direct response in the vivid present.

The required change is to enter into the immediate communion of the collectively witnessed social, without subscription to belief, metaphors or imagery of the world. Beyond the witnessed episode, knowledge and truth quickly fade to rumor, conjecture and speculation. Therefore, talk of things beyond the now, as well as abstract talk, meets with opposition, even if the situation being discussed is not fantastic, but has a real 'now' at another place. The boundary of the now is not totally defined in advance: rather it is negotiated. One visitor talked about political groups outside The Farm and was told that the talk was 'too conceptual' and 'too far from the here-and-now.' But discussion of previous life experiences, upcoming Farm plans, and ongoing events elsewhere on The Farm is not considered out of bounds. The now is identified with the simultaneity of personal consciousnesses in a social situation, but there are also boundaries to what

---

* 'Getting straight' is, for people at The Farm, the process of eliminating sources of tension, ambiguity, disagreement, conflict of situational definition, or other elements of (typically, privately held) consciousness which require the individual to maintain ego, construct lies, avoid situations, or otherwise not act freely in the social vivid present (my definition). This use of 'straight' contrasts with the colloquial use of the term in the American counterculture, where it can refer derogatorily either to a person who does not use drugs, or to someone who clings singlemindedly to a narrow definition of self as constituted by conformity with non-deviant role expectations in previously established arenas of American life. In short, the 'straight' person acts on the basis of a delineated and narrowly defined status position. On the other hand, at The Farm, the 'straight' person is 'upfront,' i.e. not hiding anything.

can become thematic in that simultaneity without objection being made by witnesses. These boundaries generally seem to be the participants' lifeworlds of direct experience.

The thrust of restricting themes of the now is egalitarian, for it limits esoteric topics. Everyone can be included in the now, regardless of breadth of experience or 'conceptual' knowledge about the world in general. One's identity does not hinge on ego, but instead on immersion in the immediate lifeworld. Such social communion is an integral feature of group life.

The now is thus constituted as a radical vivid present, available to all: it is derived from the concerns of the people involved, brought to collective consciousness, and manifested in social action directed to the 'world within potential reach' and the 'world of known contemporaries' (Schutz and Luckmann, 1973:35). Beyond the web of social relations at The Farm and the outside relations of participants (e.g. with family, friends, persons met in the course of experience) lies the unknown of other time/place, and this realm, like the purely subjective stream of consciousness, remains outside the thematic boundaries of group life.

Because the boundaries of the now are so delineated, Farm members maintain a high degree of sensitivity to each other. People quickly notice the slightest loss of rapport in the vivid present, and it immediately becomes the focus of conversation. One crew was out 'stumping' (clearing stumps for a new crop field) when one of the members began to withdraw from the ongoing talk. Another asked him if he was 'tripped out,' and the first replied that he was just tired from the heat. Certain language comes to signify withdrawal. At the sauna, one Farm member asked another:

B: 'Isn't it a rush?'
S: 'Yeah, I'm really spaced out.'
B: 'Oh yeah?'
S: 'Well, not in a bad way; just really digging it.'
B: 'Farout!'

While it is all right to have 'rushes' of personal experience, to be 'spaced out' or 'tripped out' carries negative connotations of not being 'here-and-now.' Each person submits to the social arena. Other realms of personal and world time are held in abeyance. It is not in any personal and privatized worldview that salvation can be achieved. For the individual is seen as drifting into fantasy, recollections and anticipations which provide a constitution of reality alienated from vivid present life activity. Such private time is a barrier to social communion, for it allows each individual to carry a private viewpoint without social confirmation of its 'validity.' Objectified world time as a definer of personal action must similarly be held in abeyance, for intrusion on the vivid present through 'calls to the outside' would provide a 'cover' (i.e. escape) from 'getting straight.' In like manner, the referencing of a previously established set of doctrines or rules, it is felt, would permit the individual to 'hide behind righteousness.' Any province of meaning other than the social vivid present, whether personal, doctrinal, or based on outside obligations, would detract from the invocation of the now as the arena in which meaning is to be established.

In The Farm's synchronic worldly utopia, a group rhythm of simultaneous experience provides communion. There is certainly room for personal contemplation, but the primary emphasis is on each person being 'plugged in' to collective consciousness. In that arena, people can take care of both interpersonal relations and collective projects. In such a processional synchronicity, people walk through life together. The mission at The Farm is concerned in large part simply with bringing people into the vivid present province of social reality. That in itself is seen as the communion and the salvation.

Transcendental synchronism

Not all social life is constituted through production of symbols. In the transcendental formation, symbols are regarded as epiphenomenal. While time could be idealized, as it is in produced groups, such an effort would be a symbolic reification. In transcendental synchronism, 'White man's time' is taken to be a disgusting imposition on the world. An apocalyptic insight may provide the basis for engaging in a special life. But, as in natural synchronic communes, no particular conception of time is held out as the way. Unlike natural communes, however, the transcendental formation allows for the possibility that any account of experienced time could be about a real phenomenon. It does not have to be one way or the other; multiple possibilities may exist. Symbolic representations, however, are seen as metaphors which fail to capture the richness of the experience itself. Thus time in the transcendental formation is synchronic in its shared presentness, and the experience of that presentness - in any of diverse possibilities - has a primacy prior to any account of it.

The experience of inner duration, intersubjective simultaneity of streams of consciousness, and elements of world social time each have their potential existence. The world is, before it is described, and no single, rationalized account of the world can cover all the possibilities. Therefore, in one group formed around a mystic teacher (or mystagogue as Weber terms it*), no one attempts to provide an account of time as an ethical category. Instead, group rhythm is created out of the behavior and interactions of people present. Though they could dwell wholly in personal time, this rarely occurs. Instead people create time in the running off of it all, through sounds, motion, interaction, interjections, asides, and splitting into interludes and other episodes.

> 'It's all in synch,** always. Look at it; listen to it. It couldn't be otherwise, no matter what people think.'

Time becomes a play form, since various rhythms can be created and experienced. Long periods of simultaneous experience of silence may occur, and the field of the vivid present then becomes drawn out to the point where participants experience a time stoppage.

During one discussion at 'The Cabin' about altering time consciousness through use of drugs, the 'mystagogue' suddenly interjected, 'You can stop time without drugs.' 'How?' he was asked. A silence ensued, for the teacher did not respond and the five others present had been anticipating his reply. The immeasurable silence ended when one person fainted. He later reported: 'Yellow rings started coming in concentrically. I grew dizzy. Noise started to hum, vibration. I fell slowly down.'

The 'stoppage' of time is only one of numerous possibilities. Music provides a form in which the variability of time consciousness can be experienced. At its simplest, people at 'The Cabin' use objects in the physical environment - glasses, forks, tin cans and a table - to tap out rhythms. Social time is specified neither by a rationalized time nor by any normative prescription or account of the nature of time. Instead, the events and interactions manifest as rhythms, which may

---

* See Max Weber (1968:446-7): 'He [the mystagogue] performs sacraments, i.e. magical actions that contain the boons of salvation. Throughout the entire world there have been saviors of this type whose difference from the average magician is only one of degree, the extent of which is determined by the formation of a special congregation around him.'

** Pronounced 'sink,' 'synch' is a colloquial term of film makers, viz. synchronization, the matching in 'film time' of the audio and video recordings of an event.

change according to how each participant plays. 'Getting off' then consists of playing together or playing off one another in a way that sets down a 'good beat.' Symbolic interaction may similarly emphasize form, rhythm and rhyme rather than simple content.

Such transcendental time consciousness is innately synchronic, for all other social time constructions (e.g. diachronic and apocalyptic) involve the invocation of particular schemes of time. Even other forms of synchronic time (e.g. natural and produced) involve operational assumptions about the order of the day and the construction of the vivid present. In creating and maintaining a simultaneity of consciousness, worldly utopian groups such as The Farm utilize a comprehensive model of systematized synchronicity: previously derived paths of synchronicity are provided readymade for the initiate. Synchronic time at The Farm is subsumed almost totally within a social simultaneity of fairly slow and even rhythm.

In the transcendental formation, a produced synchronic construction is seen as artificial; instead, the multitudinous possibilities of inner duration, of attention to life, and of rhythms of social interaction are taken on. Continued immersion in the vivid present, 'no matter what,' provides access to a shifting collective rhythm that feeds upon itself, carrying participants along, as it were, in a sea of time which occasionally brews to storm and occasionally subsides into total calm. In the transcendental formation, the enactment is not of a single collective time sense or a mosaic of individual time orientations, but of a simultaneous experience of time in which participants 'get off' on the moments and the changes.

APOCALYPTIC TIME IN COMMUNAL GROUPS

Groups which hold to a strong apocalyptic ideology of time tend to form boundaried sects. If sect members see the apocalypse as a decisive political struggle, the sect may seek to engage 'the beast' in warfare. In other groups, where the apocalypse is seen as already having transpired, the secular world comes to be regarded as beyond redemption, and the group provides an 'other-worldly' life of heaven on earth away from the hell of people's lives in the declining social order.

The change from the old order to a new one is recapitulated in the metanoia (Weber, 1968:1117), or change based on cognition, which the convert to an apocalyptic sect undergoes. Thus apocalyptic sects, whether other-worldly or warring, are composed of individuals who have wiped out their personal pasts and become 'new' people, with new names, beliefs and activities. The apocalyptic sect, whether it involves a communism of love or of war, transcends the old epoch; its members act in a new time and a new world.

Apocalyptic war with the established order

The communism of war as an elaborated socio-political philosophy has been formulated most comprehensively in the works of Karl Marx and Frederick Engels. It is there that themes of epoch and transition, order and revolution, are specified.

In the Communist Manifesto, 'the history of hitherto existing societies is the history of class struggles.' For the current epoch of bourgeois society, 'the past dominates the present; in communist society, the present dominates the past' (Marx and Engels, 1959:7,22). The forms of production and of interaction passed along and modified from generation to generation, as well as the increasing subjection of individuals to an anonymous institution of the market - these features of human societies have followed an iron law of development, in which classes have fought to gain and control the means of production and distribution of material goods. Such, in the view of Marx and Engels, has been the yoke of history. Individuals are trapped in 'self-activity' which responds to 'accidents' of the past and impersonal forces of the present (Marx and Engels, 1967:460-3). The proletariat, it is said, can free human society from history as domination; the history of free individuals can begin only when people united in a worldwide cooperation can control the production of both material goods and consciousness (Marx and Engels, 1967:429-30).

For Marx and Engels and true believers who follow their analysis or a similar one, achievement of true history requires revolution of people whose activity transcends their own predetermined lives and becomes directly engaged with events of world history (1967:428). As Lenin and Stalin saw it (quoted in Selznick, 1960:253),

> Insurrection must rely on the crucial moment in the history of the growing revolution, when the activity of the advanced ranks of the people is at its height, and when the vacillations in the ranks of the enemies and in the ranks of the weak, half-hearted and irresolute friends of the revolution are strongest.

In apocalyptic revolutionary war, the form of household life, like other mundane events, becomes secondary to struggle. All effort is devoted to overthrow of established powers and imposition of a new world order. Transcendence of the history of class struggles and the dawn of a new epoch is seen as achievable only in the resolution of a revolutionary war.

The warring sect pulls its members out of the quiescent masses to act in historical significance far out of proportion to the number of its members. The call is for a radical break with the past, a refusal to take for granted any longer the domination of an established order - (Symbionese Liberation Army, 1974:A16):

> We have all come to see and understand that only if we unite and build our new world and future, will there really be a future for our children and people.... We are of many colors, but of one mind, for we all in history's time on this earth have become part of each other in suffering and mind, and have agreed that the murder, oppression and exploitation of our children and people must end now.

How is it to be achieved - this transition to a new world? Here radical theorists part company with one another. Lenin, for example, might well have dismissed the Symbionese Liberation Army as undisciplined, opportunistic and adventuristic terrorists, just as more 'legitimate' contemporary radicals have. Yet such divisions turn on questions of centralization of authority and strategic timing of events, rather than on the issue of violence. In cases beyond evolutionary party socialism, the apocalyptic vision of a great transformation holds sway, and in each case this eschatology of time becomes translated, for purposes of practical action, into a protracted struggle between ruling interests and revolutionary insurgents. The image of the future may be blissful but, until victory is achieved, it is the time and events of historical struggle which hold significance.

The SLA, for all its failures and despite the criticisms of it by other radical groups, is an illuminating case of how terrorist action is intended to precipitate a momentarily growing war between revolutionary and established forces. Indeed, the very failures of the SLA seem to have been those of historic timing.

The participants seem to have had a sense of strategic time and coordination necessary for 'pulling a job.' As SLA survivor Bill Harris remarked in describing the kidnapping of Patricia Hearst, 'timing is important' (Harris and Harris, 1976:21). Each of the SLA's strategic forays went off without any significant deviation from their plans.

Where the SLA failed, by their own standards, was not in this moment to moment coordination of planned activity, but in the unfolding time of history. Surviving members of the SLA engaging in self-criticism argued that underground illegal action is not premature (Harris et al., 1976:36). Still, they admitted that in assassinating a black Oakland, California, school superintendent (accused proponent of a repressive program for policing public schools), the SLA subverted incipient spontaneous opposition to the program among students, parents and teachers (Harris et al., 1976:31).

In the Hearst kidnapping negotiations, the SLA was more attuned to the question of momentum. Protracted negotiations over the release of Ms Hearst provided the opportunity for gaining concessions from the Establishment. But the SLA abandoned their initial plan to demand release of two imprisoned SLA members as a condition for Patricia Hearst's release. To issue a demand that probably would not be met, they felt, would 'destroy momentum' (Harris and Harris, 1976:22). In retrospect, Emily Harris regards the SLA's kidnapping of Hearst and the subsequent free food giveaway extortion as 'a premature action - premature in the sense that they [the SLA] were unprepared to coordinate and bring together and organize the spontaneous momentum sparked by their actions' (Harris and Harris, 1976:22).

Interestingly, insensitivity to issues of momentum and historical timing are attributed to impatience: according to Emily Harris (1976:29), Cinque, the acknowledged catalyst of the group,

> was in a hurry. He felt like thirty years of his life were gone and now he was going to do it. In a way, impatience was one of the biggest problems for all of us, but Cin wouldn't even sleep - always thinking, writing, plotting.

SLA participants, because of their apocalyptic vision of time, abandoned their previous lives to act in a struggle embedded in historical time. In a eulogy after her 'comrades' were killed in the Los Angeles shootout, 'Tania,' the 'reborn' Patricia Hearst, said* of Cinque,

---

* During her trial for bank robbery after capture, Patricia Hearst claimed others had written the words she spoke in taped communiqués during her life as 'Tania.' At least in one instance, Emily Harris agrees that the writing of a communiqué for Tania to read was a collective enterprise (Harris and Harris, 1976:29). In any event, the source of 'Tania's' eulogy had to have been Emily or Bill Harris, or Hearst herself, for at the time it was made, they were the isolated survivors of the Los Angeles shootout.

'He helped me see that it's not how long you live that's important, it's how you live - what we decide to do with our lives' (Tania, 1974). The conventional normative preoccupation with extending length of life is abandoned: death loses its significance in the immortal rebirth of revolution. Yet the momentum of insurgents' actions must be maintained for the mystique of revolution to grow. Events and outcomes - both in momentary episodes and in unfolding historical time - are decisive for the group. In the case of the SLA, it is impatience and inability to channel momentum, perhaps because they did not choose the 'crucial moment,' which - by their own reckoning - accounts in large part for subsequent strategic difficulties.

While apocalyptic war against an established order draws its participants from those who have passed on from previous lives and feel they have nothing left to lose, sectarian groups of an other-worldly character provide a haven for those who seek personal salvation. The person who values his own skin or sees life and struggle against the established order as futile may retreat to a world of heavenly grace. Two contemporary groups provide examples of such post-apocalyptic other-worldly tableaus of heaven. While the nature of time in both is synchronic, that synchronism is enacted in an eternal way. The character of salvation and authority, we will find, sets the alternative experiences of eternality.

Krishna time

The era in which we live is a 'mere blink in the eye of Krishna's life.' Since Krishna is eternal, time in a sense stands still: the law of Krishna is eternally valid. The traditional doctrines of Hinduism spelled out in 'The Bhagavad Gita; As It Is' (the interpretation by A.C. Bhaktivedanta 'for our age') remain the only correct source of knowledge of the path to God. The way is always the same, and the source of knowledge and authority is the wisdom of the ages, handed down from teacher to disciple, through time. As it has always been, so the truth of Krishna will always be.

Mere mortals, who have not yet attained Krishna consciousness, are 'caught in a web of illusion.' We are said to be subjected to a transitory existence; we have no sense of the eternal nature of things, for in our unenlightened living we generate karma (literally 'action,' but more broadly, the consequences of action). We are always tied to our karma and thus eternally bound to the wheel of suffering ('samsara') and the eternal hell of cyclic reincarnation in this 'world of material illusion.' We are not yet one with Krishna; we have not gone 'back to Godhead,' and the path of salvation must involve such union as a goal.

Nothing less than a new construction of reality is required. While Krishna is eternal and unchanging, we only gradually begin to attain Krishna consciousness at the feet of the initiated. We may only attain Krishna consciousness by ceasing to generate karma. And Bhaktivedanta finds that 'for our age' two ways are most effective - devotional service to Krishna, and chanting of the Krishna mantra.

Service to Krishna (work, or 'karma' yoga) cannot generate new karma, for it is said to be holy action without personal motive, prescribed to be undertaken only at the direction of a spiritual master - one in authority of Krishna's will. Similarly, chanting (a meditational or 'dhyana' yoga) provides an occupation to the tongue and mind that is said to be totally pure in motive and execution. Engagement in these two activities, as well as adherence to other 'regulative principles' insures the devotee a gradually evolving union with Krishna and the transcendent eternal.

At New Vrindaban, the West Virginia farm of the International Society for Krishna Consciousness, Inc., over fifty devotees seek to purify themselves of past karma and attain 'Krishna consciousness.' There, it is held that time must be regulated in order to transcend past karma. The typical day at the Krishna farm begins early, at 2 or 3 a.m., with rising, toiletries and chanting. These activities are followed by an hour and a half of religious ceremonies starting at 4.30 a.m., followed by an austere breakfast accompanied by readings from sacred texts. Devotees then work for the remainder of the morning. The main meal of the day, at which lessons are provided from Krishna's life, is at 1 p.m., and it is followed by more work. At 6 p.m. the temple president gives a class on the 'Bhagavad Gita'; at 6.30, supper is held; and at 7 p.m. an hour of religious ceremonies ensues. At the end of the day, devotees have an hour or so to relax, and the lights go out at 9 p.m.

Simply stated, the devotee has no time to generate karma when totally occupied with the service of Krishna. While Krishna is eternal in nature, the individual, whose personal salvation through union with Godhead is at stake, must embark on a disciplined and progressive effort to embrace the eternal. God is eternally synchronic, while the mortal is only diachronic. It is thus through a regulation of diachronic life in the service of God that one may obtain union with the eternal at some future point. The now is only a waystation on the progressive path to union with the eternal. Some devotees come to wonder what the outcome of their devotional service will be.

Devotee: 'Will we always be getting up and doing "Arti" [a religious ceremony]?'

Temple President: 'Yes.'

D: 'This is it? This is the final thing?'

T.P.: 'You will be doing what you are doing now with a different purpose and a different consciousness. You do it now out of anxiety and later it will be out of love, and it will be a joy of the experience of Krishna consciousness. We get up now earlier than Krishna to wait for him to get up - to greet him. That is the life of the devotee: wake early, bathe, do "japa" [chanting on beads], greet Krishna.'

The devotee must engage in acts of devotion now in order to gradually attain union in the future with the already existing eternal Krishna consciousness.

Since we 'are not this body,' and the sensory lifeworld is 'illusory,' the attempt is to transcend the material world of space and time and merge with the eternal, timeless Krishna. Each devotee is to be engaged in a personal process of purifying consciousness of 'addiction and desire' so as to become Krishna-conscious. At the same time, the devotee is expected to work with others to build the Vedic community.

Activity in the present is thus crucial to both the personal and social future: if personal consciousness is properly directed, the devotee will become Krishna-conscious. If Krishna is served through devotional work according to direction of those in authority (who see the wisdom of Krishna), the community of devotees will prosper in the future.

On the material plane, devotion to Godhead, or 'bhakti' yoga, keeps the events of personal consciousness focused on Krishna's needs rather than on personal needs. The Krishna farm abounds with aesthetic projects of a religious rather than materially functional nature. The brass must be polished for the service. More long-range projects provide an unending outlet for devotional service. A temple is to be built for the upcoming festival. Bhaktivedanta, the spiritual master of the entire movement, has had a vision of 'seven temples on seven hills' at this West Virginia farm site, and a great deal of devotees' efforts are directed to completion of the first temple before the arrival of the spiritual master for the festival. Indeed, this is always the case: on two visits to New Vrindaban as well as a visit to a temple in Evanston, Illinois, I heard the straw bosses of devotional service exhort their workers with the cry, 'Prabhupada [i.e. Bhaktivedanta] is coming; Prabhupada is coming. We must have all in glorification of Krishna when the spiritual master arrives.' A devotee, hard at work on a road construction project, was asked,

J: 'Where's this road going?'

D: 'Off there somewhere - I don't really know. It's mostly for show, I think. We want to have it done before Prabhupada comes.'

Much of devotional service, then, is performed in anticipation of upcoming sacred events.

Such devotional service not only achieves the goals of group life; it also provides a basis for personal purification. But whether or not one is performing devotional service, he can always occupy his mind with Krishna.

Ideally, 'all talk and all effort is devoted to the glorification of Krishna and the spreading of Krishna consciousness.' There is to be no personal time. As is said in a call and response prayer before each meal, 'of all the senses, the tongue is the most voracious and difficult to control.' To completely occupy the tongue and mind, it is recommended that the devotee chant the Hare Krishna mantra:

Hare Krishna
Hare Krishna
Krishna Krishna
Hare Hare
Hare Rama
Hare Rama
Rama Rama
Hare Hare

The person who chants mantra will tell the uninitiated that chanting is a form of investment which yields certain returns: reward comes in union with Krishna. The new devotee is queried rhetorically: 'You should chant the mantra and try to attain Krishna consciousness. You don't want to be condemned to a life of suffering, do you?' 'It is recommended' that the sincere devotee chant sixteen rounds of mantra per day. At 108 mantras per round, this comes to 2,128 renditions of the mantra, or some 8,512 mentions of the name Krishna that a sincere devotee says in the course of a given day. The mantra is always on someone's lips; you wake up in the morning to the low but increasingly audible sound of devotees beginning their rounds of chanting for the day.

The accomplished devotee is able to chant sixteen rounds of mantra in somewhat over two hours, producing a rate of over one mantra per second! Less advanced devotees still chant at a rapid-fire rate. The subjective experience of inner duration is thus speeded up. Consumption of a diet high in sugar and starch further heightens the phenomenon. It is quite the opposite notion from that of 'stopping time' held by mystics (cf. Castaneda, 1972) and certain Buddhist sects. A devotee claims,

> 'It doesn't stop, and we should never try to stop it. We can only dance with it. That's why we have action and motion, both in the form of work devotion and in spiritual devotion.'

The experience of time is one both of an expansion through the rapid rate of duration, and of time passing rapidly. One devotee remarks, 'There is so much time every day, but the days just feel like they zip by.' Another, a 'blooper' who left the temple but continued as a devotee of Krishna, described his stay at the temple: 'It was the highest experience of my life. Everything was just flashing by, zoom, zoom. And it was bliss, absolute bliss.'

The ability to 'get off' through chanting provides transcendence of the everyday lifeworld and entry into a special world of eternally available timeless consciousness. The devotee achieves an attention to life which would seem to lie somewhere between full awakeness and dreaming. Indeed, chanting may well substitute for dreaming, as it typically is practiced most concertedly at the time of day (2.00 to 6.30 a.m.) when dreaming would otherwise occur. The constant repetition of a single mantra routinizes the stream of consciousness. All moments merge indistinguishably into the same moment, for it is the mantra, spoken so rapidly that words merge into a rush of syllabic sound sequence, that is constituted as the ongoing stream of consciousness. After sufficient chanting, the mantra becomes thematic in consciousness whether it is actively chanted or not. It _is_ the stream of consciousness, like the experience of a catchy tune in the secular mind. Devotees say the sound vibrations of repetitious chanting provide access to the 'third eye' of consciousness, 'seeing' that is innate to mind and prior to any sensory input.

> J: 'What's the attraction of chanting?'
>
> B: 'Well, once you have the pattern, it allows you to tune into places and sources that are beyond time because they transcend the concept of time. Once you've found the key and been to those places, your

> mind naturally goes to those places because that's where it is most natural and comfortable. And it gives you vision. It's almost like a backward time because you see a thing in its whole without understanding how it is that way, and then later on you may find the way the elements constitute it makes what you saw. But you saw it before you knew how it was that what you saw could be seen.'

Equally, chanting is an available way to remove the whole attention of one's consciousness from the social vivid present. Anxiety can be conquered through ritual.

> 'When I'm in a difficult or confusing situation, when people are making conflicting demands on me or something, it really helps me just to lay back into chanting. It gives me another way of tuning into things.'

Chanting is thus intended to provide the baseline referent point of consciousness.

Talking about Krishna and chanting are pervasive themes of group life. The expectation of a vivid present always immersed in Krishna consciousness is only rarely dropped. Simultaneity of consciousness is not achieved by any particular and unique sharing of moment. Instead, all moments are taken on equally as moments of Krishna consciousness. Synchronicity is thus achieved in consciousness rather than in the lifeworld; the vivid present may be free floating. Devotees engage in a bustle of activity and motion, moving in and out of episodes with each other quickly, freely and often. Simultaneity comes not in the depth of experience in any one 'flash' episode, but in the quick-tempoed experience of time brought by any devotee to any episode. It seems that synchronicity of time is not of the unique moment which fades from importance, but of similar constitutions of all moments in Krishna consciousness throughout the community.

Love Family time

While all communal groups I visited embraced apocalyptic ideas, the Love Family has developed a systematic understanding of apocalyptic time. In the form of the primitive Christian Church, authority is derived from Jesus Christ, as it is revealed to the chosen. The people of the world are regarded as in a state of sleep. But the revelation of Jesus Christ is that each of us gets a 'second chance,' an opportunity to 'awake' from the past, to be 'reborn' into a world in which all the old pains and 'all former things' have passed away. New life is begun in the living spirit of God. In their awakening to the new world, members of the Love Family cast aside all old things (excepting material ones, which are given over to a community of goods) (Church of Armageddon, 1971:31):

> Our former names of the past were fictitious. Our real names are eternal gifts from God, and are the virtues of Christ - real names written in the Book of Life. Everyone with a name is witnessed by the Church, and is a living example of that virtue, the word made manifest, to show mankind the meaning of Jesus Christ through each of us.

As people join the Love Family, they drop their old names and take on Biblical names. Once accepted as members of the church, they are assigned 'virtue' names such as Meekness, Humility, Honesty, and so on. Rebirth is signified through the adoption of new personal identity, just as in the Krishna society and the Symbionese Liberation Army.*

The new world that people are born into is an eternal one: 'He that believeth in me, though he were dead, yet shall he live; and whosoever liveth and believeth in me shall never die' (John 11:25, 26, quoted in Church of Armageddon, 1971:34). 'We are dead to our past by the cross of Jesus Christ. Henceforth, we are free of the past, freed from the world of sin and death.' Love Family members believe that they have ceased to age, for aging is derived from anxiety and confusion, and 'God is not the author of confusion.' Rather than living in a unique and constantly changing now, as people at The Farm in Tennessee see it, Love Family members idealize time as an eternal 'heaven on earth.' Love Family members act not in evolving personal careers and biographies, but in a transcendent interplay of their virtues.

Yet while the word of Jesus Christ is eternally valid, its manifestation is always created anew. While there is a 'Love Family way' of doing everything that is done, it is subject to modification according to the revelations of Love Israel. Heaven is timeless, but its different manifestations come down at different moments. There is no plateau of consciousness yet to be attained, as in Krishna doctrine. But neither is time constituted solely in the social arena, as it is at The Farm. Instead, deference to elders, those who are either older or among the 'first born,' requires submission and yielding on the part of women and the younger and less elect men. The elder sets the character of the moment, and each other participant

---

* When a member of the Love Family died, civil authorities were unable to notify the next of kin because the person's original identity was unknown. Everett (Washington) 'Herald,' Feb. 21, 1974, p.1.

contributes to the evocation set by the elder. The moment is not centered in personal consciousness, nor in the past or future, but in themes of heavenly imagery put forth by the elder.

Children present an eternal problem in this regard, for they do not always show the required deference. The elder may try to establish contact of simultaneous consciousness with the child, calling 'hello!' to him, but if the child is unresponsive, he will be taken from the room. Similarly, special pains are taken to usher visitors and novices into the timeless heaven by discouraging discussion of on-going world events. Especially when the newcomer worries about (anticipates) future events he is chided: 'I'm sure it will all be as God wills it.' More than once, animals have gone without feeding because people were 'so into the now.'

Heavenly time exists because intrusions are minimized; the elder can bring the focus of the moment to a reverent construction of life in which the playing out of virtue at all times appears to occur through some divine automation.

The individual at the Love Family thus lives in a world beyond the anxieties of secular times. The 'Love Family way' of doing things becomes known to all participants, and events of the daily routine can be performed quickly and without fanfare. The elder then becomes like the lord of a manor, for his ideas and demands will receive instant attention and a flurry of activity. The individual exists in an intersubjective world where submission to authority can mean an immediate change of attention.* A member of the Love Family must be ready for a new revelation to change any expectation that the future will be the same. It will be the same in that the elder will reveal the order of events as things go on. Each person will endeavor to manifest godliness in an eternal virtue. Thus, synchronic time will be attained not solely in personal union with God, nor solely in communion with others present, but in submission to a heavenly timeless interplay of virtues, focused on the present in large part by an elder's emerging definition of situation.

THE END OF HISTORY AND UTOPIAN TIMES

The rise of industrial capitalism as a form of production is inextricably linked with the rationalization of time.

---

* Similarly, at the Brotherhood of the Spirit in Warwick, Massachusetts, people are taught not to anticipate 'how things will be' because Michael Metelica, their leader, 'constantly changes his mind.'

In the rational structuring of work situations, in the constitution in consciousness of a disciplined and ascetic 'inner clock,' and in the social scheduling of life, diachronic time permeates the established order. Activity which is subsumed in this scheme of things loses its historical possibilities when diachrony approaches the limits of its development in abstract repetition. Whether historical possibilities have yet been exhausted comes down to a matter of belief. Certainly if ideologists subscribed to such a formulation, they would characterize it as the beginning of freedom. But people who hold utopian ideals not fulfilled in the contemporary situation may seek to transcend 'the illusion of history.'

The ways out of the dilemma, for those who choose them, involve invocation of new accounts of the times. When these accounts are constituted as communally shared life-worlds, they frame arenas in which actions beyond the realities of the established order may transpire.

In part social time in communal living groups is determined by the ecological characteristics of site and methods of want satisfaction. But people can organize themselves in a number of ways to take care of the needs of the day. Time-bound social relations may come, to some degree, under group control, and each particular way of constructing subjective, social vivid present and world time involves one or another ethic of 'what is to be done?' or 'how are we to live?'

In the diachronic worldly utopian account, ongoing society fails because of its incomplete rationality. The way out is to create a progressively more rational and efficient world time, so that each individual may have more control over the allocation of personal time.

In synchronic ethics of time, it is the rationalization of the world itself, no matter how efficient, that is seen as alienating people from one another. Time cannot be transcended through free and conscious acts so long as a world time arbitrarily partitions moments and dictates action. Under diachronic time, the natural rhythm of the running off of the moment is seen as succumbing to domination of the clock. In synchronic idealizations, the social arena gives the means by which necessary co-ordination of group life may occur. Shared moments of lived experience incorporate world time into the vivid present.

The character of synchronic time is set by the mode in which an ethic is enacted. In a natural mode of ethical enactment, ultimate commitments of both individuals and the group remain unspecified. It is therefore the case that no group agreement predefines the character of episodic time consciousness. The social vivid present is invoked through simultaneous, though not necessarily similar, experiences of events. The group has no hold over the individual, and thus the invocation of moment is ephemeral: there is no assurance that simultaneity of consciousness will occur, for people may simply pass through episodes while maintaining individuated internal time consciousnesses. But when the moment transpires as simultaneity, it is freely entered into and freely defined.

Worldly utopian synchronism, on the other hand, proposes that the sharing of a series of life episodes according to certain ethics of being in the social vivid present provides a way of 'saving the world.' In this produced mode of ethical enactment, certain norms of constituting time preclude individuated streams of consciousness, and enhance possibilities of egalitarian rapport and communion. A worldly utopia is achieved in the 'now.'

Transcendental synchronism holds to no such claims. The thematic concern is not with utopian solutions to problems of getting the work done and providing an amiable life for all. And the presumed plight of the established order is only to be avoided. Shared moments of time-transcendent ecstasy are found to contain the ineffable mysteries of existence, by comparison to which ordinary life pales in significance. People in transcendental association become committed to the synchronicity of simultaneous experience, rather than the individually chosen moments of natural synchronism. But unlike the worldly utopian constitution, rhythm and tension of consciousnesses are not prescribed. Instead, the experience of time is carried in the running off of sociation.

Synchronists all live in worlds of the vivid present, in large part disconnected from the push of world events beyond the door. For apocalyptic groups, on the other hand, the era is marked by an historic struggle - between the forces of good and the forces of evil, between the forces of revolution and those of reaction, between the people of light and the people of darkness, between the quick and the dead.

In revolutionary war, the synchronous moment serves as the apocalyptic focus of events in world time. Instead of a continuous running off of synchronic time, the succession of moments holds more of a field and ground relation. Certain events, both within the vivid present and on the part of allies and adversaries beyond, come to be considered decisive, while other, more mundane events form an inconsequential relief. Some broad definition of reality is seen as up for grabs, and the events of daily life hold significance only in so far as people act in the time of world-historical struggle.

But if the struggle itself is regarded as the essence of an evil world, the children of light may engage in an other-worldly sectarian life. An eternal heaven is provided by submission to the authority of God, however construed. Eternity of time is achieved in the sacred, either as a personally held consciousness or as a social enactment of grace. The synchronous moment is constituted not in its unique attributes, but as an aspect of eternity, of 'God's way, now and forever more.'

The constructions of time in communal groups thus provide frames in which social life may be enacted beyond the bounds of the established order. The personal experience of time grounds the individual in a world. Yet other components of utopian ethics are enacted in the cognitive frame of time. Under such ethics, attention is focused on one or another concern, possibility, or way of defining a situation. It is to such constitutions of time-bounded attention that I now turn.

4 The social enactment of communal life

If you would slay the Social Snake,
That brings the bosom grief and ache,
Dance while you may, dance while you may,
For heaven comes forth in social play.

Song of Fountain Grove, a nineteenth-century American community

We all gear into the world in part on the basis of tempo and rhythm, memory and anticipation, and our degree of attention to life. Entry into any social world - before one even begins to know 'what is going on' - requires a shift to the rhythms of group life, for events of the vivid present are shared only if they occur simultaneously in multiple streams of consciousness. It is in this sense that the social constitution of time is primary. An account of communal life solely in terms of time, however, would be incomplete. Communal participants subjectively experience time as an unfolding succession of events and collectively organize their activities through shared constructions of social time. But they enact the events of life in the vivid present through various ways of focusing attention and invoking meaning.

In the present chapter I examine enactments of communal life. On the basis of typological distinctions derived from the social phenomenology of Alfred Schutz, I suggest that participants in communal groups cognize reality, focus attention, and interpret selected phenomena in ways that comprise alternative meaningful communal worlds.

ATTENTION, MEANING AND THE ENACTMENT OF COMMUNAL LIFE

In the course of daily life, people continually choose to attend to particular phenomena; we draw upon schemes of interpretation for the events of perception and act in terms of both those interpretations and various motives. Though the spatio-temporal world 'out there' is manifold, we select certain phenomena as relevant to our interests and deal with them. Other immediately available experiences are excluded and passed over. People's perceptions become the bases for schemes of interpretation, while in the course of focusing attention, people take action and put the world through changes.

In Schutz and Luckmann's (1973:3-8) terminology, each individual exists in a 'lifeworld' that consists of both social others and material objects in spatial arrangement. This reality is 'primary,' if for no other reason, because it grounds possibilities of birth, death, biological existence, and movement through space. While the lifeworld is a given for everyone, each person places on it, at any given moment, an 'accent of reality.' The accent may be shifted from the primary reality of the immediate lifeworld to other provinces of reality which have 'finite meaning structures.' Such other provinces of reality include the world of science, of supernatural religious experience, of cooking, music, fantasy, dreams and so forth. In the course of everyday experience, a person shifts the accent of reality from the primary one of the lifeworld to various finite provinces as a matter of course. A person may attend to the province of cooking and become concerned with elements of the spatio-temporal world which have special uses in that province; but once food has been prepared, the accent of reality is shifted away from the special finite province of meaning. Later, in dinner conversation, the person may be carried to fantasy, to a discussion of economic matters, and so forth. The lifeworld is a spatio-temporal given of existence, but an individual operates within it through a 'cognitive style' (Schutz and Luckmann, 1973:25-8) involving a way of perceiving the elements of lifeworld and ways of shifting accent from the primary lifeworld reality to finite provinces of meaning, according to relevance and interest. In all of this, the individual takes the validity of the cognitive style for granted so long as disturbances do not intrude on the assumption that the events of experience are 'capable of explication' (Schutz and Luckmann, 1973:22).

For all of us except hermits, the lifeworld contains other persons; it is, in part, a social world. The social world may be experienced through multiple cognitive styles and from multiple viewpoints. Though people are free to select ad hoc ordering schemes, we tend, through accumulation of lived experience, to routinize and reinvoke the cognitive styles which somehow work, i.e.

achieve our intents. In any given situation, certain 'topical relevances' come to be 'thematic' in consciousness, and other relevances - motivational and interpretational - are brought into play in thematic resolution (Schutz, 1970). In social situations, themes of attention, relevances and cognitive styles may be intersubjectively invoked and negotiated. When individuals interact with each other, we may do so with more or less agreement in defining a situation.

Given a dominant mode of time consciousness, the constitution of the social world becomes an issue of how individuals, alone and collectively, focus attention and invoke meaning. People may, for example, deal solely in the vivid present, invoking finite provinces of meaning only as they become relevant to the conduct of immediate material and social affairs. With equal facility, people may downgrade the importance of immediate and 'mundane' concerns in favor of realms of meaning which are spatially and temporally beyond the vivid present.

At the conclusion of Chapter 1, I briefly described three alternative modes of enacting social life - natural, produced and transcendental. In the natural orientation, which reflects Schutz's 'natural attitude,' the world as experienced is taken to be real. Perceptions and symbolic constructions are taken on their face value, or argument may ensue as to the validity of one scheme of interpretation or another. But in any case, 'doubt concerning the outer world and its Objects is suspended. The possibility that the world could be otherwise than it appears to me in everyday experience is bracketed' (held in abeyance or set aside) (Schutz and Luckmann, 1973:36). Furthermore, though people may come to see things in the 'same' way, they do not develop and tout an explicit creed, ideology or unified scheme of interpretation as the ultimate referent of social action. Nor do they restrict themes of collective consciousness to certain prescribed provinces of meaning. Instead, various possible provinces of meaning remain in play, and no one province is taken to be the encompassing reality.

It is exactly the opposite with the produced enactment of social life. The world is not simply that which is freely experienced. Indeed, appearances may deceive; certainly they cannot be trusted as the guides to ways of biographical career and social life. Instead, a specialized construction of the meaningful world provides the relevance scheme through which experience is to be understood and action undertaken. The individual, taking on such a scheme of relevance, lives in the world in a particular cognitive style which is in part collectively socialized and legitimated. The world works because people take on cognitive styles which make it real for one another. Certain world elements come to be seen as important, while others warrant no attention at all. Some finite provinces of meaning may be excluded out of hand, while others provide a basis, maybe the only legitimated basis, for dealing with the experience of everyday life. What comprises the social world, then, is produced according to an epiphenomenal construction of how the world should be. It is this set of 'utopian' idealizations which are invoked to resolve whatever issues may become problematic.

The transcendental orientation rejects both of these approaches to the enactment of social life. On the one hand, the natural attitude is bracketed (Husserl, 1931: s.31) in the phenomenological sense: belief in the outer given character of everyday experience is suspended. It is held that all experiences are the mediated product of consciousness. But the world of everyday experience is not suspended in favor of a utopian finite province of meaning, for utopian ideational accounts are taken as intentional acts of consciousness which delimit phenomenological possibilities. To replace the everyday world with a predefined one would perpetrate a selective bracketing. In the natural attitude, the world is as one sees it because one looks at it that way. The produced stance can be taken - from the transcendental viewpoint - to be a more restricted way of seeing things, even less susceptible to experiential jolts than the natural orientation. In the transcendental constitutive process, the attempt is to get beyond a way of experiencing the world as meaningful to a totally unmediated being in the world.

These alternative possibilities are, of course, ideal types, and in no given group is life constituted solely in one mode. But since the orientations are broadly mutually exclusive, groups tend toward one orientation or another. Enactment of social life, in the context of a way of construing time, provides in each case a particular kind of situated sociology of knowledge. Each ideal-typical configuration of time and social enactment finds its expression in particular patterns of social relations and social concerns. How situation is defined, what is seen as relevant and what is treated as problematic, and what meanings may be invoked in the conduct of social affairs - in short, the cognitive character of the social world - hinges on one or another particular approach toward social enactment.

THE NATURAL COMMUNAL WORLD

In the natural attitude in communal groups, the theme of the momentary now leads where people take it, without boundaries or limitations except those which people come to agree on. The thread of conversation may move from the immediate concerns of everyday life and personal and collective problems to other provinces of reality, such as politics, science and more arcane topics of personal biography, drug experiences and the like. Fantasy and dream worlds may similarly be invoked. Though the primary reality of the lifeworld is taken as ground zero, virtually no limits are placed on the transition from that world to other provinces of meaning.

Indeed, the natural enactment of communal life rests on the absence of an ideological grounding of action. At 'URON,' the political initiators of the commune quickly found themselves surrounded by less politically motivated people. The anarchist myth of ad hoc revolutionary action came to be tempered by less political accounts.

Bank teller: '"U.R.O.N.?" What's that stand for?'
D: '"Union of Revolutionaries of the Now."'
B: 'Oh?! Well, what's your revolution?'
D: 'We live together.'

Demands of various of the group's initiators for a 'higher level of consciousness about the political implications of our actions' meet, on occasion, with outright opposition. Without a highly developed ideology, interpretation of action in terms of political values remains ambiguous, for everyone can hold a personal view of the nature of the revolution. By the same token, attempts at 'URON' (for example, by devotees of Krishna) to impose a unified religious gestalt have similarly failed. Anarchy and pluralism permit the coexistence of different ideals; the right to maintain individual viewpoints undermines efforts at ideological unification. There is no one 'way,' but people constitute group life anyway. Such a formation may thus come to be invoked at one moment as an arrangement of cooperative living, and at another, as a family, tribe, band of anarchists, and so on. It is an 'open' scene, conducive to the whimsy of drunken folly, role playing, initiative and charisma.

Any episode may totally violate the assumptions of a particular individual. The definition of the situation is in flux, as participants take what they see to be real, and invoke it as such. In private arenas, the definition of situation is less likely to become problematic, as participants typically associate intimately according to their personal affinities. But in public arenas, the touching upon a source of disagreement can quickly bring opposing viewpoints to the fore.

The irresolvability of conflict among people who hold fundamentally different tenets about the nature of the world may lead to the downplaying of themes which sound a call to intragroup conflict. Two norms of interaction come to support this development. First, it can be held, as it is in a number of groups, that 'no one can lay a mind trip on you.' Interaction then comes to focus on disagreement only when it is unavoidable. Themes of disagreement are relegated to the 'backburner' because they are seen as irresolvable: 'There's no way we can settle that tonight, so let's not talk about it.' Secondly, those who see the general course of interaction as unsatisfactory may raise objections, not in terms of specific topics but in terms of forms of sociability. At one group, a woman complained that 'all the men do at dinner is sit around and rap politics.' The attempt was to change the general definition of situation to one which held a more widespread interest.

These two norms involve, respectively, the withholding of interaction unsympathetic to another's view of the world, and the raising of topics which hold broad interest among participants. At issue in these norms is the manner in which face-to-face sociation occurs. What topics are of concern? What interpretations and motivations may be treated as relevant to those thematic concerns? And what shifts may be made to various finite provinces of meaning? The first norm is one of restricted communication; certain interpretations of events may come to be ruled out of bounds. Similarly, the second norm restricts the invocation of particular themes and finite provinces of meaning to situations where all participants maintain an interest. These norms provide for subtle structuring of social interaction. While there are, in theory, 'no holds barred,' toleration of differences in personal matters becomes prevalent (visitor to 'URON'):

> 'What you have here is reverence, a respect of each other's vision of the world and way of living in it, like the Indians had a reverence for the land. Some communes are based on love and some are based on reverence. Like Hindus have love for everything and everybody, but no reverence, 'cause it's all sacred but it does not matter. It's not easy to have reverence these days; other communes I go to, they're always pushing me, gently mind you, to take up their beliefs, whatever they are.'

It is not necessarily a question of 'walking on pins and needles,' but each person comes to engage in social interaction with an awareness of others' interests and viewpoints.

The social cognizable field begins as an open and broad one, if for no other reason, because of the diversity of viewpoints that are brought to it. In the course of social interaction, various topics are invoked as thematic by participants. These topics may be of all forms. They may treat the sphere of material events, biography (what happened), social relations, projects, fantasy (jokes, stories, possible situations), dreams, and so on. But while the possibilities are diverse, each presentation is a unique one, a promotion of a particular topical relevance into the social arena. Similarly, the responses may be of various orders. A respondent may give support, add information, disagree, bring in other interpretations, shift the thematic concern, question the whole basis of interaction, and so on. Communication about style of interaction brings to collective consciousness the awareness of a social situation's form, and may serve as the basis for modification in future episodes (members of 'URON'):

S: (after argument) 'Sometimes there's just no communication. You won't let it happen; you won't let the ideas come out. All you want to do is argue that your way is right.'

B: 'I disagree.'

S: 'That's exactly what I'm talking about.'

In the course of such interaction, participants learn (or fail to learn) to develop a collective cognitive style: problems of relevance are negotiated to the point of agreement or mutual understanding. If pluralism becomes a workable reality, the system of relevances which emerges will be quite different from other systems in which leaders or institutions define its boundaries (cf. Ogilvy and Ogilvy, 1972). As the problematic character of relevance is negotiated, members cease attempting to convince one another of the 'right way,' and begin working things out whenever they can come to agreement or operate with understanding of others' actions and beliefs. In this ongoing process of collectivizing the sense of the social, one person may provide an account of where another 'is at' or 'coming from.' Positions of individuals in the social web become further and further articulated, and come to serve as components of others' 'stocks of knowledge' at hand (Schutz, 1970) (member of 'URON'):

'I think we have come a long way in understanding where each other's at. It used to be when two people were arguing, it was just one person against the other, and there was no way to settle it. Now, since we've spent a lot more time with each other, we can tell what [part] of what people are saying is really going on and what part is just some private personality thing.'

People may come to identify one another's articulated and recurrent accounts and interpretations as 'raps.' 'Some raps just won't go down,' while others go unchallenged (visitor and members of 'URON'):

R: 'I called bullshit on him when he said that, and he agreed [that it was bullshit].'

Visitor: 'Called bullshit?! Jeez, this place is weird. I'm seeing it in a whole new light today.'

M: 'You know, we're social anarchists at Grand Central Station. They [i.e. people at other communes] might worry about whether the trains are on schedule. We just want to make sure everyone gets his connection.'

V: 'I wish I'd known that, man. 'Cause I'm seeing this place a lot different.'

R: 'You really thought we were organized or something. Had elders. We work it out.'

In part it is a question of who to 'lay a rap on' (visitor to 'URON'):

'What I like about this place is you can always find someone who agrees with you, no matter what you're thinking on a given day. If you feel like an anarchist, you talk to one person; if you want to talk about something spiritual, you talk with somebody else.'

Ongoing interaction thus provides a negotiated boundary system of relevance - not the same for all individuals, instead taking into account individual biographies and presentations of self. When issues of relevance are not taken to be problematic, the ongoing scene is one of sociability or 'hanging out.' Then, topical relevances come to be invoked in several ways. They may come to the fore in accounts of previous activities up to the current episode: the 'news' includes information about what happened to people, what current collective problems must be dealt with, what problems have been resolved, projected future events, and so on. Each of these kinds of accounts meets with other viewpoints until it is dealt with or dropped in the ongoing stream of interaction. From the same grounding of sociability, projects of an immediate nature - cooking, gardening, and so on - may be initiated. The accent of reality shifts from sociability to the project, and relevances related to the project become primary, while other potential topics are left to the available time when 'first things first' have been taken care of.

In natural enactments of communal life, the invocation of relevance shifts according to who is present, what outside concerns and interests come up, and what immediate business needs to be taken care of. Topics and interpretations are negotiated 'on line' in the vivid present. While the drift at 'URON' is toward an imagery of social anarchy, the natural enactment of communal life may give rise to a variety of other accents on reality (for example, to social forms such as communal charisma, matriarchy or patriarchy, or to aesthetics of emotionality or rationality). Whatever forms emerge, however, their existence is legitimated not by any utopian scheme, but by the ongoing conferral of attention by participants to the shifting themes of interaction.

PRODUCED COMMUNAL WORLDS

In some communal groups, particular accounts of the way things are or should be become unifying schemes for directing attention and interpreting events. The way of daily life and the concerns of that life are lived in terms of a produced utopian scheme. The scheme itself is beyond disproof, but it is feasible at the minimum only if people who believe in it live in terms of it. Such is the self-fulfilling nature of utopian prophecy.*

Several general produced configurations may obtain. In the apocalyptic construction of time, the unusual character of the era requires an extraordinary social life. Whether the mission is to save the world from the domination of evil or to withdraw to post-apocalyptic heaven far from the hell of civilization in decay, the pervasive need is for a boundaried sect which can maintain an esoteric construction of the world. Diachronic and synchronic groups, on the other hand, are what I have termed 'worldly utopian.' In these groups, the desire is not to struggle for control of the larger social order so as to implement change, nor to retreat from an intolerable world historical situation into a heavenly sanctuary. Instead, the worldly utopians live out a model of an ideal world. The

* In spite of legitimation through belief, a group may fail because participants cannot organize for provision of needs under the scheme, or because prophecy is undermined by the course of events. Kanter (1972) has described 'commitment mechanisms' which enhance success. Festinger et al. (1964) deal with the case of discounted belief. Lofland (1966) treats the prolongation of hope.

mission is to show that the world can be 'saved' if it comes to be organized according to the utopian scheme.

The diachronic worldly utopia

Twin Oaks is the most successful contemporary case of a diachronic worldly utopia. In Chapter 3 we saw how the diachronic character of time at Twin Oaks establishes an objective world structure in which moments are interchangeable. Production of daily needs is achieved through a diachronically scheduled bringing together of material and labor resource inputs. The rest of the diachronic utopian world is similarly systematized. Just as the scheme of clock time treats each productive moment as a case to which more general planning and operations conditions apply, so social life and culture of the group is routinized through the evolution of a set of universally applicable policies, procedures, norms and folkways. Since each moment is 'the same,' the rules and principles which apply must be 'the same.' The world is objectified: though any identifiable norm or policy can be modified, the 'system' attains a life of its own as an independent body of norms and procedures, separate from the subjective constructions of individuals.

The calculus of Twin Oaks's system rests on a means-end construction of the world. The system exists to provide for the needs of the group and insure its continued viability. Policies and procedures which increase productive efficiency or are felt to facilitate personal happiness and more amiable relations are valued; those which have negative or unintended consequences are identified and discarded. The assumption, fundamental to the behavioralist psychology viewpoint, is that individuals operate within a system of rewards and punishments to maximize personal satisfaction. It is thus felt that the system must be consistent in its policies and their applications, so that 'people will know what is expected of them.' And since humanitarian ideals are also valued, the system is to emphasize rewards rather than punishment. The system must then be designed so that the expected pursuit of personal gain maximizes communal goals as well. All action comes to be analyzed in terms of its benefits to the community, its sensitivity to individual rights, and its implications for other broadly established humanitarian norms.

The 'system' is designed to be fair to everyone, to operate uniformly over time in the same universalistic and egalitarian fashion towards all. For example, food is prepared for both vegetarians and meat eaters, and two types of snack food are available - less expensive free food and more expensive snacks which must be paid for out of allowance. In social relations, each individual is in principle equal in rights and stature to every other person, regardless of age, sex or race. Each person has an equal obligation to the labor credit system. Work is allocated according to a system for maximizing personal preferences. Each person has the right to a prescribed amount of personal property; and each person is entitled to equal benefits of vacations, sick leave (certified by the health manager), and so on. Equality is developed as a resolving principle in problematic areas relating to distribution of resources and privileges.

The principle of equality is justified on a rational basis: when people have equal rights and equal responsibilities as well as equal access to communal resources, they have no rational grounds for competing against one another or for feeling unfair treatment. Similarly, uncontrolled interpersonal conflict is seen as unproductive. Rational administration suggests the inculcation of norms limiting the arenas and scope of its expression. The behavioral emphasis at Twin Oaks, however, provides a special modus operandi for handling conflict. Personal beliefs, attitudes and feelings are unimportant so long as behavior remains within normative boundaries. The individual must submit, equally with others, to the rational requirements of the 'system.' The social norm of courtesy and respect for the privacy of others permits freedom of individual consciousness. But this freedom cannot be the basis for action alien to the prevailing norms.

The sanctity of the personal viewpoint is further enhanced by norms against gossip and public complaint. The everyday public arena is to be one of good conduct, if not heartfelt sociability. Violation of public norms may quickly lead to their invocation: 'If you start gossiping with someone, they can say, "You're making me feel uncomfortable," and the behaviour stops.' Behaviorally, no real distinction can be made between gossip and threats to personal worldview. The objectification of the public arena serves to suspend the validity of the presentation of subjectively held views, yet it protects their private existence. But on occasion, with interpersonal agreement, the norm may be transgressed.

B: 'I don't want to gossip, but it's really driving me up the wall.'

K: 'Yeah, I don't really feel you're gossiping. You're just really caught up in a mess with him, and you gotta talk it out with someone.'

Instead of focusing on 'negative' things, people at Twin Oaks feel it important to 'accent the positive.' Open expression of affection is encouraged, as is positive reinforcement for valued actions. Talk of discouragement, on the other hand, is met with gentle chiding and more upbeat interpretations of events.

Still, my lingering impression is of suppressed feelings of mistrust and disagreement. A duality is posed between the public accounts of situation and 'backroom' personal and factional accounts. These latter accounts become aired only privately or in institutionalized arenas: in encounter groups composed of people who find behaviorism as lacking in sufficient interpersonal sensitivity, and at 'feedback' meetings held expressly for the purpose of airing feelings without making decisions based on the discussion. When undercurrents of disagreement reach a breaking point, any person may call a feedback meeting to air grievances: 'We can come together in feedback, and at least see where each other's at, and go on from there.'

Enactment of life at Twin Oaks thus involves the sanctioning of cognitions as to their situational acceptability. In the everyday world, the individual is not to act in terms of certain provinces of meaning. Problematic topics, including interpersonal conflict and decisions concerning the operation of system policies and norms, are to be relegated to special arenas for their resolution. Other topics, those of the processes of work, are routinized according to prescriptive definitions of situation. The cognitive field that remains includes orientations of everyday action in the system and various forms of sociability. Such action and sociability transpire within previously evolved norms. So long as people operate in terms of them, the immediate tableau is one of 'good vibes.'

Just as the diachronic nature of time permits a routinization of the material world and work processes, so the time partitioning of behavior by arenas permits the resolution of problematics outside the episodes in which they occur. Individuals may hold private viewpoints while presenting normative selves in public arenas; if this requirement is met, individuals carry no personal responsibility for a given problematic state of affairs. Rather, the 'system' is to be changed to resolve the problem. An institutionalized set of 'backroom' arenas provides the situations in which participants can try to resolve such problems in the course of open and courteous discussion. The symbolic world at Twin Oaks is thus constructed in terms of a set of normalized topics, motivations and interpretations. When this system of norms and policies is found to be inadequate through the occurrence of a problematic situation, discussions in another institutionalized arena are used to create a new set of system operating conditions. Decisions on norms, policies and procedures made in the past are drawn upon in the interpretation of current problematic situations. And any resolution of a current problem sets a precedent for the future. The world is enacted on the basis of forms of public attention, interpretation and action which have been developed in the past. The diachronic worldly utopia, in having an established objective world time, engages in history through precedent.

The synchronic worldly utopia

At The Farm in Tennessee, in the absence of a diachronic world time and rationalized scheme of interpretation, it is in the immediate interplay of people in the here-and-now that all kinds of issues come to the fore and are resolved. The resolution of topical relevances occurs, not according to organizational policies of 'how things are done,' but according to 'agreements' and 'truth' which come to play in the vivid present. Collective life is entered into through use of a special shared language and special shared meanings. People at The Farm, following the teachings of Stephen Gaskin, maintain that 'we are all one':

> 'Some people say it's all one, but they don't really carry it to its conclusion: if it's all one, then there's no reason to disagree or argue; you would never want to hurt anyone; and it doesn't matter that another person works more or less. The only thing that makes any sense is to "do unto others as you would have them do unto you."'

The ideal of oneness is not achieved automatically; it is derived through a constant allusion to 'agreement' by Farm members. And this state becomes possible only when people are 'plugged in' to one another, i.e. when they intersubjectively constitute objects of attention. The first order of business, the overriding relevance, is to assure that everyone in an episodic 'group head' (i.e. intersubjectively attuned group) is 'plugged in' to the situation. To a large degree, the world of cognition must be the world of the vivid present of social others. When people feel this not to be the case, they are quick to let others know it.

B: 'You're just letting off side comments. You're not

really plugged in to what I'm saying.'

F: 'Yeah, I cop to it; I've been working hard all day.'

B: 'Yeah, but you can't cop to it on that.'

F: 'Farout, you're right: if I can dig ditches all day, there's no reason I can't stay plugged in with you.'

The primary grounding of personal cognition is thus one of shared simultaneity of consciousness. The moment must be shared by all participants in order to be real.

In the state of social simultaneity, a special language 'allows us to communicate telepathic.' The language of The Farm provides a shorthand description of collectively grasped situations, themes and relevances. To know the language is to live the world, for the words recapitulate the relevant social relations, streamline communication, and leave episodic space for non-verbal communication. A person 'plugs in' to a 'group head' and later 'cuts loose' from it (i.e. leaves). While plugged in, group head participants 'get straight' with each other and 'sort out' whatever is problematic on the 'material plane.'

Stephen Gaskin tells outside audiences that there is 'no cover' at The Farm. People devote a great deal of attention to 'getting straight,' for it is felt that acting from subconscious motive involves determinism, while acting from conscious and collectively understood motive involves free will. The holding of repressed feelings in the vivid present involves the maintenance of a 'backroom' of personal rather than collective consciousness. Such a backroom orientation is felt to permit the person to maintain an abstract cognitive map of self and world, instead of acting in terms of what is happening at the moment. The needs of the moment are thus seen as sabotaged by personal image projection which serves some sort of self-aggrandizement.

The attempt is to eliminate the subconscious, or unshared viewpoint, by bringing one's true state of mind to the fore of intersubjective consciousness in vivid present social situations. Stephen Gaskin has explained that, for example, the Grateful Dead, a contemporary rock and roll band, were a 'truth-telling tribe' for a while, and did not have any subconscious left. But they are said to have slipped from that path and allowed the subconscious (i.e. unexpressed personal viewpoints) to build up again to the point where people were no longer 'straight' with each other.

Getting straight involves eliminating whatever sources of tension, ambiguity or disagreement are felt in the vivid present. This enterprise requires, most generally, 'copping to' (recognizing or submitting to) 'the Farm Agreement.' When individuals are seen as beyond the bounds of that agreement, others will 'blow the whistle on their trip.' At one meeting of the farming 'group head,' after the business of coordinating the day's work on the 'material plane' had been transacted, people turned to a discussion of the isolation of two members.

D: 'We've been getting it on, really.'
E: 'Then why does everyone here see it differently?'
B: 'Yeah, I see you two getting kinda funky and isolated.'
S: 'We're trying to help you, but we can't if we don't have contact, and we don't, 'cause you and Keith have this isolated trip going.'
H: 'You know, while these other folks are gone to Nashville, you two could stay in our tent.'
K: 'Really, we can work it out.'
H: 'You haven't been working it out. David hasn't been to the last three farm meetings.'
D: 'I cop to that but I really believe you all are being too conservative in not letting Keith and me work it out.'
S: 'We just want to make sure you two have good tripping instructions before you do that stuff.'
D: 'But we are working it out; it just takes time.'
F: 'You could work it out faster and better if you got some tripping instructions.'
W: 'Yeah, I feel like there's a lot of ego agreement between you two that keeps you from working stuff out and getting clear.'
K: 'I have to cop to that, it's true. But I still feel like you all should have more faith in us instead of being so conservative.'
E: 'So are you going to cop?'
D: 'Cop to what?'
E: 'You know I ain't gonna tell you; asking me about what to cop is one of the things right there.' (silence)
F: 'You're gonna get the same stuff pointed out to you if you don't cop, so it's up to you.'
H: 'Anyway, you can still come live in our tent.'
E: 'Yeah, why don't you do that. Maybe you all can sort it out there.'

In this discussion, D and K have been called upon to account for 'where they're at.' D claims that their conduct has been in good faith, while E, B, S and H question this account and propose a change in households as a way of reducing isolation. D admits that there have been problems, but suggests that the others should not be 'conservative' (strict). He believes, he says, that others should in good faith allow himself and K a chance to work it out on their own. S does not deny the idea that people should be allowed to work out their own problems, but he, as well as F and W point to what they consider to be extenuating circumstances: it is suggested that D and K lack 'tripping instructions' - inwardly held codes of conduct; further, W points to existence of an 'ego agreement' - that the two individuals will mutually ignore certain aspects of the other's conduct. K admits the truth of that point but asks for trust. The others remain unsatisfied and ask D and K to change households so that they and others can deal with the issues at greater length.

Not all the 'head work' that goes on involves 'copping.' Getting straight may take the opposite course, of encouragement for actions.

M: 'Michael has been acting a little weird about that work he's been doing.'

D: 'I think he doesn't think it's very important to The Farm or something.'

L: 'We ought to do some work on him about that, because he's really saying he feels worthless, and that's the same rap he came here with.'

D: 'Farout.'

M: 'Maybe we could catch him tomorrow at lunch.'

L: 'Farout!' (they return to their respective jobs)

The intervention of third parties occurs when people regard others as unable to 'work it out' themselves. More typically, people get straight with each other in the course of daily interaction.

R: 'You've been avoiding my eyes, Jack.'

J: 'Yeah, I feel like you're beaming some kind of judgment on me.'

R: 'Yeah, I feel you don't have your thing straight with me.'

J: 'I guess I haven't told you I felt like you were hanging judgments on me.'

S: 'Yaa! A self-pumping, two-person movie!'

In this case, S has pointed to the self-perpetuating nature of the opposing personal viewpoints.

Fundamental to the process of 'getting straight' is the role of witnessing. When interpersonal relations become thematic, third parties often listen to the interaction and add their perspectives when they feel them to be relevant. No objective structure is invoked as prescribing the truth of the matter; instead, a subjective collectivism obtains. But it is also recognized that the group head and witnessing are not infallible: just as an individual can hold to an ego trip, or two people be involved in a folie à deux, so people in a group head can come to see things in a 'weird' way.

The farming crew, for example, at one point became excessively zealous in achieving its mission of getting the spring crops planted. Some members wanted to work night and day, not seeing their families until the job was done. It took the influence of another group head, the motor pool crew, to talk them out of it.

> 'So it's just like with monkeys; when you have a group head in agreement, it can still be out of line and take another group head to get it to straighten up.'

People at The Farm also maintain that the activity of 'getting straight' itself can come to excessively dominate situations. One member quotes Stephen Gaskin, as people there often do: 'You gotta start by copping to the big one, copping to the universe being there and as it should be.' The world is not taken to be a complex array of problematic conditions that have to be straightened out. In the course of 'getting straight,' the process itself may therefore become thematic.

> S: 'You guys are so into clearing out the vibes that you aren't being home folks with each other.'
>
> J: 'Yeah, I cop to that; it's like we are pumping out the trips, and not laying back enough. Not enough just plain hanging out.'
>
> P: 'Yeah, it's too conservative. It's like we're trying to work it all out on the verbal plane when we know that's not the first cause. We should spend more time just feeling the vibes.'

Although people at The Farm recognize a need to 'let it be' rather than 'picking it apart all the time,' they also generally embrace the idea that each individual must be responsive to others' viewpoints.

> 'Sometimes people get down on my case, 'cause I flip out on speed trips and flip into my own head. But it's cool for other monkeys to straighten you out, 'cause we're all just sitting on the rock, and there's no other way we're gonna get straight.'

The idea of getting straight is to reach a collective point in which no subconsciously held viewpoints interfere with the simultaneity of consciousness. The subconscious is seen as a barrier to the communion of the moment.

What would seem most remarkable is that over eight hundred people living in a community could feel the common need for the communion, and be able to work together in the same universe of discourse to achieve it. But the source of commonly held language and collectively replicated folkways is not hard to find. Almost every night while I was at The Farm large numbers of people gathered at one activity or another - shelling peanuts for seed, a potluck dinner, or just listening to music of the Farm Band. At these gatherings, tapes of Stephen 'on the road' spreading the word in some city or at some college campus were played; it is here, as well as in everyday interaction, that people learn what Stephen has to say on a variety of subjects. Everyone on The Farm 'cops to' Stephen as a teacher. Stephen, says one Farm person, 'has to be very careful about what he says and does, because a lot of people in the world are likely to do the same thing.' The teacher provides recipes for being in the world; he is not taken to be infallible, but only as a person who has thought out a lot of what is taken to be important. Stephen says, for example,

> 'People go off and do some really bad trip, and then want to be forgiven for it. But it doesn't work like that. When you've sinned against the holy ghost [i.e. the community of believers], it doesn't help to be forgiven, 'cause the bad karma is still hanging around, 'cause you've vibrated negative energy against open hearts, so you gotta fix it; you gotta make it right.'

It is through adherence to such ways of being, which explain good conduct in a community, that people at The Farm live their collective life.

Farm life consists of a processional synchronicity. The individual passes daily through a series of episodes with others in which both the business of the 'material plane' and social relations are 'sorted out.' In this process, 'getting straight' with each other is the highest priority. For it is felt that 'if the spiritual plane is together, the material plane will get taken care of.' Any hint that the 'vibes' are not 'clear' provides grounds for stepping back from the episode and 'getting straight.' So long as the vibes do not come to be invoked as problematic, the interactional stream of the present may be filled with the problems of material coordination. And where material coordination is not a concern, or where interludes in work provide an opening, people engage in a particular Farm sociability of the 'here-and-now.'

In this sociability, people talk about the events of their daily lives, recent and upcoming events at The Farm (for this is the opportunity for such information transmittal), life histories, views of the outside, and spiritual ideas. Fantasy, dreams, and grapevine accounts are ruled out. Since the community has so many people, just getting to know one another can be a full-time pastime. There are always visitors who come to The Farm to learn about Stephen's teachings, or perhaps to join; and a great deal of 'sorting out' is directed to them. Household arrangements are always changing, as people form new household group heads 'like an amoeba dividing,' says one member. Finally, courtship exists as a social category, along with marriage. The pattern is a traditional one involving a hierarchical set of statuses of association from 'seeing each other' through 'dating' and 'going steady' to marriage. Household 'group heads' may include, however, more than one married couple, as well as unmarried men and unmarried women. Such a household parallels the now all-but-eclipsed extended family unit.

Social enactment of life at The Farm is held to a very specific accent of reality. The material world is a secondary, though carefully attended, part of this world. But the consociation of people, of the others in the vivid present, is primary. It is through the interaction with others that topical relevances are interpreted according to a simultaneous (witnessed) construction of meaning. The possible shifts of the reality accent are limited: beyond its bounds lie such finite provinces of meaning as science, mysticism, fantasy, delusion, privately held constructions, and dream worlds.

The primacy of collective experience in these practices thus eliminates the private constitution of the nature of the social world. 'There's no cover at The Farm,' and through the collective experiencing of all that is sensed by individuals, the sense becomes a collective one. No individual can hold back from the collectivity without being called to task for it. Once individuals have submitted to the social present, they need no longer experience what Schutz and Luckmann (1973:24) have called the 'shock' of shifting the accent of reality - first, because the realms to which the accent can shift are limited, and second, because the shock of moving from the realm of pure sociation to work or discussion of business is 'cushioned' by the collective experiencing of it. An individual rarely takes on the shock of coming into a new situation alone. Instead, individuals, as participants in group heads, go through the 'changes' together, especially until old-timers are satisfied that others are operating with 'good tripping instructions.' The utopian synchronicity of The Farm provides a way of dealing with the cognitive field of social relations and work in a collective experience.

Other-worldly utopias

In the post-apocalyptic construction, the world of society-at-large is seen as irretrievably damned. To save oneself, the individual can only withdraw from that world and begin a new life in a heavenly society of the elect. The sect, as a way out of the times, develops a strong boundaried isolation from the rest of the world. The elect are beyond the laws and moral codes of the damned, and live in accordance with their own rules and beliefs. Admission to the sect is conditionally based on belief. The chosen person loses contact with other worldviews and draws on true belief to interpret the world. The sectarian world itself is not open to negotiation; instead, it stands as a routinized model or ritual of heavenly timelessness. The cognitive field in the sect thus exists within the finite province of meaning composed of a particular set of religious beliefs. The accent of reality always leans toward a sectarian finite province of meaning. Synchronism is not of the spatio-temporal lifeworld itself, but of a personal and social invocation of the sectarian consciousness of the eternal and paths to its attainment.

In both the Love Family and the Krishna movement, spiritual mission provides the basis for recruitment into a society of the elect. As it turns out, however, not all the people who arrive at heaven like it, recognize it as home or know why they are there (member of the Love Family):

> 'The hard thing is when someone comes here who doesn't realize where he is, you know, who doesn't respect our ways here. I was on watch [minding the place] the other day and this guy came here and was drunk and just wasn't hearing what we were saying to him, and he wasn't being with us. He had no understanding of what we are doing here. Finally he just left. But it's really hard when people are like that. I guess we want everyone to be in our family, but not everyone is ready to be in our family.'

People of many persuasions enter the nets of sectarian communal groups; such sects profess to be open to all. But belief or at least deference to the sectarian province of meaning holds as the central criterion of admission.

The Krishna temples formally require that the visitor adhere to four rules: 1 no drugs or alcohol; 2 no gambling; 3 no illicit sex; and 4 no meat, eggs or fish. But there are implicit as well as explicit rules: the visitor who trangresses boundaries of belief may also be shown the door. On one occasion I questioned the authoritativeness of Bhaktivedanta's translation of the 'Bhagavad Gita' and argued that the use of soma, a euphoric drug, was prescribed in the 'Rig-Veda,' the most ancient available text of Hindu thought.* A devotee replied,

D: 'You cannot doubt the authority of Krishna's word, for it is the authority of the way. You are engaged in mere speculation. You have no proof for what you say. The "Gita" is authority and you have nothing to offer against that authority.'

J: 'You mean that just because you have the book and I have none that you are right and I am wrong? I can't believe that.'

D: (perturbed) 'The "Gita" is the essence of truth, and we are all part of it. We are not separate from it - just as you take a cup of water out of the ocean, it still has all the elements of the ocean in it. It is separate but the same as the ocean. So we are all separate but part of the same truth, and the recognition of that is the acceptance of the "Gita" as authority.'

J: 'Well, I see no reason to take your word or some authority based on words that say that it's right and all arguments are settled in terms of it alone.'

D: (pushing on my shoulder) 'Then I will have to ask you to leave the temple. You cannot blaspheme authority here.'

It is the submission to authority and the beliefs delineated in authoritative fashion that establishes the boundary of inclusion among the elect. Once a visitor initially defers to the sectarian province of meaning, the issue of belief becomes thematic again and again. Newcomers are sized up in terms of how they regard the beliefs of the group. The processes by which this may occur are diverse, involving subtle dialogues in which sect members have anticipated other persons' doubts and developed schemes of interpretive relevance which inexorably lead down the path to belief.

The Love Family novice, for example, is told early on that 'you are a part of the family.' Revelation may have

---

* Soma is purportedly a euphoric drug. In a recent analysis, Gordon Wasson (1971) claims it to be the mushroom Amanita muscaria, a highly toxic yet common species, which when properly prepared produces a psychedelic experience. An authoritative translation of the 'Rig-Veda,' with references to soma, is contained in Max Muller's 'Sacred Books of the East' (1897).

depicted the novice in the Love Family fold. A visitor, an old friend of the Love Family, who had moved on to other associations, was told:

S: 'I had a dream about you the other night, Francis. The Love Family had just gotten another house and you were living in it.'
(silence, all eyes turn to Francis)

F: 'I'm living in another house now. Maybe it will be so someday.'

The approach at the Love Family is a gentle and loving one, but it is unyielding. The targeted visitor is defined as someone who will one day 'awaken' to the family. At some point, for the attracted person, it is easier to yield to the definition, particularly if it provides an avenue of escape from the anxieties and problems of a previous life. To join the Love Family, taking on a new Biblical name and eventually a 'virtue' name, is truly to be reborn. Though the courts may catch up with you if you avoided the draft, the Family will defend you against the impositions of both state and previous family.*

People at the Love Family become situated in a world where deference to the sectarian ways yields a sense of peaceful perfection. Redemption carries with it a righteousness purified in the living of God's chosen way. Whatever the emotional scars from a previous life, they can be cast aside, for 'all God meant for us to do is just love each other.'

The approach at the Krishna temples is psychically more authoritarian. The potential recruit is warned of a damning hell of eternal cycles of death and rebirth. It is said that Krishna provides the only avenue out of this hopeless prospect. 'Chant the mantra' and serve Krishna to be saved. Anxieties about the future and salvation are thus set up, leaving Krishna as the only alternative. Many people, called 'bloopers' by devotees, come to the temple only to leave quickly, once they have assessed the situation. But those who remain can submit to what they

---

* A perennial charge by parents is that their children have been 'kidnapped' or 'abducted,' and subsequently 'brainwashed.' One man, Ted Patrick of California, operates a 'deprogramming center' near San Diego. He is the self-acclaimed national coordinator of FREECOG, the Parents' Committee to Free our Sons and Daughters from the Children of God (a sectarian Christian group somewhat similar to the Love Family). An account of one of Patrick's efforts at 'retrieval' is given in the Seattle 'Times,' March 13, 1974, p.A15. On Patrick and the Children of God, see Cahill (1973).

call the 'spiritual discipline' of devotional life. A devout follower describes his path.

> 'I went through some heavy japa [chanting with beads] sessions that manifested pure hatred of God, real heavy feelings for my position, but like they say, you have to experience hell before you can experience heaven, or one of the spiritual planets. It's hard. Maya is testing me; she's also in Krishna's service, and she's making sure that my love for Krishna is untainted by my material modes. I can see now though: I could never leave Krishna. I serve Krishna now or I could serve demigods or demons by the score, but the highest dance is Krishna's, and the purification process is well worth the initiation.'

The process of joining provides the basis for purification. The world of the damned is left behind, and in a new life, the devotee follows God's way, as revealed by the prevailing authority. The new life takes place in a literally new world, one in which the foci of consciousness are directed according to doctrine.

For the people at New Vrindaban, the model Vedic community of the Krishna groups, and at the Love Family, life is simple and heavenly, totally disconnected from the world at large. In both groups, the sectarian withdrawal is into a specialized and finite province of meaning which provides folkways for all occasions. The Love Family province is based on love among all human beings and deference to elders, while the Krishna province involves more strict attention to doctrine on a variety of subjects.

At the Krishna farm, devotees recognize that the 'material plane' can be useful to Krishna, but ultimately material objects and other people are treated as illusory. Even one's own material existence is downgraded. 'We are not this body,' devotees claim. The accent of reality falls instead on the Krishna finite province of meaning. In the course of the day, various religious services and rituals take place in front of gaudily decorated representations of Krishna and his wife (for it is stressed that Krishna is a person like us, but the transcendent person-spirit of the universe). Classes are held on various texts made available by the spiritual master, A.C. Bhaktivedanta, and during meals a devotee reads aloud from the texts while others eat. In the Krishna world, one sensory input comes to be emphasized:

> 'The ears are very important; they are the least illusory of our senses, all of which are full of error. As you spend time here, you must learn to attach more importance to what you hear than to what you see, for

> you only see the material world, but you hear the chanting and the words of the spiritual master.'

Chanting, devotional service and ritual leave little time or place for other conversation, and that which occurs is usually devoted to testing of novices on doctrine, stories about Krishna, news of the movement, and so on.

In the idealized form of being in the Krishna world, the constitution of the vivid present moves between three levels. The most basic and pervasive theme is that of chanting mantra. When people are not chanting, they are expected to be spreading Krishna consciousness through talking about the glory of Krishna. Finally, the realm of immediate concerns is invoked only as necessary. While the need to do 'first things first' (Schutz and Luckmann, 1973:47-50) takes precedence over thoughts of Krishna, completion of business ideally signals a return to thoughts of Krishna. Similarly, any deviant conversation is dismissed in favor of Krishna.

> (Two devotees are crosscutting firewood; another arrives.)
>
> B: 'I hear —— has been chosen by swami to head up the incense distribution business.'
>
> L: (still sawing) 'Is that so?'
>
> B: 'Well, those are the rumors.'
>
> L: 'We wouldn't want any rumors going around; tell me what you know of Krishna.'

As a devotee becomes immersed in the cognitive field of Krishna and in the chanting, the thematic kernel of consciousness shifts from the conscious ego operating in a lifeworld to other realms of experience. Psychically, the change parallels that of sexual arousal. The focal point of consciousness comes to be centered in one or another of the bodily 'chakras' or nerve ganglia which have been delineated by Eastern metaphysicians as meditation centers. But the experienced shift of consciousness from ego is not interpreted in physical imagery. Instead, each chakra is represented in a cosmology as one or another spirit force; the devotee who has been steeped in the Krishna cosmology may journey to 'other plants,' encounter spirit forces, and so on. The lifeworld of everyday action becomes less and less significant. Time and place are not conceived in terms of material coordinates, but in terms of spiritual ones. Beyond this limited material universe which our bodies inhabit, as a pamphlet (ISKCON, 1973:1) advises:

> there is a transcendental world. The top-most planet there is Goloka Vrindaban, in the shape of a limitless lotus flower. This is the abode of Lord Sri Krishna - the Primeval Lord, the Original Personality of Godhead. There he engages in eternal, blissful pastimes with His innumerable devotees.

In conversation, devotees muse about the possible existence of 'planets' so far removed from Krishna consciousness that they are immersed in darkness. The cosmology of Krishna provides a 'road map' for the interpretation of psychic experience which transcends the external sensory world.

While the prevailing accent on reality invokes the province of Krishna belief, devotees do not live their whole lives in transcendent consciousness. Indeed, some devotees merely 'front the rap,' as con artists would explain it. One Boston underworld figure, an intermediate-level dealer of illegal drugs, hid out at a temple for several months when 'the heat was on,' without ever being challenged as less than a sincere devotee. But such cases must be rare. Eventually, 'it would catch up with you, because people would see through it, and point out to you where you were failing to make it.'

Even among true devotees, lapses in Krishna consciousness occur, but only under certain conditions. When the temple president is not around, devotees may fall into idle gossip, only to tell him when he appears that they have been busy 'thinking of Krishna.' And impure conversations may be held in certain zones of the material plane. While invocation of the Krishna reality may never be transgressed in the temple sanctuary itself, the bath house provides a spatial zone where intimate aperçus and jokes can be shared.

D: 'You know, I had a really hard time getting up this morning.'

E: 'Yeah, it's that end of the week burnout.'

D: 'I was sleeping and Bhakti Govinda came up and said, "Hare bole!" [a greeting], and I said "Already?"' (laughter)

The primary accent of reality is on Krishna; in the purest form of the devotees' life, all thought and action is to be devoted to Krishna. But this requires daily involvement in mundane affairs, and occasionally the world of material objects breaks down. Even when the cream separator fails to work, the novice claims, 'If Krishna wanted it to work, it would work,' but a Brahman (statused devotee) has the good sense to invoke worldly knowledge: 'Well, obviously if you buy one at an auction, it isn't going to work.' While sectarian withdrawal into a utopian scheme of interpretation may be pervasive, when devotees become more secure in their belief, they learn to make the shift from the finite province of meaning to other provinces of meaning, while maintaining the special spiritual sector as encompassing.

It is all Krishna, but in some matters of devotional

service, belief alone will not make it. All worldly talents are worthwhile if they are performed in the service of Krishna. On the other hand, speculation and other personalistic provinces of meaning are frowned upon. The symbolic world is thus subtly structured to utilize other, more pragmatic provinces than that of pure Krishna consciousness, while excluding provinces which might conflict with the dictums of Krishna belief. Speculation is out of the question and the technical knowledge can be used only in the service of Krishna. Only the advanced devotees are steeped enough in the spiritual discipline to take on the hard decisions not covered by the Krishna universe of discourse. Newer devotees must concentrate on purifying their consciousnesses of worldly motives. For them, work orders are to be taken on without question, while personal initiative must be eliminated. For them, work is not so important as the activities of chanting and worshiping the deities. The mundane activities of life are downgraded, while the system of belief becomes the world.

At both the Love Family and the Krishna farm, specially constructed symbolic worlds of belief provide schemes of relevance which increasingly circumscribe individual consciousness. The novitiate comes to take as real the finite province of meaning which creates the definition of daily life as that of heaven. At the Love Family, those who do not subscribe to Love Israel's scheme of things are characterized as doubters who 'sow confusion,' to be given short shrift since 'God is not the author of confusion.' In each group, an account is readily available for those who do not see the rightness of the utopian vision. While extensive effort may be devoted to 'saving' the fallen person, a failure to do so generally results in exclusion from the community of the elect. Those who remain are thus the hard core of true believers. While worldly utopians focus on outer world relations, either of an objectified system or of social relations, the focus in sectarian withdrawal is on internally constructed systems of belief. The new world exists not necessarily because of any utopian changes in material and social relations, but because belief legitimates a state of affairs as heavenly.

Apocalyptic sectarian war

For some sectarian groups, no amount of submersion in an alternative world is taken to counterpose the existing order. Individual salvation seems irrelevant in a world where the masses are seen as having fallen prey to the apocalypse. On the basis of more or less developed critiques of the social order, ideological primary groups and 'quasi-ideological' street gangs and revolutionary cadres organize for direct struggle with the established order.* Such incipient conflict with an established order almost never poses an actual threat to the existing structure of domination. Nor is it intended to. Instead, violence usually has other purposes: to provide publicity and a symbolic rallying point for insurgent forces, to demonstrate the vulnerabilities of a state and the feasibility of guerrilla-style warfare, to sabotage institutions felt to be particularly reprehensible, to precipitate repressive action on the part of a state, to bring a war of nerves upon the enemy, to extort specific concessions, and so on. Such violence against the existing order of things, whether destructive or simply symbolic, falls into the category of terrorism. As Brian Jenkins (1975:1) has suggested, terrorism is violence for effect.

Cases of state-initiated and 'psychotic' terrorism aside, ideological belief provides motive. But because belief dictates a dramatic struggle in historical time, the nature of struggle - rather than its ultimate goals - frames a particular province of meaning. A war of insurgency, whatever its scale, must be concerned with military discipline and strategies. Boundary definitions of the warring sect have to be much stronger than in otherworldly sects, for secrecy requires a style of organization in which infiltration can be guarded against: members must be able to trust and count on one another totally. Under a wartime discipline, immediate death is often the penalty for treason. And, as in war, participants must be concerned with the logistics of supplies, communication, intelligence and propaganda. Like people

---

* See Edward A. Shils (1966). Shils describes the ideological primary group as an organization in which ideology is accepted as sacred by group members, giving sufficient grounds for transcending other differences. Shils maintains that the concept is best exemplified by separatist political and religious sects, though it would seem broadly applicable to worldly utopian groups as well. He also links the idea to Schmalenbach's (1961) concept of the 'Bund.' But the basis of the 'Bund' would seem of a different order, cutting across the dimension of ideology. For Schmalenbach, the 'Bund' is an affinitive loyalty of individuals based on the ephemeral experience of communion. Ideology may comprise one, but certainly not the only, sacred theme of communion.

at the stock market, members of a sectarian revolutionary group have a Machiavellian concern not so much with what should be, but with 'how it's going to be.' Though belief provides motive, strategy is based on projections of 'what will happen if ...' a planned action is performed in a particular way. The sect engaged in struggle thus comes to focus on the immediate lifeworld and sequences of action in it, alternative immediate results, contingency plans, and the mediated effect of actions on the general public. Like the gang of thieves, members of a revolutionary sect want to 'pull a job' without getting caught. But unlike thieves, revolutionaries are concerned with the effects that actions will have in furthering a revolutionary state of affairs.

The SLA tried to engage in selective terrorism with strategic goals. Though they were not as successful as other terrorist groups such as the Weather Underground, it is for this very reason that we know more about their operations. They chose to assassinate Marcus Foster, an Oakland, California school superintendent, because they felt him to be guilty of crimes against the people. They chose to kidnap a Hearst family member partly to exploit the media empire owned by the Hearsts. Emily Harris maintains that they chose the daughter, Patricia, rather than one of her parents because they thought 'it would be more important to have influential figures like Randolph and Catherine Hearst on the outside, working to get a release' (Harris and Harris, 1976:22). And, according to Emily Harris, they chose a food giveaway program as a condition for Patty Hearst's release 'as a way to involve a lot of people in a guerrilla action- to have them take part in the results of that action so that revolutionaries could begin to be seen as a valid part of their everyday lives' (1976:21).

Overall strategy is open to debate. In retrospect, Emily Harris says the SLA 'misjudged the way the community would respond to the assassination of Marcus Foster.' And Russ Little, one of the SLA members in jail for assassination at the time of the Hearst kidnapping, believes Randolph or Catherine, rather than Patty Hearst, should have been kidnapped: 'it's always better to snatch someone who is a righteous pig' (Harris et al., 1976:31). The thrust of SLA survivors' self-criticism is that terror should be selective. But hindsight is usually better focused than foresight, especially when survivors at the time of self-criticism still faced various trials for their terrorist actions.

During the unfolding action itself, what Erving Goffman has called 'strategic interaction' would seem to obtain.

Following Goffman's (1969:86) analysis, a 'party' with a 'unitary interest to promote' can draw on any individual to be, among other possible roles, a 'player' exercising intelligence on behalf of the party, and a 'pawn' (hostage). Strategic interaction, when it is between two parties, transpires as a game in which each party has turns and makes moves which result in positions where - at subsequent turns - certain conceivable moves become viable, and others, non-viable. In this perspective, the actions of the SLA can be interpreted as a series of some 'good' and some 'bad' moves. Certain moves yield information to the opposition and force the group to significantly alter its strategy. The SLA's initial choice of a 'safehouse' in a middle-class neighborhood was a bad move because SLA members did not fit in; the subsequent attempt to burn the safehouse and its clues during a hurried departure was a poorly executed move: the fire failed to take. Similarly, the shoplifting episode at Mel's Sporting Goods in Los Angeles was the genesis of the deaths of six SLA members: a parking ticket in the van that had to be abandoned at Mel's helped the police locate the SLA hideout. Some of the SLA's moves - the assassination, the kidnapping, the robbery, and the food giveaway - were more 'successful.' As intended, the negotiating demand for free food for the poor showed tacit support for the group by those who would take the food. Though newspaper columnists lamented the fact that people would be willing to reap the benefits of such extortion, the 'Washington Post' (1973:Feb. 23, A16) reported that those who took the food were undeterred by its circumstances:

> One welfare mother summed up the universal sentiment with the statement to a reporter: 'Man, I been out of food stamps two weeks now, and I got six kids to feed. I feel sorry for the lady (Patricia); but if that's the way they have to get food for the people, then I don't mind taking it.'

Even successful moves can constrain the 'game': though the intent of the SLA had been to manipulate the media, survivors believe the SLA became so successful in dealing with the media that they 'lost all contact with reality outside of an artificially staged media context.' The saga of Patty Hearst as 'Tania' epitomizes this difficulty. According to two sources that often contradict each other in other respects (Kohn and Weir, 1975:I,46; Harris and Harris, 1976:28), the possibility of 'turning' Patty Hearst from SLA-held pawn to 'Tania,' player for the SLA, developed out of interactions between Hearst and

Cinque, the charismatic catalyst of the group.* At that time, say both sources, most SLA members opposed the move on tactical grounds, e.g. of decreased mobility because of Patty's widely known appearance. But Cinque and Patty prevailed, in part out of deference by others toward Cinque, but also because the 'conversion' would be a propaganda coup, an 'inspiration' demonstrating 'the potential in everyone to change.' In retrospect, Joe Remiro (Harris et al., 1976:34) termed the move 'another example of the media effect taking precedence over more important considerations.'

The SLA's difficulties had less to do with their planned actions than with their evaluation of strategic options during a series of unfolding moves. They made moves which left their security weakened, either out of simple error, or in order to exploit media advantage. Still, the SLA exemplifies the character of terrorist communal action. Apocalyptic doom spells out a strategic battle in historical time. A group may attain de facto legitimacy by having its demands treated in good faith by an elite, and by dramatizing the needs of the 'poor and oppressed.' So long as the insurgents cannot be brought under control, doubt is cast on the abilities of police and intelligence agencies of the established order. And if the strategic interaction results in extermination, the vanquished group may attain martyrdom in the minds of sympathizers. The real and ongoing effectiveness of a

---

* Whether Patricia Hearst actually 'turned' or not is a continuing subject of debate. SLA members believed she did, and 'Tania' apparently did not avail herself of numerous opportunities to escape. But at her trial for bank robbery, Patty Hearst only admitted to fraudulently convincing SLA members that she was one of them, while she claimed that the SLA, even in accepting her as a convert, still considered the possibility of using her as a hostage ('Washington Post,' 1976:Feb.21, A6). After her 'conversion,' Hearst thus may have been a player for a party consisting of herself, and both a player and a continuing pawn for the SLA as a party. In this view, her conversion was an operating misunderstanding based on strategic advantages for both parties threatened by an external party - police forces and the FBI. Alternatively, Hearst could have been a pawn who believed in her conversion (at the time), while at least after they had first 'turned' her, SLA members continued to regard her as a pawn. But it is doubtful that the SLA would have continued to take the risk of 'fronting' a pawn as a player.

current elite's rule is not seriously challenged by this expressive and non-instrumental form of political action; the intent is to create a situation in which violence becomes more widely accepted as a viable and necessary focus of revolutionary action (cf. Fanon, 1968). The myth of revolution advances by the play of symbolic events.

TRANSCENDENTAL ENGAGEMENT IN THE PHENOMENAL WORLD

In the transcendental formation, the relevance of meaning is downgraded. Instead, importance is placed on attending to phenomena themselves, as primordially given and experienced. The approach encompasses various forms of mysticism and ecstatic spiritual experience, as well as certain Eastern religions such as Zen Buddhism and Taoism. Fundamental to such viewpoints is the perception that meaning is epiphenomenal and, as such, only impedes access to the essential character of existence.

Since meaningful interpretations are regarded as inessential and inaccurate accounts, few writings explicate the transcendental position. Those that do take a broadly enigmatic form: deep insight is attached to few words (cf. Weber, 1968:545). Witness the Buddhist koans or riddles used as meditation devices in Zen monasteries. 'What,' the initiate is asked by the Zen master, 'is the sound of one hand clapping?' (Reps, 1957). Essential comprehension is a state of consciousness, not one of meaning. 'The Mystery of mysteries is the Door of all essence' (Lao Tzu, 1961:3). In the unfolding of action, meaning and motive only impede the realization of conclusion. Thus the archer is advised to avoid an 'I' who 'aims' at the target. When the target, archer, bow and arrow are 'one,' and when the release of the arrow from the bow is an occurrence and not an act of volition, then the archer will never miss (cf. Herrigel, 1953). The mystery is that no mystery exists; the answer, that no answer will do: 'Tao [the way or path] never makes any ado, And yet it does everything' (Lao Tzu, 1961:53).

Introduction to the 'mysteries' I have called transcendental is achieved through social interaction. Books may provide signs of the path, but the path can only be found in life itself. Quite independently of the transmission of institutionalized religious doctrines, mystics, shamans, magicians and monks pass on their understanding of the ineffable.* The transmission may take place in a

---

* The institutionalized religions may all have their genesis in the explication and interpretation of

variety of circumstances. The student may visit the recluse master and receive introduction to the mysteries (Castaneda, 1972), or a more rationalized monastery organization may provide the arena (Suzuki, 1965).

In either event, a boundary exists between novitiates and those who have 'seen.' And these two categories are set apart from the rest of the world - people who are either unaware of the possibility, or otherwise fail to seek it. The course of events among the unaware is of little importance. An apocalyptic understanding pervades the view of the outside. At 'The Cabin,' the charismatic master has described the state of contemporary society thus:

> 'American society is like a 1950 Cadillac rumbling out of control down the side of a mountain. Ideologues sit in the back seat assuring their companions that they are on the right road. Liberals outside try to jump in and steer, while conservatives dig pits, hoping to trap the car. Meanwhile the revolutionaries place bombs in its path. Some of us have come to the bottom of the mountain. We are sadder and wiser, and not on the road.'

In this group, it is felt that all Americans have become afflicted by the 'diseased' society which spawned us. We all carry the burden of American socialization and education and face the untenable prospect of working in the maintenance of American institutions and the alienated production of material needs (person at 'The Cabin'):

> 'To be "sane" in an insane world is to be insane. The boundaries of the insane world exclude the bad and the good, and keep people from getting freaked out by the universe. Wolves surround the fire, and there seems to be little hope for escape, but once beyond, the forest swallows us up. There is no trace, but there are signs.'

Since the American drama is seen as 'horseshit,' the need is to get beyond its definitions and pretensions. This is to be accomplished by debunking the world that is taken for granted. What is taken for granted has to be rendered problematic. In coming to the remote site of this group, visitors find that whatever may be imputed as 'the way things are' is challenged. Definitions of self brought into the situation receive little support if they are

---

mystical experiences for a wider audience, from whom the experiences themselves are withheld. Wasson (1971) points to this possibility for Hinduism, while John Allegro (1970) makes much the same case for Christianity.

considered 'horseshit,' and abstract beliefs and ideas will be similarly challenged. The visitor who exhorted people to recycle their beer cans for ecological reasons was told, 'If people didn't put so much shit in our lives, we wouldn't have to recycle our minds.' The catch phrases, 'u-pump-it,' (derived from the self-service gasoline motto) and 'anything you say' signify that the visitor constructs reality with words and a personal outlook on life.

Visitors who stay any length of time either acknowledge and embrace the transcendental viewpoint or 'freak out.' In the latter case, they typically take on a 'sick role.' Immediate departure from the site is not always easy, and the 'sick' one may instead withdraw from the ongoing social arena. This 'sickness' prevalent in many visitors came to be identified as 'woodticks.' Woodticks were considered to infect those who were reluctant to go along with the group, who failed to trust what was happening, no matter where the situation led. The disease came to be diagnosed by a 'doctor' and his 'competent staff' (people at 'The Cabin'):

F: 'Bob, it looks to me like you have woodticks.'
B: 'No, I'm doing fine, really.'
F: 'Well, you seem to have all the symptoms. Maybe you should have a checkup and an exploratory operation.'
B: 'I don't need any checkup and I don't need any operation. I don't have woodticks, I tell you.'
T: 'Doctor, I think the patient needs an operation; we can't take any chances - the health of the community is at stake. Why if the county health department finds out about this, they'll close us down in no time.'
B: 'I don't have woodticks, damn it!'
F: 'See how he denies it; that's always a sure sign. The fever's causing delusions. We'd better operate immediately.'

Though such operations, usually held late at night, were profusely guaranteed by the doctor, they were rarely successful, and the need for another operation soon became apparent.

The 'operation' and other enactments based on absurd premises served to point out the social nature of the construction of reality. Not only are the outsider's predefinitions of self and sociability challenged, but these predefinitions are replaced by other assumptions totally ungrounded in anything except the caprice of the actors involved. In the course of such hazing (to make things hazy), the visitor-turned-novitiate comes to abandon previous constructions of the world and ways of presenting self. What is learned, then, is not a particular set of rules or regulations (as in the diachronic worldly utopia), nor an ethical code of conduct (as in the synchronic one), nor still a system of beliefs for interpretations of the world (as in the case of apocalyptic otherworldly sects). Instead, the individual gradually comes to understand the multiple possibilities of cognizing reality and acting in the social sphere.

The recruit's personal cognitive organization of the world must be undone, if the group is to provide a new way for the recruit to be in the world. 'Abandoning the history' of previous definitions is the first order of business (Castaneda, 1972). All manner of staged 'inversions' of reality may be used to achieve this effect. It is then possible to offer an alternative, transcendental acçount of the world. In one instance, a mystagogue and his followers engaged in an extended session of acting out manifold social constructions of reality (person at 'The Cabin'):

> 'He then said, "This is the church," holding his index finger pointed out at nowhere in particular; and at that moment I had what was similar to an acid flash, where the whole presence of the room - log walls, his finger and body, the floor and ceiling - attained a crystalline floating wholeness.'

The initiate then takes on the particular social production of reality that is unique to the cult, secret organization or monastery. This production of the social need not be keyed to particular schemes of interpretation in a finite province of meaning. Its comprehensiveness is contained in the group's succession of experiences themselves, in cognitions produced in the unfolding stream of vivid present interaction.

In the transcendental orientation, the lifeworld, the socially constituted vivid present, and all the potential provinces of meaning available through individuals' stocks of knowledge, as well as possible cognitive frames and accents of reality - all these aspects of living in the world are available prior to any systematization of them. For example, the essence of holding 'power' in the desert is an ability to survive the onslaught of alien forces. The 'warrior' cannot learn any rationalized meanings of signs in advance, but he learns to be able to discern the signs and their meanings as they 'appear' in the desert (Castaneda, 1972). It is the submersion into established provinces of meaning and schemes of interpretation that is seen as alienating from existence (Lao Tzu, 1961:3):

When all the world recognizes beauty as beauty, this in

itself is ugliness.
When all the world recognizes good as good, this in itself is evil.

The way of being in the world is all. With it, the one who has nothing is said to be wealthy, and without it, the one who has met all desires is poor.

In this perspective, the enactment of the lifeworld is open and beyond systematization. The initiate learns to 'let it be,' to exist in the world without needing any account for that existence. What 'is' will be what 'was' and can never again be available as a moment of experience. Thus the precept, 'You should be digging it while it's happening, 'cause it just might be a one shot deal.'* In the socially shared vivid present, any topic may become thematic and provide the reference point of association for the introduction of relevances and whole other themes. The commitment is to begin in the moment and follow it wherever it may lead, with the highest degree of attention possible. The remainder of the lifeworld and the social worlds beyond the thematic kernel are totally bracketed. It is the submersion into this cognitive approach when focused on Christ's return to earth which constitutes what Mannheim (1936) has called the 'intense expectation' of chiliasm, particularly in its ecstatic forms. But the close attention to the thematic constitution of moment may be played out in other ways as well, depending on what is thematic. It provides the possibility, through the suspension of belief in the world 'out there,' for entry into the internal stream of consciousness. Music as well as special sports in which good performance can be accomplished through a high degree of synchronous engagement (for example, archery, darts, pool and pinball) are activities in which this possibility may easily be sensed, but all social interaction and action in the lifeworld is equally open to this same possibility. The moment is derived via improvisation on the available themes, and group life among initiates is taken to be no more or less than this enterprise of 'letting it happen.'

SUMMARY

The realities of communal life may be understood as ways in which the lifeworld comes to be enacted. Communal life need not necessarily prescribe a utopian way. In a

---

* A quotation from a rock and roll song by Frank Zappa: 'You should be digging it while it's happening.' 'Waka/Jawaka.' Bizarre Reprise Records, 2094.

natural approach, the lifeworld shared with others does not come prepackaged. What is to be thematic is in play and open to the incursion of any event upon which people focus. In produced groups, on the other hand, communal life is lived in terms of a utopian scheme of interpretation which holds precedence over other interpretations as the ultimate definer of reality. For worldly utopian groups, the scheme of interpretation is touted as a basis for living in terms of which all society could be organized. The diachronic worldly utopia exhibits a rule-based scheme of interpretation in which problematics are resolved through further rationalization of the interpretive scheme. In the synchronic worldly utopia, ethical precepts provide interpretations of conduct that allow for vivid present resolution of issues without further modification of the precepts. In the diachronic utopia, personal provinces of meaning may extend beyond the social scheme of interpretation so long as they do not infringe upon its rules. Rationalization of system functions and normative behavior permits a pluralism in the areas of cultural and social life. But in the synchronic utopia, the 'now' is delimited to that which is characterized as real in the ethical scheme of interpretation. The result is a conformity in the cognitive style of social life.

Other produced groups do not seek to provide a model for transforming the world so much as they respond in a sectarian fashion to the perceived apocalyptic condition of the world. The utopian impulse may then be one of changing the world through terrorist action, or withdrawing from it to embrace the right path of personal salvation. In the case of terrorism, social action is directed toward an unfolding strategic situation. On the other hand, the other-worldly sect puts forward a tableau of life in 'heaven' in which a finite province of meaning sets the boundaries of all social life.

Finally, the transcendental approach consists of a mystical engagement with the phenomena of the world. Both the natural attitude and utopian constructs are regarded as focused partial accounts. In the natural orientation to enactment of social life, symbolic constructions are taken as real, and multiple definitions of situation may coexist. The produced orientation restricts such situational interplay of definitions by advancing a particular finite province of meaning as the encompassing relevance structure for cognizing, interpreting and dealing with events of everyday life. In produced enactments of utopian life, 'In the beginning was the word, and the word was God,' whether God is the labor credit system, 'getting straight,' the Holy Ghost, an authoritarian father, or a revolutionary ideology. In the transcendental formation, 'Before the word' and before interpretation, there exists a phenomenal world. Words are always 'about' other things; at most they are taken to be 'honest lies,' which may be used to attempt to mirror remembered, present and anticipated worlds of experience. The transcendental process of initiation becomes one of learning to 'see' the phenomenal basis of life experience, devoid of any scheme of interpretation or meaning.

In each communal formation, then, participants enact collective life via one or another cognitive map. The world of everyday existence - manifold in its possibilities - is conventionally circumscribed as to the ranges of perception, ways of focusing attention, and styles of interpreting the events which bear attention. In each communal group, participants establish a unique nexus between a sense of time, cognitive assumptions about reality, and the relation of action to that reality. The sociological temptation is to establish conceptual distinctions between ideology, social structure, norms, action, and so forth. But in communal enactments (just as, we may suspect, in other social situations), these distinctions are embedded in one or another encompassing 'reality' which is cognized, acted upon, and objectified only in the course of participants' ongoing attention to it.

5 Needs, want satisfaction and work

You can't always get what you want;
But if you try sometime,
You just might find,
You get what you need.

The Rolling Stones

Above all else, communal life would seem to unfold as one or another kind of consciousness. Still, the collective life takes place in a spatio-temporal world where, at the minimum, people eat, sleep and excrete. The transcendent fantasy of an ideal world must be reconciled with the daily material wants of people. Moreover, people bring various affective and symbolized wants, such as those of love, emotional support and communion, to the communal world. Indeed, an overriding reason people often give for seeking out a communal lifestyle rests on the inability to satisfy non-material needs in other situations. Dissatisfaction with the established material scheme of production is mirrored in personal dissatisfaction with life. The search is for a more meaningful life, which at the same time must involve a workable construction of the material plane.

Once consumerism has been eschewed, numerous alternatives open up, some of them out-and-out hustles, others sacredly legitimized ripoffs, and still others, sincere attempts at 'living the life' or implementing utopian visions. Each alternative requires a new specification of needs and delineation of new purposes, missions or enterprises in terms of which meaning can be ascribed. Moreover, social action required for satisfaction of wants must somehow be organized and legitimated. Since communal organizations are generally restricted in the use of coercion, commitment to participate in the satisfaction of shared wants is contingent on personal identification with the specified wants and chosen methods of realization. If the communal group does not always give its members what they thought they wanted, people must at least become convinced that they are getting what they really need. In the present chapter, consideration is given to the various ways needs and wants are redefined and provided for in communal groups.

OLD AND NEW BASES OF WANT SATISFACTION

Rejection of the work-consumption equation

The modal scheme of want satisfaction in the USA and the rest of the industrialized world is bound up in the wage or salary job, the institutionalized production of goods, and the household as a unit of consumption. Under industrial capitalism, tasks are removed from the household economy and placed in the nexus of mass production and servicing. Patterns of consumption are brought down to matters of 'taste,' and aesthetics of lifestyle are manufactured, marketed and purchased. Consumers may purchase frozen dinners in a variety of ethnic categories more easily than they can find the ingredients to make a meal from scratch. The marketplace remains the primary source of want satisfaction in the industrialized organization of material life, but the options within the marketplace are increasingly rationalized under the domination of corporate organizations. Money earned in wages or salary mediates between corporate production and household satisfaction of needs and wants, and individuals gradually lose the capability of 'doing it' themselves.

As Max Weber (1968:202) has remarked, 'In a market economy, the striving for income is necessarily the ultimate driving force of economic activity.' Aside from the independently wealthy minority, people must keep full-time jobs to avoid being crushed economically. Even in the days of perceived affluence in the 1950s and 1960s, most Americans had little freedom in their choices of consumption - a house mortgage, cars and other major bills imposed severe constraints. Display of lifestyle status through consumption remains important, but in the consumer society, self-reliance becomes an ability to keep the credit company off one's back. The job is a crucial asset; moonlighting is not unusual; and more and more 'working wives' enter the labor force.

Rejection of this scheme of things seems to be a pervasive part of every communal formation. The talk is of 'turkeys living in a plastic society.' The shoddiness of industrially produced goods is attributed to the mode of production and the capitalist scheme of marketing in which 'people out for a buck are ready to cram all the worthless goods they can down your throat.' To adopt the communal life is almost universally to accept a standard of living which is 'lower' than the prevailing one in terms of cost per person per unit of time. Though the contemporary American communal movement emerged during the perceived affluence of the 1960s, communalists anticipated problems of long-term scarcity which have become more widely apparent in the 1970s. They freely embraced the ethic framed by Buckminster Fuller, that 'less is more,' while others have been forced by circumstance to come to terms with it. The cost of the American standard of living is seen as too high in terms of its one-dimensional work requirements, use of natural and energy resources, and unabashed materialism. If for the General Electric Corporation, 'Progress is our most important product,' for the communard, in the words of one visionary, 'Poverty is progress.' At its simplest, communal life may be regarded as a cheap and expedient way of surviving the hard times of inflation and unemployment. Especially in self-avowedly religious communal groups, material needs may be played down in favor of spiritual ones; but in all communal groups there is a spirit of escape from the alienated modes of production and the status aspects of consumption prevalent in the society-at-large.

Communal groups exist at the margins, beyond the conventions of established society. For this reason, as Weber (1968:507) noted in a similar context, they stand at 'the point of Archimedes' with respect to all aspects of social life. They are capable of innovation in want satisfaction and organization of work, while others are 'locked in' to previously established formulas. 'Windfalls and welfare' (Berger et al., 1973) are the first basis of simple subsistence for many loosely organized communal groups, while the ethic of self-sufficiency leads to development of appropriated means of production. In some groups, hip business enterprises or cottage industry are developed to appeal to a well-established and sizable market based on 'hippie' aesthetics. In rural groups, gardening and animal husbandry become important avenues of want satisfaction. Even in urban communes, taking on a full-time job in the 'straight' job world is often regarded as only a last ditch, up-against-the-wall option. The communal transition is from a model of earning as much as possible for the practice of consumption to one of consuming as little as possible to reduce the need for alienated work. It moves from participation in a job world where the mode of production and social interaction in relation to it are largely predesignated to a communal world where participants may organize to satisfy wants in a variety of new ways.

Redefining needs

If people in communal groups are to successfully reject a job-consumption model of want satisfaction, they must open up alternative ways of construing the material grounding of social life. Just as other status groups develop styles and levels of consumption congruent with their perceived social positions, so communalists arrive at new aesthetics of wants which exploit their new household situations.

Gone is the equation that consumption confers status. More likely, the individual who spends money on useless novelties is taken to be a fool. The aversion to straight jobs requires avoidance of styles of consumption which can only be maintained with steady income. Fashion is transposed from the revolving door merry-go-round of 'in' and 'out,' headlined by Paris, New York and Hollywood designers in slick magazines and movies, to other aesthetics that do not require 'keeping up.' People in communal groups are more likely to implicitly establish collective aesthetics of fashion marked by inexpensiveness and a gradual rate of change.

As it is with fashion, so it is with other possible avenues of consumption. Under the 'natural' aesthetic, less extravagant foods are prepared from raw materials. Household items such as stoves and washing machines are used more intensively. And the consumption of books, TV, movies, art, records and other items of mass cultural production is often downgraded in favor of on-site folk cultural production. Whatever functions it may have for group integration, folk culture mitigates the impact of mass culture as well as the social identities and consumption patterns promulgated through it.

Whether the communal aesthetic is oriented toward asceticism, the 'good life,' the 'natural' life, or the 'hippie' life, material wants can only partially be satisfied by a system of mass production. In spiritual asceticism, any pursuit of material gratification is denigrated as a motive. Indeed, there is no personal outside consumption anyway. And the needs of the 'good life' (Nearing and Nearing, 1970) and the 'natural' life are such that localized, small-scale production and community exchange are valued above mass production.

In the 'hippie' aesthetic, more than in other ones, consumer needs persist. A quality stereo system may be an unconditional requirement for some communes. The desire to create communal music or copy 'other people's music' in a 'hippie' band (cf. Bennett, 1972) may lead to purchase of expensive musical and sound amplification equipment. But certain hippie wants cannot be satisfied even in newly emerging markets of mass production. Marijuana and psychedelic drugs, for example, are often an important basis for communion.* In one formulation of the countercultural ethic, 'It's easier to go through times of dope and no money than to go through times of money and no dope.' Drugs must either be purchased through underground channels or produced on-site. Aside from such technological and mystical 'necessities' of hippie life, just as with other communal aesthetics, the hippie impetus is toward 'doing it' rather than 'buying it.'

Communal definitions of wants thus encourage minimization of mass consumption. Wants come to be treated not as products of mass culture but as products of communal sociation. And the forms of sociation which create wants come under the reign of alternative communal legitimations. Material wants are minimized in return for greater freedom in modes of want satisfaction. While the consumption styles of middle-class life demand either wealth or a steady job, the reduced level and alternative patterns of wants in communal groups cannot be satisfied merely by spending money, but can be achieved by other means. Abandonment of the job-consumption scheme frees the delineation of lifestyle from its established economic base.

At the same time, members of communal formations take on new values and new wants. Some of these wants, such as those of land, require initial investment capital unnecessary for a life of work and marketplace consumption. Others, such as the requirements of organic farming (cf.

---

* There is an almost complete absence of drug use in diachronic groups (ostensibly for legal reasons) and in apocalyptic sects of war or piety. Synchronic groups, on the other hand, almost universally accept the use of marijuana and psychedelic drugs. At the worldly utopian Farm in Tennessee, marijuana and natural psychedelics are used in communion and production of ecstasy (cf. Gaskin and The Farm, 1974). Members of The Farm, including Stephen, have served jail sentences after an unsuccessful attempt to have their use of marijuana adjudicated as a legal sacrament of religious communion.

Rodale, 1971), involve marshalling of raw materials in ongoing rural economies that parallel those of other rural households. Manure is a precious commodity in a farm enterprise. No matter how much alternative values define wants that differ from those of a job-consumption ethic, the ecological and social location of the communal group dictates some kinds of needs.

And aside from material wants, members of communal groups may define social wants in quite different ways. Personal 'spiritual growth' as well as various missionary enterprises can come to be treated as wants that are as important as, if not more important than, material wants. The process of living out communal life thus involves an ideologically and materially based reconstruction of the wants and needs of everyday life. The ideological aspect may be characterized by the degree of social organization involved in satisfaction of wants, while the material aspect is related to group construction of ecological situation and its exploitation. Each of these aspects will be discussed in turn.

Social integration and want satisfaction

In communal groups, social relations are in part bound up in the degree of personal autonomy as opposed to personal dependence on the communal matrix for satisfaction of wants. Three broad alternative models of want satisfaction - anarchism, socialism and communism - sketch the possibilities. While Weber (1968:153-4) defines household communism as uncalculated consumption in religious and military communal groups as well as in families, here I treat communism, like anarchism and socialism, as a model of production for satisfaction of wants.

In the model of anarchism, the collectivity of individuals bears no responsibility for defining wants or satisfying them. Just as the state is seen as illegitimate, so the collectivity is prevented from usurping individual prerogatives in economic life. Individuals maintain private property and personal means of survival. They may, on occasion or regularly according to agreements, cooperate with others in enterprises which benefit all (such as the purchase of land), but such action need only be sporadic. Group projects arise as problematic occurrences for which the specifics must be hammered out each time around. Nevertheless, individuals need not become hermits. Instead, they are immersed in a web of social commerce in the course of taking care of business. Their positions in an economic community may become tied to political decisions of reciprocal association and cooperation. When individuals possess special talents and resources, sharing of such arcane knowledge may be customary, and return 'in kind' is to be expected. Such cooperation may provide mutual benefit to both parties. Equally, it is possible for one individual to prosper more than another through the clever negotiation of exchange agreements. Economic action is unregulated by any collective agency, and the course of anarchical relations may result in the domination of key resources by one or several persons in a collectivity of individuals. The anarchist arrangement is an unstable one, unless it becomes routinized as a 'feudal' set of mutual obligations and rights, or, in production for exchange, as a capitalist formation of owners and producers. Such tendencies, however, only become possible with the passage of time. The more idealistic vision of development entails an interdependent and collectively viable network of free individuals.

In the socialist model, while some portion of want satisfaction is left to the individual or to nuclear association, major features of wants, especially material ones, are defined and satisfied through collective action. While the styles of agreements and ways of apportioning labor are diverse, satisfaction of collective needs requires a giving over of the aesthetics and mechanisms of want satisfaction to collective decisions and regimes of action. Individuals may still engage in private want satisfaction, but they are required to submit to the social structure of wants as well. Private property may continue to exist, but production and utilization of communal resources become major group concerns.

Finally, under pure communism, all needs are taken to be defined by the collectivity, the many who act as one. Individuals hold no property other than personal effects, and certainly none which produces economic advantage. Instead, the group controls both the means of production and the allocation of individuals' efforts to meet needs.

These three models of social integration specify the degree to which wants and their satisfaction are treated in communal organizations as collective enterprises. How are such models utilized by communal groups with varying orientations toward time and social enactment?

Anarchism is based on the rejection of a collectively derived relevance structure in favor of symbiotic interpersonal relevance structures. It could thus only serve as a vehicle for want satisfaction in groups with a natural or transcendental mode of social enactment. In the natural case, anarchism reflects the pluralist ethic in which diverse personal time and meaning orientations remain in play with each other. In the transcendental formation, any rationalized system of want satisfaction contradicts the drive toward an unroutinized world. Anarchism certainly allows for this transcendental immediate transaction of wants. But spoils communism - anarchic in process, but communistic in spirit - is a more likely form.

Communism requires a degree of social integration unlikely in the pluralist, natural formation, certainly possible among worldly utopians, and practically required among apocalyptic sectarian groups. The maintenance of private lives in the pluralist formation precludes total domination by the collectivity, while the specification of a total belief system in sectarian groups requires that the mode of satisfying all wants come under collective domination. In the other-worldly sectarian case of withdrawal from the secular world, individuals specifically submit to the unified heavenly gestalt; they have no 'personal' needs, only ones which make them more fulfilled participants in the spiritual community. Similarly, the group concerned with Manichean battle with the forces of evil cannot afford to cater to individual whims. Personal life is given over to total service in the organization's pursuit of its objectives. Wants, in sectarian communal groups, are collective wants for collective operations.

Socialism provides a middle ground between anarchism and communism. It may occur in natural groups where participants wish to collectivize a certain portion of material want satisfaction, as well as in other groups, both worldly utopian and transcendental, which do not require total submission on the part of participants to a collective belief system.

Types of want satisfaction

Apocalyptic sectarian groups, as well as worldly utopian ones, are especially predisposed to satisfying wants through a high degree of collectivization of needs and labor organized for meeting such needs. But this says nothing about the ways in which wants are actually satisfied. While minimization of the collective economy in more anarchist formations precludes certain ways of satisfying wants, in general, communal groups may, at any given degree of collectivization, employ one or more of several strategies of want satisfaction.

Max Weber (1968:348-50) has suggested five ideal-typical ways of satisfying wants: 1 the 'oikos' 'with its collective natural economy' in which goods and services are produced from the communally organized raw materials and labor, not for exchange, but for the self-sufficient community, as in a manor or royal household; 2 'market-oriented assessments' in the form of taxes, dues or fees used to purchase goods and employ workers, charged either on the basis of equity, services rendered, or simple political power; 3 'production for the market,' with profits surrendered to the group of which the enterprise is a part; 4 the 'maecenatic type' of unconditional voluntary contributions by those, whether members or not, who have an interest in the enterprise; and 5 'contributions and services linked to positive and negative privileges.'

TIME, SOCIAL ENACTMENT AND WANT SATISFACTION

Any communal group is likely to use a mixture of want satisfaction strategies. Nevertheless, it is apparent that the degree of social integration in the constitution of wants (anarchist, socialist or communist) and the type of communal formation (in terms of time and social enactment) determine the utility of one or another strategy. Each formation may be considered in turn.

Natural synchronic want satisfaction

As I have already suggested, owing to the tendency of pluralism, production-oriented communism is an unlikely basis of integration in the natural commune. If it is to occur at all in such a formation, communism is based on household consumption paralleled by participation in a market economy. More likely to be found in natural synchronic groups are the less unified modes of anarchism and socialism. With sufficient capitalization, however, moves may be made in the direction of the 'oikos' of self-sufficiency or some cottage industry or other commercial production.

The natural commune typically occupies an ecological niche like those of similarly situated non-communal groups. The urban commune has fixed rental or mortgage costs, as well as those of energy and food. Rural communalists often find their neighbors working at steady jobs and farming on the side; for both non-communalists and their communal counterparts, some form of monetary income seems necessary. Individuals living in the group may be assessed for expenses on some agreed-upon equitable basis, with outside jobs providing the source of money.

Or patrons - those members and outsiders who are wealthy or have excess profits from personal economic activities - may bankroll various capital expenditures. In such 'maecenatic' tithing, communal groups are reluctant to grant special privileges on the basis of donations. But services and contributions in kind linked to special privileges may be permitted, especially for transients and the destitute. Alternatively, the collectivity may come to be organized for some unified role in the outside economy, most easily in wholesale trade and distribution, or in a small retail business. Profits can then be used to subsidize group life.

The type of want satisfaction employed in natural synchronic groups has implications for subsequent development of the communal household economy. The assessment approach, tied to individual outside sources of income, makes the transition to a more self-sufficient 'oikos' difficult. At issue is the way in which a division of labor comes to be legitimized. Egalitarian principles may require the sharing of financial burdens and inhibit transition to alternative economies of self-sufficiency or production for exchange. On the other hand, a division of labor can create other problems. If certain individuals carry the financial burden because of wage earning capabilities while others are responsible for self-sufficient activities or those geared to production for exchange, political cleavages may form on the basis of perceived divergent 'class' interests. The 'maecenatic' approach and various forms of household capitalism, on the other hand, create no such basis for class conflict and permit easier transitions to household-centered production of commodities.

Worldly utopian want satisfaction

While want satisfaction in natural synchronic groups may involve diverse strategies, groups which promote utopian symbolic constructions of the world are more restricted in their methods. The worldly utopians hope to provide a model of how the entire social world could be. They must therefore be concerned with types of want satisfaction which have some basis in production, either for internal use or for exchange. Donations and profits from promotional activities may serve as secondary sources of income. Assessments and gifts may have been important during initial stages of group life. But the ongoing group has passed any point where such sources of income could provide for wants.

Efficient use of labor and material resources thus becomes the overriding issue of concern in worldly utopian groups. Whether oriented toward a self-sufficient 'oikos' or production for the market, such groups are faced with the prospect of supporting collective life principally through the organized efforts of participants.

The forms of production are generally those of socialism. Anarchism, as a mode of integration, while suited to regions where occasional outside work is available and subsistence possible (e.g. in certain agricultural and raw material ecologies), is of little use in situations where maximization of production is the key to economic survival. A purely communist mode, on the other hand, rests on a highly collectivized set of wants. In general, for worldly utopian groups, a socialist balance of collective and personal want satisfaction provides a middle road whereby collective want satisfaction can be achieved without invocation of sectarian schemes of true belief.

The character of socialist want satisfaction in worldly utopian groups rests on the nature of group world time and its correlate, the organization of work. In the diachronic worldly utopia, such as Twin Oaks, a system to maximize personal preference for work is calculated in terms of 'labor credits.' The more, in quantitative terms, individuals prefer a particular type of work, the fewer labor credits they receive for it. Each person at Twin Oaks gets from 0·6 to 1·6 labor credits for each hour of work performed and must 'earn' a standard quota of labor credits each week. Available labor must then be allocated to labor needs specified in terms of routine tasks. Work serves not as a self-contained job, but as a segmented episode of a more inclusive productive process. Such a form of organization is particularly suited to the requirements of the assembly line, and production for market exchange becomes an important basis of want satisfaction. Since time is rationalized, available labor is a calculable productive input, and the maintenance of individual labor accounts becomes a relatively simple matter. The individual's 'fair share' of contributing to want satisfaction becomes specifiable in terms of hours of work at a given rate of credit for a task. The example of household capitalism cited by Weber (1968:376), in which individuals' relations to the collective household economy are specified in terms of monetary accounts - this form is paralleled in the diachronic worldly utopia by way of labor accounts. The labor credit substitutes for money, and an accounting obligation displaces a personal one, thereby maximizing personal freedom (cf. Simmel, 1963).

In the synchronic worldly utopia, the absence of an

objectified world time leaves no opening for individual labor or capital accounts; indeed, there is ideological resistance to such an approach and work is communal. At The Farm, the spiritual community in Tennessee, specification of work is achieved synchronically, in crew 'group heads' tied to want satisfaction functions. The emphasis on crew formations makes routinized participation in assembly line processes difficult; but industrialized production of sorghum, soy milk, lumber and books is still possible. As Weber (1968:153) has observed, the assurance of effectiveness for such unaccounted communal work is to be found not in calculative optimization of labor time inputs, but in the value-based commitments of mutual solidarity. Nevertheless, the worldly utopian demonstration of a viable social model requires that work be organized efficiently enough to provide for collective needs. The style of organization must be rational, but it need not involve rationalization of labor time.

Apocalyptic sectarian want satisfaction

While organization of work and its benefits are central issues for worldly utopian groups, the apocalyptic sense of living in unusual and transitional time leads to a downgrading of materially productive work as a dominant theme of concern. In the case of Manichean war with the forces of evil, the specification of wants becomes tied to the logistics of mission; in the case of sectarian withdrawal, emphasis on spiritual purpose makes material wants a subsidiary issue. The methods of want satisfaction cannot interfere with primary directions of social action, whether they be of warfare or of religious invocation.* The requirements of a self-sufficient 'oikos' or production for market would be too great a burden on participants' missionary endeavors, while any kind of tax

---

* Weber (1968:153-4) does not make a distinction between worldly utopian and other-worldly apocalyptic sects. Instead, he ties all 'communities based on religious belief or some Weltanschauung,' including monasteries, utopian socialist communities and sects, to special want satisfaction of communal labor or patronage. Here, I maintain a distinction: groups with a strong apocalyptic vision, either of war or of other-worldly withdrawal, embrace special methods of want satisfaction, while worldly utopian formations, even spiritual ones, involve more routine, everyday patterns of want satisfaction.

assessments would limit participation to those with sufficient resources.

Instead, apocalyptic purpose becomes the consuming raison d'être, and the collectivity - however organized and construed - becomes the total arbiter of allocation of resources under a pure communism. A variety of unobtrusive economic activities may be used to satisfy wants defined in a communist manner.

The apocalyptic warriors draw on a charismatic spoils communism: resources are distributed according to the needs of the group. So long as participants can maintain 'fronted' identities above ground, underground activities may be financed through 'straight' jobs. But once a group is forced totally underground, once its members are 'on the run,' donations from sympathizers and booty from pillage, robbery and extortion may become the only sources of income. No matter how money is obtained, the warring sect has extraordinary needs - for 'safehouses,' a support network of sympathizers, bombs and weapons, printing presses, vehicles registered to non-traceable persons, faked identification papers, disguises, and so on. In the name of an apocalyptic holy war, insurgents appropriate the skills, social contacts and material resources necessary for the waging of terrorist action against an established order.

The other-worldly apocalyptic sect tends to engage in a communism of love. Here, the creation of a heavenly plateau requires that want satisfaction and work not be intrusive. This condition rules out any labor-intensive drive toward total self-sufficiency or production for market. At the same time, the resolve in an other-worldly sect to be, at least in principle, open to all comers regardless of their financial statuses, excludes any equitable assessment basis of money procurement. Still, the population of spiritual seekers may be advantageously directed to minimizing needs and raising outside support through solicitation and proselytization. The tableau of a spiritual community composed of former drug addicts, street people and others with and without portfolio working in harmony to achieve union with God, whatever its basis in fact, is a crucial image. It is here that construction of temples, achievement of perfection in physical appearances and accomplishments of spiritual salvation convince both the initiated and the newcomer of the righteousness of the divine mission. The concomitants of such a tableau provide the basis of want satisfaction.

At the Love Family, for example, the giving over of personal property to a community of goods permits the sorting of goods useful to the community, and the barter or sale of surplus goods can be used for acquisition of special resources available only externally. This demonstration that 'the Lord provides' is held out as the basis for further proselytization and attraction of outside patrons.

The Krishna movement employs more strictly calculative and routinized methods of want satisfaction, similarly based on proselytization. The wholesale distribution of incense, oils, shampoos, books and music, as well as the distribution of religious materials in the streets in return for 'donations' provide monetary income and a chance to proselytize. In addition, the missionary appeal of an enterprise with 'good consciousness' attracts patrons who identify their support of a worthy cause as 'good karma.' Thus, George Harrison, a former member of the Beatles and Krishna supporter, has been told that he can do the movement more good from the outside than from within. Though benevolent support may be of the 'maecenatic' type, devoid of any special privilege or dispensation, it may also be associated with specific benefits, such as rights to visit, live at, or retire at a spiritual community.* All of these approaches, whether or not linked to privilege, rest on the aesthetic and moral appeal of the spiritual enterprise, and the ability on that basis to attract further recruits.

Want satisfaction in transcendental groups

In the transcendental formation, the concern with immersion in phenomena devoid of interpretation precludes proselytization on the basis of a belief system like those prevalent in apocalyptic sects. Rejection of continuous economic enterprise of self-sufficient or market production is as important in the transcendental formation as in the apocalyptic one; but drives of proselytization to expand the community of goods involve a calculation generally held in disrepute. The transcendental formation therefore more closely approaches the type of charismatic want satisfaction described by Weber (1968:245):

---

* The Krishna farm in West Virginia at one time launched a membership drive with different statuses attached to size of donation. For $500, the donor receives a ten-year membership in the community 'with full guest privileges'; for $1000, a lifetime membership; and for $5000, 'the status of patron' with 'a private cottage, which can be used as a home, retreat or retirement [sic]' (New Vrindaban, n.d.).

> From the point of view of rational economic activity, charismatic want satisfaction is a typical anti-economic force. It repudiates any sort of involvement in the everyday routine world. It can only tolerate, with an attitude of complete emotional indifference, irregular, unsystematic acquisitive acts.

Such want satisfaction may take a number of forms, all communistic in consumption and devoid of any ethic of work asceticism. People bring to the social arena what they can, and these resources, both monetary and material, are used by participants as they see fit to provide wants. No privilege is associated with the provision of material resources, nor does the inability to make such provisions affect the standing of a person otherwise enmeshed in the collective life. Specifically, money cannot buy the services of a shaman or the socialization into seeing provided by the mystic (cf. Castaneda, 1972:21-2), though donations by grateful recipients of healing or knowledge may be accepted. People of independent wealth may form the cornerstones of transcendental organizations, and money for special expenses may be raised from well-to-do visitors. But whether the basis of financial support is one of independent wealth, assessments, donations, extortion, or occasional outside work, the transcendental enterprise of providing an alternative experientially based understanding of the world is the thematic concern. Satisfying material wants is of secondary importance. In the more specialized work of shamans and medicine men, some required resources may be quite unique and only obtainable through non-economic means. Mushrooms and herbs can only be collected by walking in the countryside. Whether the required resources can be obtained in the market or only in the forest, their preparation for use in satisfying wants is accomplished not through any rationalized or authoritarian work structure, but instead in the course of the collective living of 'the life.'

STRATEGIES OF RESOURCE ACQUISITION

Whatever methods of want satisfaction communal groups employ, they still operate to acquire material resources outside the communal site. At less technocratic rural groups (the vast majority) the general ethic is to decrease dependence on the 'System.' Emergence of a self-sufficient association of communal groups, each concentrating on a particular resource, may be contemplated. But even those groups closest to self-sufficiency do not escape the interdependent character of present-day social life: tools, hardware, parts and machinery are but the most noticeable of market economy resources used by even the most independent of groups. And even where an autonomy based on hand-crafted technology is praised, groups use outside resources to approach such autonomy. The horse-drawn plow and the woodburning stove are still made of metal, and the contemplated solar energy system may actually call for plastics. It is here that some of the hard political choices are made by communal groups: whether to exclude certain cultural items on ideological grounds, use them under a rhetoric of necessary evils, or 'cop to plastic as a good thing.' The resolution of such an issue to some extent determines the kind of commerce with the external world: the subsistence orientation allows for a falling away from dealings with multinational corporations and their distributors. But no matter how close a group comes to self-sufficient subsistence, some outside needs are still satisfied in quite conventional ways: money obtained by whatever means is used to purchase them.

However dependent they may ultimately be on purchase of some outside resources, communal groups generally seem to reduce levels of needs and employ special strategies for meeting such needs. These strategies are made possible both through economies of scale and through the creation of a household social arena where surplus time is available for work. Four strategies of resource acquisition seem particularly important to the maintenance of communal life. They include: 1 theft and scrounging; 2 direct commerce with wholesalers and producers; 3 barter and exchange; and 4 participation in an alternative community economy.

Theft, scrounging and salvage

Resourceful communards quickly find that certain unusual situations permit happenstance acquisition of material resources at bargain rates - either free or tied to labor-intensive commerce. Outright theft may be the basis for procuring food from supermarkets, building materials from construction sites, and other commodities not nailed down, particularly those from corporations. Such activity is not widespread, especially at more ideologically grounded communal sites. But its use, when it does occur, comes to be justified under two alternative ethics, both related to the concept of property. Under the first rationale, property owned by corporations, especially large ones, has been acquired through exploitation and oppression of the labor force, in order to produce profit. Corporate possession is treated as an illegitimate fiction of profit ownership, and the act of removing such goods unlawfully may be referred to as an 'act of liberation.' During the heyday of radical political collectives in the early 1970s, some people boasted that they 'shop at Safeway just like everyone else. We just don't pay.' Theft may also occur at non-commercial sites. In such situations, the rationale of removing goods produced through exploitation is supplanted by a second rationale, the 'property belongs to those who use it.' Material goods such as hardware, plumbing parts, and lumber may be 'liberated' from those who have no apparent use for them. Inherent in such theft is the idea that proprietary rights are not to be ascribed through any system of social legitimation. Instead, they are to be seized. Such charismatic want satisfaction is seen as a revolutionary act.

Most groups find, however, that the 'karma' of revolutionary appropriation comes back to haunt. One communard found immediate 'cosmic' retribution: the case of eggs he thought he had successfully 'lifted' turned out to be a decoy of egg cartons filled with gravel. In most communes, theft has become passée. If material goods are really not being used by others, members of communes often find it possible to socially establish proprietary rights. Thus, one group acquired a greenhouse for a nominal cost plus the labor involved in dismantling and reassembling it. During housewrecking operations, free salvage wood is there for the work involved in sorting and removing it. The settlement of an estate may produce goods for which only the most intransigent hippie artisan can find a use. And the members of communards' original families are often all too eager to unload some of the hodgepodge of possessions they have accumulated over the years.

The smart hippie learns to establish use values for goods and sort accordingly, but less suspecting groups can find themselves overladen with a void of useless junk. Diligent acquisition, however, may produce the prerequisites of small-scale farming with the technology of a bygone era. Praise comes to be heard for 1948 International Harvester tractors made when steel was still 'strong stuff.' Pride comes to be taken in making use of goods that others had long since written off as losses. The 1950 Ford three-ton farm truck with a two-speed differential and hydraulic dump is alternately cursed and praised when a mysterious animism seems to govern its operation.

The salvaging orientation may also be directed toward food items. Members of communal groups on occasion haunt the produce sections of supermarkets looking for free food that would otherwise be thrown away. The president of a Krishna temple instructs a group of devotees to be sure to beg for food as shoppers come out of a supermarket. And members of the Love Family and other groups take advantage of the abundance of food at harvest time by 'gleaning' fields for potatoes and other vegetables missed by machine harvesting. Fruit trees on abandoned farms are picked clean, and may even be pruned as earthly recompense. And those who do not subscribe to vegetarian practices may fish and hunt for food.

In sum, a variety of material goods, from building materials to food, may be acquired by communal groups through activities such as theft, salvage, scrounging and begging. The use of such strategies indicates a substantial difference between the communal and more conventional modes of want satisfaction. An understanding that goods are available through irregular channels is substituted for the assumption that all wants must somehow be satisfied through purchase of goods at a store or commercial outlet. Like the gypsy, the communard comes to look at the careers of material goods as a flow whose channels can be altered to the benefits of the community. The categories of acquisition are broadened from the bourgeois ones of purchase and gift to various schemes of 'manifesting' which sweep away the rationalized treatment of material goods and their proprietary linkages to social actors.

Entering the wholesalers' and producers' markets

Especially in the early stages, and always to some degree, a communal group depends on the purchase of goods to satisfy wants. A nuclear family or other numerically small unit of consumption must depend, for the most part, on retail outlets. In this retail market, producers and manufacturers of basic goods exploit conditions of high turnover of low volume per unit goods to maximize profits. A number of marketing devices such as additional processing (e.g. in frozen TV dinners) and convenience packaging serve to expand the dimensions of value added from which profit may be extracted. Manufacturers may also seek to maximize profit by decreasing the production costs per unit of goods through minimizing material and labor costs, often giving consumers 'less for their money.' So long as most companies competing in a given sector of the retail market act on such a basis of economic rationality, the quality of goods seems to suffer a decline. Especially when zones of retail commerce are closed to entry of new kinds of competitors, as in shopping centers or market sectors with high barriers to entry, consumers are left continually shrinking roles in the preparation of material goods and in selection among alternative strategies to satisfy wants.

Both for ideological and economic reasons, communal groups seek to bypass retail markets, particularly those of profit-taking corporations. Whatever ethic of self-sufficiency prevails, most communal groups at least seek to shun politically unacceptable producers. At the same time, communal groups seek in an economically rational manner to increase the purchasing power of their scarce financial resources. Such maximization of money value is a natural consequence of the economies of scale inherent in communal life.

The larger size of communes, in comparison to other available household units (excluding such institutionalized ones as housing cooperatives, the military, mental hospitals, certain universities and nursing homes) allows for exploitation of economies of scale. By purchasing larger quantities of goods and developing adequate storage facilities for semi-perishable goods such as grains, the communal group may obtain goods at a lower per unit cost.

Such savings begin in the retail market with purchases of the giant economy package. But this is just the beginning. Further searches for economies of scale lead to direct business with wholesalers, and ultimately, producers. Savings of 15 to 40 per cent off retail prices may be achieved in the purchase of food, and more spectacular savings may be realized in purchase of specialized goods. One urban group actually maintained the cost per person per week for food over three years (1971-4) when the prices of food were continually increasing. A rural group realized a savings of over 60 per cent in purchasing fertilizers directly from producers. Under a cooperative purchasing principle, the tendency is to maximize economies of scale by purchasing in quantity and dealing more and more with wholesalers and producers, thereby bypassing retail and middleman profits.

Mutual aid, barter and exchange

In the course of their activities, communal groups which are more than simple cooperative housing arrangements come to possess scarce resources and commodities, and are thereby able to enter into transactions of barter and exchange with other communal groups, neighbors, and others. Skillful negotiation may produce benefit for both parties involved: wants can be satisfied at a mutual saving which avoids the perils of the market, conserves scarce money, and eliminates third-party profits.

Groups come to possess excess resources in a number of ways. Establishment of a community of goods, as in the Love Family and similar sects, immediately provides a wealth of televisions, stereos, automobiles and all manner of other property - either communally useless or duplicative. Other groups come to possess property through other means - those of theft, scrounging and barter. In addition, the acquisition of certain equipment which has a service use - such as welding equipment, tractors, chain saws and special tools - also gives a basis for exchange. Finally, the productive communal groups will have on hand a surplus of certain products and commodities, for example, cottage industry goods, marijuana, craft items, food and agricultural products and byproducts such as hay and manure.

Such surplus resources may be disposed of in three ways short of selling them. They may simply be given away to whoever wants them. Secondly, in the case of mutual aid (Kropotkin, 1914), the communal group provides goods and services to other groups, families and individuals without directly negotiating exchange. In this approach, following the tradition of certain Pacific Northwest Indians and others, a set of mutual obligations is set up. 'I'll scratch your back if you scratch mine.' The group that has an extra 250-gallon fuel tank will 'lend' it to another group with the understanding that such a 'loan' can be collected at some future point, either by repossession when the recipient group no longer has need of the tank, or alternatively, through provision by the recipient group of some other resource needed by the original lending group. While the loan is materially unconditional, it occurs only with the understanding that other loans in the opposite direction would be similarly unconditional. The concept of 'use value' is substituted for one of 'market value.' A community of resources beyond the boundary of any one communal group is thereby established. In this resource community, proprietary rights are based on need rather than ability to pay. So long as equity is felt to be approached in the long run, participating groups benefit through their maximization of use value of free resources. Mutual help between a communal group and neighbors may be unsentimentally based on an expected future return (cf. Weber, 1968:361), but between two or more communal groups, the unprovisional, unroutinized basis of exchange supports development of a mutual solidarity.

The more calculative institution of barter requires direct exchange of goods or services on the basis of some market value equivalence rather than the more particularistic sentiments of mutual aid. An urban group may bankroll rural organic farming efforts with the negotiated expectation that the harvest will yield foods at below market prices. Hay can be traded for the right to store it. The hay producer can thereby hold the goods off the market until benefits can be reaped from increased demand, while the warehouser receives a share of goods at below market prices. Similarly, the artisan or cottage industry group can avoid the middleman by trading products for needed items available from other groups. A selling producer would typically incur third-party costs that involve getting goods to market and paying for middleman profits in the purchase of other goods. Under such conditions, barter is a rationally profitable enterprise. Moreover, it allows the group to use money - a scarce resource obtained only outside the communal 'oikos' - for wants that cannot be obtained in any other manner. And the calculative spirit of barter already extends beyond boundaries of inter-communal solidarity found in mutual aid, for it treats goods as having a market value which must be maximized. Mutual aid thus tends to be invoked, at least as a metaphor of exchange, in transactions where there is an impetus toward solidarity, while more calculative barter may be reserved for transactions with producing neighbors, alliances of communes where a basis of mutual solidarity is absent, and wherever an unsentimental impersonality similar to that of the market is desired.

The alternative community economy

Particularly in geographical areas in which a sufficient number of rural and urban communal groups and peripherally associated households exist, a relatively autonomous community economy may begin to operate. In the ideal-typical construction, such an economy is based on external wholesale transactions, and internal mutual aid, barter, and non-profit transactions. Retail marketing to non-associated consumers is treated as 'foreign trade.'

The process of exploiting economies of scale used by individual communal groups is recapitulated in a community-based union of consumers. Both communal and other households band together to form consumers' 'conspiracies' and cooperatives. Though the initial impetus for such cooperation typically is focused on food, the cooperative concept is easily transferred to provinces as diverse as health care and automobile maintenance. Especially in the food economy, a cooperative approach may lead to the development of a cooperative wholesale organization. Such an organization, for example, the Cooperating Community of Seattle or the Common Market of Denver, can engage in barter with local producers and direct wholesale purchases from more distant producers and cooperatives. A complex but fairly direct 'food chain' is thereby established.

In the playing out of cooperative consuming groups, the continual ideological tension is between pure economic self-interest of participating households and the emergence of mutual solidarity based on value agreements and the experience of shared work. If cooperative membership is extended beyond an ideological community base, peripheral consumers 'just in it to save money and get good organic food' may press for sacrifice of ideals in favor of efficiency and cost minimization. On the other hand, the ideologically 'pure' formation of a cooperative group is limited in its expansion-based increase in purchase power, and must rely more heavily on members' labor, a higher price markup for non-members, and the economics of barter to compete effectively with corporate food distribution economies of scale.

Whatever relations obtain in a given organization, the community economy of communal and other households, cooperatives, 'hip' businesses, producers and wholesalers serves as one basis for further community organization of want satisfaction. In the urban situation, medical and dental clinics, crisis centers, resource networks and other organizations may be supported in part through community labor, and, as in Champaign-Urbana, Illinois, Madison, Wisconsin and other university towns, through a community 'tax' charged by retail stores and cooperatives. Social service functions, previously the domain of the state, come to be provided by indigenous community organizations.

Such consequences of community economic organization are a subject for analysis in their own right. So far as their consequences for communal life are concerned, the existence of community economic institutions permits groups to satisfy some wants by dealing with alternative marketplaces, both saving money and increasing the viability of the organizations involved. In the course of development of such community interdependence, a communally based division of labor may emerge. One rural organic vegetable farming group may depend on another rural group that specializes in seed production; the vegetable group's initial capital costs are provided by an urban group which receives produce in return, and the excess of harvested crops may be exchanged for other goods.

The emergence of a community economy allows a communal group to minimize the costs of obtaining externally supplied goods, while at the same time placing money or resources in the hands of those with similar commitments to communal enterprises. It is in this arena that communal organizations with diverse worldviews, folkways, and internal organizations may enter into commerce with one another. It is here that pagans and Marxists may do business with spiritual ascetics, and utopian anarchists may rub shoulders with sectarian Maoists. Whatever political and spiritual differences people may have, they are bridged in an alliance of economic folkways which establish a dimension of mutual solidarity, of a community of exchange relations which parallels and opposes the mainstream models of retail consumer want satisfaction.*

LABOR SUBSTITUTION AND PRODUCTION OF GOODS

The communal group, however tied to outside resources, serves as the ultimate link between wants and their satisfaction. Certain groups - simple housing cooperatives and those groups with special missions - may rely heavily on a cash-based outside resource procurement. The ability to make money, either at outside jobs or in a communal enterprise, often overrides the savings that can be achieved through communal work: if more capital is generated through outside jobs or a communal enterprise than can be saved by communal labor, the group remains active in market and community market economies while streamlining the internal satisfaction of wants.

In most communal groups, however, there is a surplus of people who do not find the income benefits of 'straight' jobs commensurate with the perceived social costs. In such groups, labor substitution for capital becomes both an expedient basis for survival and an ideologically

* As Reinhard Bendix (1974:152-4) observes in a review of Marx's and Weber's theories of class and status groups, in the economies of privileged groups, status considerations of social honor may be maintained and elaborated as a means of solidifying attained economic advantages. Contemporary developments of intercommunal economies indicate this process may be used in parallel fashion by negatively privileged groups.

justified way of 'doing it.' Salvage, barter, and wholesale purchases are paralleled by internal processes of labor substitution. Movement away from retail consumption leads to marshalling less processed or finished resources. Increasingly, raw materials are processed through labor substitution to satisfy wants. Communal participants in labor substitution probably do not add value to the degree that they could by participating in the external economy. But they do reduce cash outlays and provide a quality of life unattainable through retail consumption. Such labor substitution can function in two ways: to produce finished goods from raw materials for internal consumption, and to produce goods for market.

In the first approach, materials needed for finished goods are bought in their raw components. Instead of purchasing bread, people bake it. Communal groups have similarly begun producing their own yogurt, sprouts, granola and other food items. Special means of production are sometimes bought and used for developing an internally-based satisfaction of wants. Tools permit the servicing of equipment, machinery and cars; special equipment may enhance productivity of a garden; goats, chickens and cows may be kept to provide milk and eggs. And buildings may be constructed in part from internally available raw materials. The communal site comes to serve not merely as a locus of consumption, but increasingly as the site where goods are produced by participants for their own use. These strategies bring on a diversification of communal enterprises: since time is more available than money, it is put to use in ways that have an internal marginal utility.

In the second alternative, production of some particular item becomes routinized to the point where economies of scale permit production for the market. Whether the goods produced be those of cottage industry, services, or agriculture, the successful development of an exchange commodity or service leads to the downplaying of self-sufficient enterprises. At Twin Oaks, for example, where hammock production and editorial services provide an outside source of income, gardening increasingly becomes economically irrational.

ORGANIZATION OF WORK

All communal groups (aside from household cooperatives) draw upon some parallel ways of producing material goods and entering into exchange with the external economy. Situational features - the availability of a household labor force and economies of scale tied to household size - make possible external forms of acquisition such as salvage, barter and exchange, wholesale acquisition, and internal labor substitution for monied purchase. But the organization of work in which such dynamics come into play parallels more specific strategies of want satisfaction. Just as communal strategies of want satisfaction are grounded in various constructions of time and social enactment, so the organization of work reflects such orientations. That this is the case may be seen by examining the various ways communal groups organize to produce goods and satisfy wants on-site.

A diachronic organization of work

In the diachronic construction of an objective world time, the organization to meet needs is rationalized and whenever possible, routinized. At Twin Oaks, all need areas are specified by area managers as to their monthly labor requirements and associated schedules of performance. Both community enterprises of production for exchange and self-sufficiency and household requirements (such as cleaning and cooking) are represented in labor budgets hammered out at group meetings. Individuals in the labor force are assigned slots every week according to an internal market system of preference maximization. Other work may be 'self-assigned' at a going labor credit rate. The original organizational form was simply one of area managers and workers. More recently, people who specialize in certain occupations such as construction and cooking have pushed for the allocation of labor budgets to work crews which then take responsibility for satisfaction of wants through collective decisions. Whether work is performed according to preference system assignment, self-assignment or crew assignment, individuals accrue labor credits for hours worked to satisfy communally budgeted wants. On the other hand, work that has not been budgeted seldom gets done. Time off is free time and the diachronic organization of work is thus based solely on a monthly and weekly planning system in which available hours are allocated according to budget requirements and individual preferences. It is the worldly utopian example of a bureaucratically organized, planned socialist economy.

Increasingly at Twin Oaks, there is dissatisfaction with the planned economy of labor. While some people treat assigned work as a burden and just barely meet their quotas each week, other individuals become so enthusiastic about their tasks that they accumulate a considerable surplus of labor credits. The system enforces a minimum contribution of hours to community work, but in so far as people treat putting in hours as satisfaction of community obligations, the quality of work suffers. In the cottage industry jobs, quality control becomes a necessary component of work organization. In other areas, the care with which work is performed does not always indicate pride or personal investment in the quality of the job. The system of reward solely for budgeted work discourages these personal touches. One disgruntled Twin Oaks resident was led to comment: 'Around here it's not how good you are that determines your [labor credit] rate; it's how much you hate the work.' The job of building an intentional community verges on a labor for credits rather than a labor of love.

This can easily be seen by the visitor who compares the main community at Twin Oaks with one of its branches, Merion, a small household of people who chose to live together while participating in the Twin Oaks community labor system. At Merion, the very details which are absent elsewhere at Twin Oaks come to the fore. Social relations are ultimately personal, rather than universalistic, and the household life represents emergence of a common aesthetic of living. People have quite obviously gone out of their way to do their work well rather than just getting the job done.

In the larger Twin Oaks community, assignment of labor slots, even according to individual preferences, does not encourage development of esprit de corps in the work situation, though it may develop anyway for other reasons. Individuals guided by compasses mapped weekly interact with each other in the course of a day according to work preferences. Increasingly, the labor assignment process has been taken over by managers, and in certain kinds of work such as cleaning, construction and cooking, by crews. The Merion branch takes on a household labor quota which members allocate among themselves. These tendencies toward crew and household allocated labor indicate a dissatisfaction among some members with the universalistic and egalitarian labor credit system of allocating work. More and more, diachronically-based planning of work is supplanted by synchronic forms of work initiation: officeholders and crews begin to usurp the rationalized and policy-based specification of wants, according to their individual and collective prerogatives at the site of work. The ideologists of scientific management are thus challenged in their defense of a rational organization of work by those who care less about procedure and form than about doing work well and enjoying the engagement of it.

Synchronic work organization

The diachronic work organization in its ideal-typical form can be identified by a partitioning in time, consciousness, and often place, between planning of work activities and their execution. In this situation the worker acts under what Mannheim (1934:14-16) calls the 'functional' rationality of a footsoldier involved in a more encompassing 'substantive' rationality of captains and generals.

At urban cooperative communes composed mostly of persons with outside jobs, the horizon of world social time is sometimes similarly organized via a weekly schedule, with responsibility for various tasks assigned on a rotational basis. Such a schedule is meant to ensure that shopping will be done, meals prepared, and so forth. When anticipated (scheduled) events fail to occur, responsibility may be affixed in terms of a previously established objective matrix. At more communal groups - both urban and rural - such a schedule is typically rejected. Instead, in a synchronic formation, when things are going smoothly, the collective temporal horizon of the day is understood by all, and people act in terms of it, working out the details at the moment. Whatever the authority structure of work may be - whether of the charismatic lead man or lead woman, of patriarchical authority, office holding, or work democracy (cf. Reich, 1970), little division in time or among people is maintained between the conception of work projects and their execution. The obligations and rewards of work (and standards of censure for shirkers) are contained not in any externalized, rational and equitable system of conscription, but in the collective sentiments of communal participants. While work in the diachronic construction is allocated labor, the synchronic concept is of joint projects.

In natural and transcendental formations, the tasks of the day are woven into the flow of other activities according to whims of participants. Work is not assigned, but rather negotiated on the spot; people count on each other to 'do what needs to be done.' At 'URON,' for example, the primary recurrent events of want satisfaction that constitute a world time revolve around meals. It is understood that a communal meal will be held each evening, and that the kitchen and dishes will be cleaned afterwards. As the time for dinner draws near, one person or another may start cooking. If no one has begun the meal, someone will ask (members of 'URON'):

L: 'Has anyone done anything about dinner?'

F: 'Jim was going to, but he had to pick up Ann at work.'

L: 'I'll get something started. How many people do you think there'll be?'

F: 'Well, Bill's eating out, and Mary and Carol are at yoga class, so I guess there'll be around fourteen. Probably a couple guests - make it sixteen.'

N: 'I'll come help as soon as the news is over.'

In other natural communes, particularly rural ones, the events on the horizon of world time are more complex but, because people are less involved in outside activities, world time still need not require a schedule. Instead, the want satisfaction events of the day may be handled either through the taking on of chores as individual responsibilities, or totally synchronically within the vivid present. In the course of a day, people may decide on various activities: two intimates may work in the garden while another person maintains machinery. If someone needs help, other people can easily be pulled away from their activities for a few minutes. During a break, the status of various projects and future plans may be discussed. The open-ended course of synchronic work can be understood by examining the day's activities at a commune.

One day at 'Free Union,' an open land community, the talk was of taking the cabin structure off an old truck, converting the cabin to a dwelling, and putting a flatbed on the truck. Other more immediate concerns involved finishing the dome roofing and insulation, and making a trip into town for supplies. When it started raining, we went into town, and on returning, we spent the afternoon inside, drinking and smoking, and patching clothes. By the time the rain let up, it was too late to get much done outside, but Tex was drunk enough to want to patch the roof. He and Three Paws went up to the top of the dome, and Three Paws tied a rope around Tex's leg, let him down the curve of the dome with patches, roofing nails and a hammer, and held tight to the rope. Tex did the job and they came down for more beer: 'Brother, let me tell you, you was carrying it all up there; if you'd have gone, we'd both be gone, 'cause I was already gone!'

At another group, the day's main project of building counters for the kitchen was interspersed with meals, a hike, motorcycle repair, working out a deal with another group for loaning a truck, and playing music.

Rather than trying to plan work, people do it as they

go along. Hardly anyone wants to be straw boss; hardly anyone wants to work under direction of a straw boss. Depending on the degree of coherence in work communication, people may engage in work that is counter-productive to efforts of others. The absence of a formally rational scheme requires greater on-site communication. With such communication, work is defined in terms of sequenced episodes of projects rather than as labor in rationalized time. Momentary tasks come to be taken care of without being raised formally as wants, and other tasks are accomplished on the basis of individual and collective priorities. A 'backburner' approach may emerge: certain wants are tabled until materials, situations or expertise make possible or require the activity. Similarly, a particular goal (e.g. harvesting hay) may provide an agenda and rough timetable for the accomplishment of necessary prior activities such as repairing equipment. It is in the execution of such complex and contingent operations that loosely organized synchronic groups are most likely to encounter difficulties.

In large-scale worldly utopian groups such as The Farm, work relations are more complicated and closely coordinated, but retain a synchronic character. At The Farm, work is divided into various functional areas - farming, gardening, food preparation, child care, vehicle maintenance, and so on. The individual takes on a vocation of working in one or another functional area, and thereby comes to participate in a crew 'group head.' The person who 'knows the most' is accepted as crew leader and exercises authority on technical and operational matters with the advice and consent of other crew members. The leader, however, is to receive no special deference in 'spiritual matters.' The crew group head comes together immediately after breakfast, and the tasks of the day and how they will be done are settled in a rapid fire 'telepathic' style of communication. At one such meeting, of about forty people in the farm crew, the leader 'sorted out' required work, necessary resources and available people. A goal of planting fourteen acres a day had been set. The leader determined what tractors were free and where they were needed, asked another person to 'make closure' on fertilizer, and pointed undirected people to the need for pea pickers. The leader of the stump clearing operation was told to get in touch when he needed a tractor, and 'we'll try and free one up for you.' At the end of this interaction, the leader asked if everyone was 'plugged in' and whether anyone needed more folks. We then broke briefly into work sections - tractor operators, stumpers, pea pickers, and so on. Further arrangements for the details of various projects were quickly made, and we moved off to work.

Almost all work at The Farm is done in such crews, and a work rhythm is established by the participants. A worker may be chided by peers both for 'laying back and not doing a fair share' and for the zeal of being 'more into the work than into the people.' It is thus that the collective vivid present rather than an objectified system establishes standards of work participation. Individuals know where they stand by the feelings of work solidarity which occur on the spot.

Such crew work is not the only means by which needs are satisfied at The Farm. Household 'group heads' take care of their own needs, and work-oriented parties may be held in the evenings. As with other synchronic groups, the attempt is to blur any distinctions between work and play (cf. Csikszentmihalyi and Bennett, 1971). What is done is to be accomplished with a sense of enjoyment, and any feelings of ascetic self-sacrifice, self-righteousness, or the like are usually challenged.

Apocalyptic work

In the apocalyptic construction, special missions are dictated by a special time. This is especially apparent in warring sects, where strategies of terrorist action require special skills and special resources. If such a group has an adequate basis of financial support, apocalyptic work comes to involve procuring necessary material resources (safehouses, transportation, weapons and the like), and using these resources skillfully to advance group goals. Thus participants train in martial skills and discipline, develop plans and strategies, engage in 'dry runs' for planned actions, and take actions themselves, either for spoils or for terrorist effect (cf. Harris and Harris, 1976; Harris et al., 1976; Kohn and Weir, 1976). Daily life becomes permeated not only with strategic concerns, but also with sexual communism (Harris and Harris, 1976:24) and struggles with bourgeois conditioning (Tania, 1974). For apocalyptic sects, life itself becomes apocalyptic work.

In other-worldly sects, the mission does not involve direct Manichean struggle, but work and want satisfaction are similarly tied to the importance of mission. In the Krishna groups, distribution of books and incense provides monetary income and nets recruits for the organization as well. Similarly, the Love Family community of goods depends on attraction of propertied believers. In both cases, work itself attains a symbolic importance, for only the demonstration of a heavenly utopia can attract more followers.

For both groups then, a large part of daily life involves proselytizing. At the Love Family, it is not such a compelling duty, for the 'children will come home to their family' in any event. Love Family members, out in 'the world,' seem to meet up with the lost, homeless, lonely and disenfranchised. They will tell such people that 'God has a family waiting for you with Love.' By direct contact and through reputation, the existence of such a group becomes common knowledge among the young. Some who hear of a group through one incident or another are drawn into the web of group involvement.

> 'People know when they're part of the Family - we go out on missions and find them. Like when I first came here. I had seen Jesus several years before: He had come to me saying he was the way, to follow him. But I didn't have the spirit in me to follow, even though I had received the word. And so I had been searching. And I and a buddy had gone out to Vashon Island - we were just drifting around. I didn't have a job; I was just searching. And a guy told us we could spend the night with the Love Family that night. I didn't think much of it until we got back on the ferry late and didn't have any place to go, so I came up here and I've been here ever since. It's my family, and when I came here, I knew it was home.'

The projection of important symbolic work is maintained by a 'backroom' of calculation behind the front image, itself a construction of material appearances and the 'raps' of devotees. On the way to 'samkirtan,' or street worship, where pamphlets are distributed and donations requested, the talk among Krishna devotees is of how to present materials in such a way as to make a sale or convert. The acquisition of goods and productive resources is accomplished by operators who proselytize outsiders ranging from the uninformed public to believers in various stages of initiation. Recent converts, less secure and more fanatical in their belief than old-timers, find their identities as devotees further strengthened by dealing with outsiders.

> D 1: (driving back from street worship) 'How'd you do? Pass up your money and materials.'
> D 2: 'Not very many people today.'
> D 3: 'Not very nice either. One man scowled and knocked the book out of my hands.'
> D 1: 'Out of your hands! What a devil! These people are so sad. There are so many devils in this world.'

D 4: 'We're really in a minority.'
D 5: 'No we're not! Three-quarters of the spirits in the universe are Krishna-conscious, but they don't have an existence on the material plane.'

At the site of the Krishna community, the presence of potential patrons leads to special preparations and more elaborate services of worship. All the while, devotees whisper back and forth about the rumored wealth of the visitor.

At the Love Family, action is taken to establish proprietary rights over goods that are 'loose.' The newcomer is wined and dined, often at the table of Love Israel himself. And when an outside associate of the Love Family left to live in another state, Family members were sent to say 'goodby.'

'Love wanted Richard to give them a cow, and Richard didn't want to. Love felt it was theirs because John had bought it for Richard while he was staying out there so that Richard could give milk to the Family. But Richard offered the cow to them once and they didn't want it. Then Love changed his mind and sent Strength, Cooperation and Logic out to get it; but Richard had changed his mind by then and didn't want to give it to them, because he said the Bible says that a man who doesn't care for his own family first is worse than an infidel. It was really heavy because the Love Family people hadn't succeeded in their missions and were going to have to go back to Love empty-handed.'

The dual activities of proselytization ('souls' and skilled people are important) and acquiring goods may be directed toward any individual, from the total outsider to one who has 'wandered from the flock.' In the playing out of such hustles, the believer becomes more skillful in 'selling' the sectarian package, and the cooperative 'mark' begins to feel a union with the holy, while the less open target comes to be dismissed as a hopeless sinner.

Such tactics toward outsiders, from street people to wealthy patrons to devotees, are used to assure a steady flow of resources and recruits to the elect, those 'chosen by God' to set up the kingdom of heaven on earth. It then remains only to make the most of what resources become available, and organize internal work necessary to the presentation of a spiritual tableau of material life. Here again, religious belief can be played upon to serve the operational needs of the community.

The assignments of work, at both the Krishna farm and the Love Family, are usually made by elders. Women are to 'honor and serve' men, as well as take care of the household and children. Men, according to their status in the spiritual community, are assigned roles of varying responsibility. In the more traditional Krishna organization, roles are routinized: one man is a woodcutter, another works the fields, and still another handles incense distribution. The straw boss makes assignments at the beginning of the workday for those who do not yet have an established job. Work of the Love Family tends to be more communal and happenstance; the elder of a household and other household members may work together on a project; but always the lower statused men and women are to anticipate the Lord's bidding in the execution of mundane affairs.

In both of the other-worldly apocalyptic sects, the work of the community encompasses resource acquisition and proselytization, as well as the everyday tasks of sustenance. Instead of relying on bureaucratic management or crew coordination, apocalyptic sectarian groups bring to bear a hierarchy of spiritual authority for the specification of tasks.

WORK DISCIPLINE AND LEGITIMATION

Rarely in communal organizations do workers receive any monetary rewards. In some groups, they may not even receive equal benefits of community life, and in no case does a legal contract obligate the participant to work. Communal groups can thus only survive through the acceptance by workers of their roles. Such acceptance seems contingent on exploitation of incentives, the self-interest of participants, and symbolic legitimations of work relations. These features are determined by both the kind of communal organization and the nature of work involved (cf. Weber, 1968:150-3).

In the natural commune, typically a small-scale farm or urban household, no special ideology or belief system specifically legitimates work. Initial legitimation may be derived from the apocalyptic imagery of a need to band together to survive independently of the larger economy, but this charismatic basis of work must be routinized once the apocalyptic threat loses its potency. In lieu of apocalyptic legitimation, the incentive to work must come from another source. It may most typically be found in mutual solidarity. Quite simply, people understand that the communal tasks of material maintenance and provision must be accomplished if the collectivity is to continue.

If there is a basis for domination by a charismatic or traditional leader, or a consensual decision arena, individual work roles and the discipline of work are legitimized through that focus. At one patriarchical family living at 'Free Union,' a subservient woman spoke her allegiance to the patriarch's lady: 'When Donna's here, what she says goes, and that's cool with us.' Donna herself rules with the threat of psychic violence: 'You're damn straight [i.e. right] they'd do it [tasks listed to be done in her absence], or find out they'd better do it. We've got too much that has to happen.'

In more anarchic groups, such heavyhanded tactics would be doomed. Among equals, domination by those with special skills or aptitudes is frowned upon. Instead, each person is expected to do a 'fair share' of the work agreed upon. Yet what constitutes a fair share remains problematic, especially if an ethic of marginal self-sufficiency (prevalent among hippie types as well as spiritual ascetics) is countered by 'unlimited willingness to work' (Weber, 1968:152) on the part of agricultural virtuosi wishing to maximize economic return of a land holding. If work asceticism and guilt come between those with differing work ethics, inequalities broaden until differential rewards, a strike of the virtuosi, or a purge of slackards come into play. The social economy of work may take various directions, depending on what interpersonal relations are invoked (member of 'Uronearth Farm'):

> 'You can either have it where "I won't do this for you because you didn't do that," and then the other person won't do anything for you 'cause you didn't do that for him, or you can do things for people knowing they are doing stuff for you.'

Though outcomes are diverse, they all depend on the politics of mutual obligation and exchange. Only the solidarity of individuals who accept one another's contributions as equitable or at least sufficient can sustain an anarchic collective level of effort.

In worldly utopian groups, the organization of work is more complex, and its formal legitimation becomes more an issue. At Twin Oaks, the bureaucratized system of labor planning and allocation requires submission of the individual to a system which defines work roles and maximizes personal preferences among alternatives. As in most bureaucratic industrial organizations, many work roles are specialized rather than broadly specified.* Though the

---

* In Weber's (1968:140ff) terminology, specified work involves interrelating a variety of tasks to produce something, while specialized work, in a division of labor, involves performance of a single function enmeshed in a more encompassing productive process.

individual can maximize preferences among the available work, the system itself and especially the rational organization of work define the scope of available work roles. The typical individual submits to some routine jobs. In a theoretical sense, legitimation is based on the exercise of preferences among alternatives by workers. Since each worker submits to the same system, no workers' displeasure should be greater than anyone else's. Operationally, managers of functional areas, themselves seeking to maximize productivity, must balance efficiency of labor use against the costs of making the work generally unpopular (thus raising the cost of attracting workers to the area, thereby devaluing the area's allocated labor budget). But incentives for workers are less straightforward. Short of incurring a labor deficit and being hounded from the community, the worker is beyond reproach. The incentive to perform quality work efficiently must therefore be based not on direct self-interest, but on an internalized collective interest. The individual obtains no purely personal benefit for work done, benefiting instead in equal measure with others from a prospering community. Each individual, then, has an interest in collective efficiency.

> 'The way I look at it, it's a question of efficiency and more important than that, happiness, which can't happen if things are an inefficient hassle. So I want things to be as efficient as possible because it means more free time for me to learn to play the guitar.'

Purveyors of ideology strongly tout the notion of progress. Hard work now, it is said, will pay off in a better future for all. The dream, then, is of a twenty-hour week, paid vacations, and other benefits which will justify the highly rationalized system of work.

The synchronic case of a worldly utopia, The Farm in Tennessee, depends on a structure of less specialized occupations. The ability of workers to enjoy crew work itself obviates the need for strong external legitimation. Indeed, work itself is a kind of communion. At a work break, for example, the members of the crew come to sit in a circle together. At first all is quiet, as people settle crosslegged into places of stillness. Someone may produce a marijuana cigarette, which is smoked by all as they relax and look around to each other, experiencing their presentness, and looking one another in the eyes. What legitimation does occur is based on a synchronic sense that work serves as its own reward and has ongoing benefits to the community as a whole. Worldly asceticism of the early reforming Protestant sects (cf. Weber, 1958), while rationalized and stripped of its sacred character at

Twin Oaks, is completely rejected at The Farm. Instead, more affectual sentiments are emphasized. Stephen Gaskin, The Farm's spiritual teacher, says,

> 'It doesn't matter where you put the energy in; if it's for a good cause, you'll be covered. But you can't have any attachment to the fruits of your labor - that's the whole trouble with just doing it on a material plane - you're always fighting for more, a pension plan, higher wages, that trip.'

In large part people work (sometimes too zealously even for 'elders') to support Stephen's mission of 'saving the world.' But they also believe what he says, that people with sincere motives can support each other by enjoying the work they do, without invoking future rewards or punishments. Indeed, achieving that viewpoint on work is seen as a crucial aspect of 'saving the world.'

In the withdrawing apocalyptic sects, true belief legitimates work. Devotional service at the Krishna temple is both a duty and a principle avenue to Krishna consciousness.

Devotee:	'I'm tired of working on the road. Why can't I do milking? That's what I'm most qualified to do.'
Straw boss:	'Sometimes Krishna asks you to do other work so that you don't become conditioned to one material plane mode.'
D:	'Yes, but I'm getting conditioned to road work if I'm getting conditioned to anything.'
L:	'Do you want to become Krishna-conscious?'
D:	'Yes, of course.'
L:	'Then you must accept Krishna's authority in doing devotional service to him.'

Beyond the spiritual legitimation of work, the ultimate form of religious domination mirrors St Paul's dictum. The slackard at the Krishna temple is told, 'If you don't work, don't eat' (cf. Weber, 1968:245). Projected future rewards and punishments by God (Krishna) may become much more immediate if the structure of legitimation is pressed.

At the Love Family, on the other hand, the extensive reliance on a community of goods inspired by the charismatic mission of Love Israel leaves less need for direct legitimation of work. Work is not an overbearing requirement of community life, and it becomes incorporated in the broader perfectionist sociability of demonstrating the kingdom of heaven. Deference by females to males, and 'younger' people to elders ties legitimation of work to status deference, which in turn is grounded in religious belief. But since the kingdom of heaven is at hand, the member of the Love Family does not 'work'; certainly no future rewards could be greater than those of ongoing heavenly life. The Love Family member is a manifestation of God, and must 'manifest' good works both as a deserving member of the elect, and as one grateful to God for the abundance received. To do otherwise would be to potentially subject oneself to the gentle chastisement of Love Israel, an embarrassment too great for most family members to even contemplate.

In the transcendental formations - of mystics, shamans, and the charismatic communities of their followers - absence of routines and roles, as well as aversion to epiphenomenal symbolic accounts leaves little basis for legitimation processes. Want satisfaction occurs on a happenstance and providential basis. The person who acts out of a sense of duty or fair share of work would implicitly take on an abstraction of meaning in a 'structure' of social relations beyond the vivid present. No exchange relations can be developed; no deals can be struck; no transactions can be rationalized; in the absence of money, personal obligation remains important (cf. Simmel, 1963:552). The recruit is resocialized to a view of the world in which the experiences of the social and the world make sense in and of themselves. If work activities are legitimated at all, it is only paradoxically in the shared understanding that they are beyond any legitimation which might be constructed. While in the synchronic worldly utopia, work is its own reward, in the transcendental formation, life experience is not to be compartmentalized into work and leisure. It is all play (in the sense of engagement). Though no normative system of deference sustains sociability (as it does in the Love Family), the transcendental experience similarly involves a weaving of diverse activities into the 'running off' of everyday life.

EFFICIENCY AND EFFECTIVENESS

Communal groups organize in a variety of ways to support themselves, depending upon both the type of group formation with its social and ideological requisites, and the material and labor resources which can be exploited at a given site. Satisfaction of wants may be assessed in two different ways. First, we may consider the purely economic question of efficiency - the degree to which an organizational formation with its strategies of want satisfaction and work maximizes output in relation to resource and labor inputs. Second, we may ask about effectiveness - the ability of a communal organization to maintain motivation of participants and other social conditions of survival.

Extraordinary want satisfaction

The latter issue - of effectiveness - is particularly relevant to those transcendental and apocalyptic groups which make no pretense of supporting themselves through production. While efficiency of consumption may become an important issue in such groups, especially as they increase in size, survival does not depend on efficient satisfaction of wants alone. Instead, it depends in large part on the ability to produce and maintain either a spoils communism of war or a communism of love which attracts recruits, patrons and supporters. The Love Family, for example, must continually search out social channels of want satisfaction for its community of goods. And the Krishna groups rely on similar devices, as well as on the sale of incense and oils to those who associate such purchases with good consciousness or support of the movement. Apocalyptic groups, it would seem, can only remain effective in satisfying wants so long as the invocation of extraordinary circumstances convinces outsiders to throw resources in the desired direction. If they are particularly resourceful in amassing resources during the 'apocalyptic' era, those who retain organizational control and their adherents may be able to survive on the spoils long after the images lose their force. Otherwise, the end of the apocalypse requires routinization of want satisfaction in a transition to a church formation or a more productive communal organization. If a group has already developed a rational economic enterprise, the transition may be relatively easy. The Krishna group, for example, has already begun to distribute products devoid of any religious connotations. The more charismatically styled Love Family employs no specifically rational form of economic enterprise. As the effectiveness of apocalyptic want satisfaction declines, transitions to concerns of productive efficiency will be easier for the Krishna group, in which nascent economic rationality already exists.

The transcendental formation is less tied to an expanding following than groups of apocalyptic formation. A strict division may be maintained between arenas of economic activity and the tableau of communal life in which the reformation of consciousness is the only concern. But such a division already undercuts the simultaneity of consciousness which is at the heart of the transcendental enterprise. The more travelled course is therefore to depend on the independent wealth of participants or the patronage of associates. Under such conditions, any loss of charismatic powers to marshal resources must similarly involve either some kind of routinization of economic life or failure (cf. Weber, 1968:1119). Both apocalyptic and transcendental groups may survive for a time on the non-economic basis of a spiritual mission which categorically rejects material concerns. But such approaches to the satisfaction of wants, whatever their pretenses concerning lilies of the fields, offer no solutions for ongoing satisfaction of wants.

Natural synchronic dynamics

It is in the natural synchronic and worldly utopian groups that efficiency as well as effectiveness of want satisfaction becomes an issue. Anarchist and pluralist groups can only marginally attract resources through purveying 'good consciousness,' and are thus subject to more ordinary issues of economic survival than apocalyptic and transcendental groups. And worldly utopian formations specifically represent attempts at demonstrating the viability of ideally prescribed social forms. Among natural communes, the particular relations of communal site to modes of production determine economic viability, while in worldly utopian groups, the social relations and legitimation of work become increasingly important.

Often natural communes, particularly urban ones, depend upon participants' outside jobs for a money-based economy of household communism. During hard times, efficiency may be attained through labor substitution for outside expenditures. But so long as outside work is available and desirable, efficiency of group want satisfaction may not be an overriding concern. The group which depends upon outside work need not be particularly efficient to realize economies of scale. Depending on the austerity of lifestyle, the cost of basic food and shelter per person per month may range from about $75 to $150 (1974 dollars). As the marginal savings decrease in comparison to outside earning capabilities, internal production of goods can be maintained only on the basis of economically non-rational sentiment such as the desire to bypass corporate channels of want satisfaction. On the other hand, if a collective economic enterprise is the basis of support, the efficiency of that enterprise becomes important. Want satisfaction in this case is tied to problems of maintaining a profitable and satisfying enterprise. The group whose members depend on outside jobs may be more stable, in that it can exploit heterogeneous contacts with other economic channels, but mutual solidarity may be more difficult to maintain with such segmentation through outside occupations. The collective enterprise can be the basis of a stronger solidarity so long as it does not succumb to the economic crises which are the bane of small-scale businesses.

In rural settings, the natural synchronic formation takes quite a different direction. Typically small farms (from 10 to 200 acres) may be developed according to highly efficient use of resources and byproducts to eke out a living in an ecological niche which would not be conducive to large-scale rationalized agriculture. In part, the 'back to the land' movement is based on exploitation of such marginally productive land. While self-sufficiency can probably never be fully realized these days, 'godsends' or occasional outside jobs, together with maximization of productivity can produce a viable style of life. The model of small-scale communal farming, so long as it uses marginal lands and rests on anarchism or pluralism, is only open to expansion through duplication. But such a form, as it becomes widespread, can make a significant contribution to the agricultural economy, particularly as economies of scale in agribusiness reach diminishing returns (currently because of increasing chemical fertilizer prices) and the worldwide pressures on food supplies increase.

Worldly utopian models

Both diachronic and synchronic worldly utopian groups take on the problem of how to organize a collective economy on a large scale. While hippie farms may efficiently exploit marginal economic situations, their styles of production are too labor-intensive for use in producing the needs of large social units. Worldly utopian groups come more and more to rely on machinery and large-scale production to meet their needs. At Twin Oaks, goods (hammocks) are produced for market according to a highly rationalized and efficient process. The development of such production and other means of obtaining income results in a money economy: investment capital necessary to maintain production or yield future returns is readily allocated. So long as enterprises remain profitable, the benefits of self-sufficiency are less than their costs, and money-based production for exchange continues to develop.

At The Farm, on the other hand, the incipient organization of work on a basis of broadly specified operations rather than specialized ones is suited more to production of commodities (e.g. sorghum) and unfinished materials (e.g. lumber) than to manufacturing. Income produced from such activities is not so spectacular, and a highly monied economy is less likely to develop. Additionally, synchronic work organization in crews rather than by bureaucratic scheduling permits more efficient use of labor in activities of self-sufficiency. A review of the financial records shows that the income needed to support each person at Twin Oaks, a community of forty in 1973, comes to about $1200 per year, about the same as that of urban communes where members take outside jobs. Costs per person per year (1973) at The Farm are only $365. While part of this difference in the cost of living at the two groups can be attributed to The Farm's program of austerity and its economies of scale in a population in that year of over seven hundred, a major financial savings is derived from production for the self-sufficient 'oikos' rather than emphasis on production for exchange and purchase of other items from outside.

Implications for a new ethic of work

The Twin Oaks formulation - that efficiency is a product of rational organization - has its limits. It opens group life to greater dependence on a money economy as needs are increasingly satisfied with profits from rationalized production. Efficient development of resources is abandoned in favor of profitable utilization of resources. And these developments are paralleled by more and more challenges to the legitimation of work and its benefits. People at The Farm accept a more self-sufficient and austere life coupled with crew organization of work. So long as they are motivated to work for the communal good and because of the enjoyable character of work, there are fewer problems of work legitimation or quests for fringe benefits than at Twin Oaks.

Two problems limit the applicability of The Farm model of crew organization and work specification (as opposed to specialization). First, its applicability to industrial forms of production is only beginning to be understood. Some work may be accomplished more efficiently through specialization and separation of tasks. Yet The Farm employs crew organization in several industrial processes (e.g. a soy milk dairy and a publishing company). The bureaucratic tendency of industrial management has been to rationalize work to a point where worker alienation may counteract rational economies. The success of Volvo factories in moving toward crew organization of automobile production shows that the benefits of such work organization could be usefully pursued. The limits of synchronic work organization have not yet been fully tested.

Second, work at The Farm is based on an ethic that runs counter to contemporary union concerns with wages, conditions of work and fringe benefits. Under the collectivized ethic of The Farm, work and its benefits for the community serve as their own reward. As in the People's Republic of China, collective production becomes a sacred enterprise. Exploitation of The Farm's organization and legitimation of work thus depends upon both a collectivization of life and a synchronic legitimation of work. Collectivization is a political question, but the basis of a synchronic work ethic is already abroad in the contemporary young generation of Americans. The current wave of desires for immediate gratification are bemoaned by bourgeois publicists as the antithesis of the Protestant ethic. The promise of future rewards and progress of the social order currently seem empty words to the alienated young. Synchronic work legitimation would no doubt require modifications in the organization of work in American society, but it would permit the transference of sentiments for immediate gratification from the realms of leisure to those of productive activity.

6 Government

> It didn't take me long to make up my mind that these liars warn't no kings nor dukes, at all, but just low-down humbugs and frauds. But I never said nothing, never let on; kept it to myself; it's the best way; then you don't have no quarrels, and don't get into no trouble. If they wanted us to call them kings and dukes, I hadn't no objections, 'long as it would keep peace in the family.
>
> Huckleberry Finn

The desire to move beyond authority structures and corrupt politics of the established secular and sacred orders has always been one of the primary bases of the utopian impulse. In a society where one has to 'play the game' (i.e. act within an already established structure of authority) to get ahead, youth are encouraged to 'work within the system to change the system;' later they may discover a less idealistic ethic: 'to get along, go along.' Among communalists, the way out is variously depicted as changing the game, starting a new game, or avoiding games altogether. For some, the problem is simply one of personal salvation in an age beyond grace; others seek to demonstrate the possibilities of life under good government or without government; still others seek a radical transformation of the sources and manifestations of power and domination in society-at-large. The political process in communal groups may thus be the vehicle for a mission, a demonstration in itself, or the expedient basis for resolving the problems of everyday life. The forms that action in the political sphere have taken in communal groups range from personal rulership based on tradition and charisma to bureaucratic administration, to less structured cases of anarchy and collegiality. In some cases these forms are carefully legitimated as utopian ideals, said to represent social advances over the secular constitution of power and government. In other cases, de facto power is beyond question and legitimation is a remote issue. In short, the character of government and political action in communal groups does not provide a unified contrast to authority and political processes in the established order.

Given such variety, three concerns are of primary importance in the understanding of communal government. First, we must understand the sources and types of governing formations. Second, we should elaborate the processes of political action and legitimation under various formations, and third, it is important to consider the consequences of various operating models for group stability and the incursion of crises of legitimacy. In this chapter, I suggest that each of these issues, for a given communal group, is circumscribed by the organizing time construction and mode of social enactment of communal life.

SOURCES OF GOVERNING FORMATIONS

Communal groups may be understood as political communities. In Weber's terms (1968:902):

> a separate 'political' community is constituted where we find (1) a 'territory;' (2) the availability of physical force for its domination; and (3) social action which is not restricted, in the frame of an economic group, to the satisfaction of common economic needs but regulates, more generally, the interrelations of the inhabitants of the territory.

Weber went on to note that in certain cases, as with the Quakers, violence may be rejected on principle, and he further suggested that actual organization for the use of force may be entirely absent. Elsewhere, he (1968:54) observed that coercion may be of a hierocratic type, where religious benefits are distributed or denied. This would seem to be the case with the vast majority of communal groups: while sanctions up to and including expulsion from the communal group may be applied against individuals in the name of a communal group, except in warring apocalyptic sects, enforcement rarely involves violence. While even in religious communal groups, physical coercion may occur on occasion, for the most part, coercion is more psychic. Even though membership in communal groups is ultimately voluntary, ongoing participation involves action within what may be considered political communities: even in cases where administration and decision-making are intermittent, people expect conflict to be resolved through collectively legitimated social action. In this regard, the housing cooperative represents a transitional case from communal to purely economic association where decisions are almost exclusively limited to economic wants and their satisfaction, as well as entitlements based on economic participation.

In a political community, politics may be said to be the art of influencing the outcome of problematic issues, particularly those relating to allocation of scarce resources and resolution of scarce decisions. According to Weber (1968:943), domination can have two diametrically opposed sources. It may be achieved either through a mastery of a constellation of interests or through authority, however legitimated. In the first case, resolution of problematic issues in a manner favorable to the dominating power occurs simply because the force of circumstance makes such action the self-interested best solution for dominated persons or groups. In the latter case, self-interest, though a factor, is not the ostensible compelling force: a command is obeyed because it is considered legitimate. Where it occurs, the transition from domination by virtue of a constellation of interests to domination by authority is a process of formalization. If interest becomes more and more determinate because of the emergence of a successful monopolizing power, the power may be institutionalized into a legitimated structure of authority.

The distinction between the two sources of domination differentiates, in the political sphere, between communal groups which have a natural approach to social enactment and those in which a normative relevance structure of produced enactment is imposed. Specifically, the produced approach of worldly utopian groups as well as apocalyptic sectarian ones in each case poses ideological justification of a way of life as a mission. Authority is used by persons in positions of dominance both to enforce adherence to the way of life and to otherwise protect the interests of the promoters of the communal enterprise. In natural synchronic groups, on the other hand, mission seldom extends to the promulgation of a single, encompassing purpose.

Just as with most other kinds of groups, the genesis of natural synchronic groups can only be considered as charismatic: inherently they involve breaking previous ties of association and previous ways of life in order to form a new household. But the charismatic solidarity of embarking on a new mission cannot be sustained simply through the playing out of 'normal' or mundane social life. Since no straightforward legitimation of authority is available beyond the initial loosely charismatic one, the politics of group life becomes subject to the play of competing interests and values. On the face of it, no one image of authority can command more credence than another, and the emergence of a structure of authority may be totally problematic. Change seems inherent, for, as with charisma, commitment is contingent on success, and as with democracy, the way is open to succession toward other formations. Individuals, factions, and the entire collectivity may on various occasions invoke one or another image - of anarchy, cooperation, democracy, family, the act, truth, wisdom, and all manner of other ideals. Whether one or another image comes to be institutionalized as a structure of authority depends on the interplay of individuals. The owner of the land may come to be able to exact deference as a patriarch; charismatic allies may lead the group into mission, or the process of recruitment and departure may sift membership to a point of working consensus, anarchy or chaos. Whatever the historical outcomes, the pluralist character of a natural group assures that the initial dynamic of politics will be based on constellations of interests, however the problematics of interests may be construed.

In groups with produced enactments of social life, whether they be worldly utopian or apocalyptic, the virtuosi of collective life seek to avoid subjecting a legitimated structure of dominance to the play of interest constellations. To do so would be to allow the incursion of non-legitimated and potentially threatening powers. Even in the case of charismatic authority, and more especially under other forms of domination, protection of the 'party line' in produced social enactments requires symbolic legitimation and, ultimately, the subjection of malcontents to various forms of coercion. Yet such coercion cannot be so extreme as to arouse opposition to its methods. The proponents of utopian schemes may thus find themselves caught between matters of principle relating to their vision and the pragmatics of providing a program of group life capable of inspiring adherence of believers.

If mission necessitates authority, then the specific type of mission and its basis of formation underlie forms of domination. In worldly utopian groups, such as Twin Oaks and The Farm in Tennessee, the mission is to provide an operational model of how social life can be constituted on Earth, the difficult issues of want satisfaction and human imperfection notwithstanding.

The mission of good government is closely intertwined with the genesis of the worldly utopian group and the consciousness of time invoked in work and social relations. Weber (1968:1117) has suggested that the two great sources of social change involve respectively charismatic 'inner' change and 'outer' change through rational organization and rationalization. The two worldly utopian groups I have described in detail recapitulate this distinction. The Farm ultimately devolves from the charismatic mission of Stephen Gaskin to 'save the world' by awakening people to a 'higher' order of social relations, while Twin Oaks depends specifically on the creation of a utopian order through the development of more rational social institutions.

At Twin Oaks, the institutional disposition of collective life turns on rationality. Organization of work is dependent to a large degree on repetitive functions in a diachronically coordinated whole. Coordination and planning of such an operation's productive capability requires policy. Social concerns of equality and justice similarly depend upon an institutional form of government in which universalistic administration of situations can operate evenly over time. Particularistic considerations cannot hold sway, for they represent incursions of irrationality and sentiment. The structure of dominance is thus one of legal authority, administered by managers and monitored by planners, with the advice and consent of participants.

At The Farm, it is the 'change of heart' that makes utopia possible. So long as a change is assured for each newcomer to the community of participants, to focus on institutions and policies as mediators for situational decisions makes little sense. While the genesis of The Farm is contained in the charismatic mission of Stephen Gaskin, that charisma in its increasingly routinized form turns on the synchronic resolution of problematic issues by the relevant constituencies. The original charismatic formation becomes transformed into a labyrinth of collegial relations (cf. Weber, 1968:271-83). The resolution of problematic matters is attained through the deliberations, called 'sorting out,' by individuals who bring to bear not the body of law as at Twin Oaks, but the amalgamation of collective ethical and social concerns.

In apocalyptic communal formations, the nature of the mission differs from those of the worldly utopians', and the governing formation varies accordingly. Whether a group's mission is warring or other-worldly, it is the participants' belief in the sanctity of mission which legitimates an order of authority. The actual form of that authority is dependent on the specific nature of the mission. The SLA, for example, rejected the monopoly of legitimate coercion claimed by protectors of the established order and became charismatic warriors against that order. Whatever the specific nature of authority they invoked, the SLA had to have engaged in a discipline of war.

Apocalyptic withdrawing sects similarly base government on a specific mission. But the character of that mission is to present a tableau of the kingdom of heaven. The form of government is theocratic. In both the Love Family and Krishna groups, authority rests in the hands of those sanctified by God - in the former group, elders confirmed by Love Israel's prophetic revelation, and in the latter, priests chosen through traditional authority. Differences in the ambience of government in the two withdrawing sects stem from the specific character of religious belief. The Krishna groups are quite involved in the doctrines of sectarian dogma which are presented as having a long and involved history devolving from numerous ancient sacred texts, newly translated with extensive commentary and purport by the present spiritual master. Issues of authority and justification of action are thus interpreted in terms of scripture. The Love Family similarly bases its charter on doctrine - the New Testament, particularly as it relates to the formation of the primitive Christian church. But Love Israel's prophetic revelation, especially in its more recent phases, emphasizes the spiritual sustenance that the community of the living elect provides its members. Just as members of the Love Family characterize Jesus as living according to the law of his heart, they similarly maintain themselves to be beyond either secular law or the need for an ascetic devotion to the law of the Bible. A charismatic feature of the new revelation is embodied in the idea that 'we are all manifesting the best we can as we go along.' The ideals of love, charity and forgiveness are invoked as necessary to the maintenance of a heavenly family.

Such differences in the form of government - based on degree of reliance on doctrinal discipline - all occur in the context of an overriding similarity between the two withdrawing apocalyptic sects. In each case, authority is based on 'nearness to God.' The basic form is theocratic, and as Weber has commented, revolutionary, to the degree that it calls for domination of secular affairs by religious authorities. No matter what the allegiance of the theocracy, the effect of its operation is to transfer any political inclinations from a class to a religious (status) sphere. Authority and grace are, for the participant, bound up in the religious leader and doctrines. The religious leader may covertly or openly support the secular order or maintain a revolutionary religious mission which counters state authority. In either case, the action of participants is neutralized in the secular world, except as residents of the old order make status passage to a new world.

Transcendental formations, unlike apocalyptic and worldly utopian groups, do not involve allegiance to a specific mission. Neither the development of a utopian model, nor a seizure of state power, nor the establishment of a heavenly kingdom falls within the transcendental province of action. Instead, the ecstatic experience and action in the immediately available phenomenally constituted world is the domain of shamans and mystics, magicians and gurus. In such domains, legitimation is not directed simply toward authority, but rather, to the whole point of view. Authority is not bound up in any ideational legitimation, but simply in the ability of those marked by charismatic powers to convince disciples that possession and mastery of power are bona fide - based not on fraud but on insight and engagement. The transcendental form is inherently a purely charismatic one: authority based on some claim of legitimacy devoid of particularistic qualification has no standing. In heretical Christian sects of the Middle Ages, certification of official capacity (office charisma) was regarded as insufficient to change wine and bread into the body and blood of Christ. Heretics held that such an act could only be accomplished by one who is filled with the 'spirit' at the time. Similarly, the ability to perform 'magical' acts is not guaranteed by any training or certification. Instead, to maintain charismatic validity, the mystagogue must be able to invoke powers successfully at the appropriate times. In certain situations, for example, in Buddhist monasteries (cf. Suzuki, 1965), charisma becomes routinized, but to the extent that such routinization does not contradict the original mystical concerns, authority continues to be vested in those persons whose charisma is acclaimed by a preceding virtuoso or the participants.

Governmental formations in communal groups, as I have tried to demonstrate above, are especially bound up in group orientations to social enactment. In natural formations, a pluralist free market of interest obtains; groups with a produced mode of social enactment, whether worldly utopian or apocalyptic, rely on symbolically legitimated authority of missions; transcendental formations provide a charismatically unified momentary field of authoritative action.

THE POLITICAL PROCESS

Given broad relationships between orientations toward time and social enactment and the legitimated character of a communal group as a political community, the political process takes one or another direction in the ongoing resolution of problematic concerns. Certain interactional motifs and stratagems of domination constitute power in one kind of communal group, while they would never occur in another one.

Constellations of interest, non-legitimated action and collegial authority

The natural communal group typically begins in a wave of charismatic enthusiasm which eventually fades. It may evolve toward a loosely accepted balance of powers based on some form of authority such as collegial consensus, direct democracy or patriarchy, or less institutionalized domination by personae, through control of material resources and the like. Whatever the outcome in this free market play of interests, certain stratagems of both the endowed and the dispossessed become prevalent.

The overall character of political pluralism turns on the problematic nature of legitimation. Pluralistic divergence of worldviews can be largely avoided through an early and consistent use of a consensus or direct democracy model, under which differences are 'thrashed out' by reasonable people open to compromise. But even under such a regime, lapses in bringing issues to the political arena and absence from meetings by one or another member can create problems. Unless total continuity in consensual decision-making and administration is maintained, conflict between diverse viewpoints may come to dominate the political arena. While members of one faction may claim a working consensus, others will argue that decisions have not taken into account their points of view. The issue of what constitutes a meeting in which decisions may be made remains problematic. Those who are absent claim the decisions have no force. But even when a meeting of the whole occurs, people may not agree on what, if anything, has been decided. At one group, a decision concerning where to locate a planned building was changed even after the foundation was begun, because some people came away from a meeting with one sense of the decision which had been reached, while others construed the decision entirely differently. In another case, an individual who had not attended a 'discussion' concerning a problem in relating to an outside organization took action which undermined the approach discussed.

Individuals living in a pluralist situation may adopt one of several broad approaches to politics of unlegitimated action. In one approach, individuals simply avoid involvement in issues where their interest is only peripheral. Instead, they engage only in action which is unproblematic within the group, either because it is a routinized and legitimated communal course of action (e.g. milking the cow) or clearly a personal action devoid of communal implications. The actual ranges of such an orientation are, of course, socially negotiated.

When group legitimation is more problematic, such a line may be difficult to maintain. Frustration with inabilities to constitute an arena of legitimated consensual decision-making at once leads to and is further reinforced by faits accomplis. Unless individuals develop with each other a collective sense of what decisions can be made individually, by interest constituencies (e.g. people engaged in a particular enterprise such as gardening, or those affected by the results of the enterprise), and by the whole, what could function as a form of collective anarchy lapses into more individualistic competition of approaches. Participants may purposely withdraw from meetings where key decisions are at stake and refuse to abide by others' decisions. Conversely, they may purposely avoid bringing an issue to the collegial group and present others with a fait accompli. Justification may fall short of altruistic communal interest: 'I knew it would create a lot of hassle if we tried to reach a decision about it, so I just went ahead and did it anyway.' And if the propensity to countermand such decisions (where possible) is brought to bear unevenly, either because of substantive support for the non-legitimated action or personal deference to the actor, the precedent of unlegitimated action further undermines any push for a legitimated structure of authority. While such ad hoc individualism will find its limits in some woefully stupid or misdirected deeds, it remains the basis of much action, both of propriety among those who see what needs to be done and do it, and of righteousness among individuals propelled by true belief in their cause or viewpoint.

Other people, more timid or perhaps simply cagey, use less controversial ploys to legitimize personal provinces of discretion. Such stratagems are diverse in form and content, but several bear mention for their widespread appearance. Establishment of precedent and expectations provides one way of maintaining a personal province of power. The individual 'broadcasts' information through words and actions: it becomes well known that the individual will hold others accountable for certain actions, or will not allow incursion by others within certain 'personal' domains of influence. Precedent becomes established as customary expectation, for which an account is readily available: 'Ed doesn't like others disturbing him while he's meditating,' or 'Susan doesn't have time for long, involved projects, so she helps out more everyday in the kitchen.' In some cases, the expectation may involve an individual's territorial control of collective concerns. At one group, a woman, with some support from allies, imposed her personal aesthetics upon the purchase of food. Whether the province of expectation is personal or collective, certain ethics come to be invoked as rationalizations of action. Generally, these ethics are logically derived from an ideal of non-interference with others because of rights to privacy or personal freedom of action. Thus, the individual may be 'laying a trip on everyone' if an alliance of opposition to action forms, but more typically, the personal province is protected by an inverse application of the same ethic. In the latter formulation, the group does not have the right to 'lay a trip' on the individual, or 'step on a person's toes.' Such ploys and stratagems for controlling the ongoing social definition of situation are particularly successful if others have built up similar precedents. People who resist having their 'toes stepped on' may form alliances both with those who agree with substantive positions and with those who have a vested interest in maintaining the ethic. They are opposed, if at all, by persons who perceive socially unlegitimated action as threatening their right to a voice in decisions.

The strategy of alliance formation may as easily be used by those who claim to represent the interests of the group as a whole as by diverse individuals with personal domains of discretion. If consensual decision-making and some form of direct democracy fail to legitimate collective actions, then those who feel frustrated by obstruction or indecision which plague natural synchronic collegial groups may increasingly depend on 'backroom' decisions and administration to take care of business that seems to them necessary for group survival. Either this alliance of those who can 'count on' one another is exposed by opponents as alien to public norms, or it remains unchallenged because of its effectiveness. Other group members, 'sitting on the fence,' may throw their chips in with the alliance as the only available constitution of a political community. If the backroom alliance remains open to inclusion of others, it may effectively constitute a dominant working consensus of the group. The arena of politics then becomes what Marx referred to as 'the administration of things' rather than the politics of opposing factions. Alternatively, the backroom alliance may become that of a closed group which increasingly controls material and social interests of others - through property rights, attachments of sentiment, and the like. If one person sufficiently monopolizes the interests of others, that person may become the 'natural' leader of the group, and effect a collegial structure of domination with a preeminent head (cf. Weber, 1968:272).

While the possible emergences of the pluralist political arena are diverse, each depends on the resolution of competing factional interests and consolidation of a collective sense of the group. Unless a collective decision-making process of collegiality, consensus or democracy is strictly maintained, domination of events falls to those who are able to exercise power without legitimation.

Political process in symbolically legitimated groups

Pluralist groups with natural approaches to social enactment may attain working consensus in the 'administration of things,' become mired in factional conflict, or submit to domination by the powerful. Such emergences are grounded in an initial free play of political interest. Produced social enactments of communal groups, on the other hand, begin with ideological constructions of how political decisions and conflict are to be mediated. For worldly utopian as well as apocalyptic groups, the idealization of government defines both the arenas of decision-making, rules for access to positions of authority, and normative bases for the resolution of conflict. However public such institutions may be, their existence is the work of founders who are committed, above all, to the elaboration of the incipient forms.

Such commitment of true belief to the ideologically legitimated forms places virtuosi in the position of maintaining the overall structure of the status quo. At one newly formed group, based on a behavioralist ideology similar to that of Twin Oaks, a virtuoso told other true believers in other groups,

> 'I have decided to become a planner and get immediate one year and five year plans going so that some newcomer won't think the place is up for grabs and stage a takeover. It's hard enough to get a place going when even Robert has doubts about egalitarianism. But I figure you can mold people to it, if you give 'em a

reason for doing it and lots of attention.'

Especially in initial stages of collective life, and continuing so long as admission to the group or positions of power in the group is limited to those who assert personal belief in the ideology of group formation, the entrepreneurial virtuosi of true belief can establish norms, policies and operating procedures which are conducive to maintenance of legitimating ideology and personal authority connected to belief in ideology.

While the unarticulated bases of legitimacy in pluralist groups can turn any problematic issue into a crisis of legitimacy, the construction of authority in symbolically legitimated groups forces any problematic issue into a normative political matrix in which the ideological virtuosi hold the upper hand. So long as the basis of domination remains unchallenged, the ruling minority can act concertedly to deal with any opposition. The exercise of such power of domination varies according to the sources, structure and time consciousness of domination.

1. Political process in a diachronic worldly utopia

In the diachronic worldly utopian group, social relationships are mediated through the elaboration of a rationalized system of 'law' formed through the rule-based legislation of policy and precedents resulting from previous applications of legislation. At Twin Oaks, planners are chosen by incumbent planners.* They serve at once as mediators of conflict, judges, and leaders in various public decision-making arenas related to community, household, labor, finance and 'feedback.' Individuals occasionally come upon ways to 'beat the system.' In other cases, policies provide no clear and straightforward interpretation for new problematic situations. In such cases, the planners develop policy to 'close the gap.' Material issues are to be resolved in terms of rational analysis. Social issues are to be resolved in terms of justice: a planner described the need for a legal basis of action in a meeting about application of group policy to an individual case in the following manner:

> 'We have a policy to ensure that all persons are treated favorably under the law, so that a person like Jane, who we all really dig, will not get special treatment.'

---

* Though members of the community have power of majority veto over the selections by incumbent planners, this power has rarely been used to date.

Social issues may involve both the development of policy for generally problematic situations (for example, whether an allowance accrues during a legal leave of absence) and in the application of policy (for example, whether a person's leave of absence is legal). In resolving such issues, and in ad hoc decisions as well, various principals to the issue have their say, other interested members of the community contribute their views, and planners try to arrive at some resolution which satisfies the precedents of law, the specifics of situation, and the parties to the issue. 'We ask,' says one planner, 'what is the effect of a particular policy?'

Some heretics may challenge the system of decision-making as a shield for covert motivations:

> 'I say we should do away with the rules, 'cause we're just ignoring them anyway. We would be better off to be straight with each other. Who are we kidding - if this were a new member instead of Jane, we would have [made an unfavorable decision] months ago.'

But planners and adherents of the system maintain that a 'rule does serve a function: it tells the person where co [i.e. he or she] will stand if co behaves in a certain way.' While all kinds of sentiments, backroom politics and coercion may be involved in the formulation and application of policy, its formal and ostensible basis remains that of a special public institution distinct from everyday life.

Though those holding the office of planner hold formal power in these public institutions, they are limited in both the degree to which they can strictly interpret and apply policy and the extent to which they can actually engage in the function of planning. On the one hand, they must take popular sentiments into account in the judicial resolution of specific cases and, on the other hand, the political alliances opposed to a strong planner concept limit the degree to which strategic planning (as opposed to interpretive judicial 'planning') can be practiced. Whatever the formal legitimacy of the office of planner, it is limited in power by popular checks against its exercise.

2. Political process in a synchronic worldly utopia

In the synchronic worldly utopia, government is not limited to a special institutionalized arena. Nor does it function on the basis of rules and policies. Instead, at The Farm in Tennessee, the 'Committee,' a collegial group hand-picked by the charismatic leader, Stephen Gaskin, exercises power in areas beyond the everyday operations of various functional 'group heads' such as the gate (i.e. the administered entrance to the communal site), the motor pool crew, and the farming crew. The governing 'Committee' is bipartite in form, following the presbyterian model of democratic government. 'Elders,' initially selected by the charismatic leader, deal with overall direction of 'spiritual affairs,' and 'deacons,' qualified through expertise, deal with the functional management of everyday matters. In both the functional group heads and the Committee, collegial decisions are made on the basis of circumstances, wisdom and pragmatic solutions. If, for example, money is needed to plant crops, the Committee may decide to recruit a work crew to go to a nearby metropolitan area to earn money. A decision of this kind, once made, must be implemented through careful presentation to the community. Members of the Committee 'talk up' the decision and its benefits, and recruit community members to participate. In one case, a member who resisted recruitment was told, 'Yeah, I agree. You're being drafted for a worthy cause.' The entrepreneur of the Committee's decision then elaborated on the logic of the endeavor, the goal of a self-supporting farm, The Farm agreement, and the need for consensus before the action could be undertaken. The still reluctant draftee was then told, 'I feel you're resisting this without good cause.' A witness then rebuked the Committee member: 'I feel like you're pressuring him to cop when he ain't but just had it laid on him ten minutes ago.' The Committee member then agreed to let the recruit 'think it over.'

In other cases, the same pattern is reflected. The Committee or those representing The Farm agreement single out those they feel to be dissenting, and 'work on their case,' until they submit. While The Farm agreement is never made completely explicit, it is used as a pressure for consensus. The individual is never right or wrong in any objective sense, but only because of his or her stand in relation to the agreements of the whole group, or some relevant group head. The Committee members and the overwhelming majority of the community use The Farm agreement and other ideological formations as a basis for coercing conformity in matters regarded as of collective importance. Unresolved dissent and the private maintenance of contrary viewpoints are not tolerated at The Farm. Social control transpires as the establishment of a group consciousness. Unless collective agreement concerning the issue can be reached, the promulgated viewpoint cannot be regarded as 'true.' The continuing pressure is therefore 'to cop to the agreement.' The character of government is thus of the same form of interaction used more generally in the 'sorting out' of interpersonal relations at The Farm. The group head establishes agreement on the truth of a course of action, and then implements the decision. People at The Farm would rather not consider this system of government as an exercise in domination. Instead, it is to be treated as a manifestation and instrument of the 'school' where Stephen Gaskin is teaching.

> 'They (the Committee) are all enough into The Farm and what's going on with it, and enough into each other, that they can meet and make policy - actually it's not exactly making policy; it's like telepathic. It's not so important what things are decided; what's important is that the group head is together.'

The ideal of government in this approach is not to produce some balance of power between conflicting interest groups, but, through continual elaboration of agreements, to prevent emergence of factions and maintain a continual development of the collective interest. The checks and balances of this system rest in the processes of truth-seeking and witnessing which occur within and between various group heads, rather than in any legislated relations of power or compromise between opposing factions.

People who live at The Farm have 'copped to' Stephen as a teacher. They therefore adopt his teachings about creating and maintaining a unified group head, based on 'straight' social relations and a search for agreement. It is in the adoption of such principles of interpersonal relations that potential conflict is drawn out at its inception, and dissipated before it can attain factional standing. So long as people submit to the social process of reaching agreement in group heads where previously socialized members legitimate boundaries of possible action, belief is recapitulated in the arenas of social intercourse, and legitimacy remains unproblematic.

3. The political process of apocalyptic war

In apocalyptic sects, just as at The Farm, belief in the righteousness of mission legitimates a structure of domination. But apocalyptic groups, whether warring or other-worldly, regard their mission as a special one which must not be tainted or denatured. The exclusive mission reinforces the authority of those who can claim to represent it through either a traditional legacy or charismatic revelation. Those who assert their dominance as carriers of the true mission can exercise authority without succumbing to democratization and influence of peripheral believers and seekers. Thus, in the Symbionese Liberation Army, anyone who, after becoming associated with the group, rejected its missions or tactics, was dismissed as a traitor marked for assassination.

Little is known of group workings of the SLA, and little more will ever be known since most of the participants were killed in a shootout with a Marine-trained team from the Los Angeles Police Department SWAT (Strategic Weapons and Tactics) division. But certain speculations should be dismissed. Brainwashing techniques, the solidarity of love or a cult of personality - whether or not they were important for symbolic integration of the group - could in no way provide sufficient strategic capabilities for the execution of group plans. Donald DeFreeze, the black man known as Cinque, was the acknowledged original catalyst of the group. According to Emily Harris, after Cinque had escaped from prison by walking away from an unwatchful guard, he was sheltered by Willie Wolfe ('Cujo' in the press, actually Kahjo) and Patricia (Mizmoon) Soltysk. It was with them that Cinque had originally shared ideas about forming an underground terrorist group (Harris et al., 1976:29). But Emily Harris, in her self-criticism after capture, went on to suggest that good leadership is leadership by example. The idea, popular in the press, that Cinque was a sexual tyrant who exercised hypnotic power over the group's women was dismissed by her as 'ridiculous.' Since women in the group were concerned with issues of women's liberation, the popular account of Cinque's role would seem distorted. Bill Harris notes that people 'looked up to' Cinque because of his sense of survival. As Kohn and Weir (1975: I,46) have suggested, Cinque was probably treated as a guru because of his 'street knowledge.' But while Cinque may have received deference at times (as with his proposal for 'turning' Patty Hearst), he could not have been considered to have held authority. In advocating the 'turning' of Patty Hearst, Cinque had to go to other SLA members to get their agreement (Harris and Harris, 1976: 28). According to Joe Remiro (Harris et al., 1976:34),

> 'we all just exercised leadership in areas where we had the most practical understanding, and we didn't feel any need to call anyone the "leader".'

In her 'eulogy' (perhaps written collectively with Emily and Bill Harris), 'Tania' noted the special political and tactical skills and personal qualities of each of the dead SLA members. Though the communiqués of the SLA had the flavor of a hierarchical military organization, this may well have been a propaganda bluff to portray strength and size (see Harris et al., 1976:34). The militaristic tenor of the communiqués to the contrary, Remiro's account seems plausible. The success of the group had to have depended on collective agreement as to strategy and the full use of the knowledge and abilities of each member. Though Cinque may have been a charismatic initiator whom others held in esteem, the group would seem to have operated as a charismatic community of virtuosi. Each individual seems to have submitted to various kinds of disciplined training; each person seems to have taught others by ethics and example. The group ultimately depended on the ability of persons to count on each other in moment-to-moment co-ordination as circumstances changed. The basis of discipline seems to have been a charismatic sharing of warring comradeship rather than submission to autocratic dictates of a visionary idealist.

4. The political process in other-worldly apocalyptic sects

Other-worldly apocalyptic sects, whether founded on tradition or charisma, have none of the moment-to-moment strategic problems of a paramilitary organization. In the face of the perceived collapse of the secular social order, those who become true believers leave the secular order's domain to live 'according to the law of the prophet.' At the worldly utopian Farm, Stephen Gaskin provides an exemplary prophecy in his charismatic teachings, hoping to inspire actions like his own by others. In quite a different formulation, both the traditionally legitimated Krishna groups and the Love Family require adherence to religious authority. The leader of the theocratic group establishes ethics of behavior as the basis for attainment of spiritual enlightenment or grace. The follower is told not to 'be like me,' but rather to 'honor and obey me.' In each case, a status hierarchy is maintained between the 'more spiritually evolved' and the less elect, including newer members, women, and others who for reasons of alleged competence or untested allegiance, are not trusted to fill spiritually symbolic roles.

In the Krishna groups, A.C. Bhaktivedanta, the leader, is said to be the last disciple in a direct succession from the most recent reincarnation of Krishna. He reigns over a set of priestly 'temple presidents,' who in turn exercise hierocratic authority over their domains. A hierarchical system is maintained using the Hindu vocabulary of caste: devotees, promoted to Brahmin status after 'about a year' by the temple president on the basis of 'sincerity,' engage in priestly, scholastic and managerial functions. A laity provides labor for the work of the community; and novices begin at the bottom of the heap. But this status system is permeated with direct hierarchies of authority established in patriarchical form by the temple president. Various Brahmins are given priestly functions to perform, or serve as part of the personal staff of the temple president, performing managerial and public relations functions. And in conduct of daily work, a lieutenant to the temple president acts for him as a straw boss, assigning work to the lay associates and novices. Want satisfaction and production are organized on a community rather than household basis. Theocratic domination is therefore played out in a centralized priestly form, in which peripheral households do not serve as loci of political domination per se. Instead, all authority and work is centered in the temple and its administrative organization of Brahmins and their straw bosses.

In this hierarchy of authority, those at the 'bottom' must be careful not to overstep their mandates. In one case, the lieutenant chastized a lay brother for exercising authority over a novice.

Lieutenant: 'You have no authority to give orders!'

Woodcutter: 'Well, I did the way I said it; he was working for me.'

L: 'Working for you!? Working for Krishna!'

W: 'Well, yes, of course, but he was supposed to be chopping wood under me, and he didn't do anything in the morning, so I said, "do you plan to do anything this afternoon?" and he said, "no," so I told him, "if you don't intend to work, don't eat."'

L: 'Well, I still don't think it was your place to say anything. If we had everyone giving orders like that, a very unfortunate situation could develop.'

Though the lieutenant is the straw boss of devotional service (i.e. work), the temple president takes a daily tour of the premises and exercises the political authority of dispensing control over resources and jobs, counselling people with special problems, promoting devotees in status, and elaborating the spiritual doctrines of Krishna consciousness.

A similar theocratic form of government is employed at the Love Family, though it is tempered by a less doctrinally based belief system, a more patrimonial form, and the casting of the leader as a kingly shepherd of his flock rather than the priestly representative of doctrinal regulation. Love Israel's vision of a return to the charismatic form of the primitive Christian church allows him to supplant Biblical authority with the benevolence of a good father. Like the Krishna temple president, Love Israel is served by a personal staff. His prophetic charisma must be protected from tainting by material affairs, and so his lieutenant, Serious Israel, handles matters of finance, problems of public relations, and legal squabbles. Love Israel himself has all of the participants at his service and, like the temple president in a Krishna group, may dispense favors and benefices according to his wisdom.

At the Love Family, functions of want satisfaction are at least to some degree distributed according to household. One house serves as the 'front door' and food storage facility, another as the dormitory for newcomers, another as a sanctuary, and so on. Even where no special function is served by a household, its affairs are run by an appointed elder who acts in the household role of patriarch and is beholden, in patrimonial form, to the head of the organization, Love Israel. Because of the patrimonial form, household elders picked by Love Israel exercise some autonomous spiritual and material authority. The spiritual hierarchy has a decentralized household basis, but otherwise parallels the status distinctions of Krishna groups.

Differences between the two groups stem not so much from the degree of centralization of authority as from the source of all authority. Each group operates as a theocracy, but Krishna's Bhaktivedanta may be considered a guru of tradition, and the temple presidents under him as priests, while Love Israel has taken on the imagery of a kingly charismatic prophet. His followers are his personal subjects: he maintains a 'royal' style of life while that of his followers is more austere; and he holds 'court' as a sovereign arbiter of conflict and benevolent bestower of grace. Followers are to emulate Love Israel's manifestation of Christ consciousness, but they are not to take on the trappings of Love's status position. Rather, on the basis of Love's righteousness, followers are to become the virtuous carriers of a heavenly ethic. It is held that everyone can and should become an 'elder' but only in the sense of taking responsibility within the flock, and not in the sense of becoming a household patriarch.

While Bhaktivedanta and his priests initially receive obedience because they represent the doctrinally legitimated authority of Krishna, Love Israel is considered a holy man in his own right, one who can establish the way not solely on the basis of scripture, but more because he 'manifests' the will of God in his own revelations and actions. Bhaktivedanta and his appointed priests exercise domination through the authority of Krishna, and direct ritualized worship to the stylized representations of the deities. Love Israel, on the other hand, receives deference because he is seen as an unparalleled avatar - an embodiment of God. He thus acts politically not as the delineator and interpreter of paths to salvation, but more directly as the bestower of grace and salvation. While the Krishna priest receives deference because of his office, Love Israel receives deference because of his personal qualities.

Since the Krishna priest rules on the basis of scripture, he maximizes this avenue of power through authoritarian domination. Love Israel is not limited in this respect. Structurally, his power and that of a Krishna temple president both involve use of a patriarchical staff, but the imagery surrounding Love Israel's position is that of a binding love between a shepherd and his flock. The Krishna temple president must act in terms of the higher authority of Krishna, and exploits this authority in exacting devotional service. But Love Israel may rely on the ideology of communal love and virtuous living on the part of followers to maintain a personal religious devotion conducive to the revelation of special missionary purposes and the rewards of a directly bestowed grace. Even within the form of theocratic patrimonialism, the character of political domination of subject stems from the form of legitimation of authority.

The transcendental political process

The whole thrust of the transcendental social enactment is to avoid invocation of institutions or social forms as bases of power. Don Juan, the Yaqui Indian mystic, for example, in taking on Carlos Castaneda as a student, maintains that power is a quality of the persona. It can only be obtained, Castaneda (1972) reports, through a personal quest involving such processes as 'erasing personal history,' conquering fear, and learning to 'see.' For don Juan, power - the ability to control the outcome of events - need not be categorized according to its objects: the world is one, the available field of being for the person of knowledge. Power cannot be based on authority, for authority in itself cannot be used to trap an animal in the desert. Instead, power requires a charismatic engagement of the actor with objectives. One may learn something about power from a teacher; still, ultimately it is the manifestation of the individual's engagement with the world.

This sense of power devoid of social institutionalization is paralleled in other transcendental formations, for example, those of Zen Buddhism and of Tao. In Zen philosophy, it is the loss of ego involvement - the shedding of the sense of an 'I' that acts - which enables the individual to 'hit the target' (Herrigel, 1953). In Taoist philosophy, it is recognized that 'bad government' can be sustained through use of force, but 'good government' is accomplished by the wise ruler through the practice of 'Non-Ado' (Lao Tzu, 1961). In each of these idealizations, government is best when it has no apparent manifestation; true power derives from a direct and conscious engagement with the world.

How, then, are the events of social life in transcendental formations governed? The case called 'The Cabin' and other accounts all involve the relationship of a teacher or master and students or followers. The relationships are based on a desire on the part of students to be taught to 'see' as the master sees. The master thereby receives an immediate deference within the situation. He may direct the consciousness of the student as he sees fit. The student who tries to justify action on the basis of socially derived authority or culturally derived theoretical knowledge is likely to incur derision from the master. Failing these stratagems, the student learns to deal through direct action with the events of the day. Some episodes of collective life are solely concerned with the transference of knowledge of power. Other episodes, however, not only serve educational purposes, but also provide the everyday needs of sustenance and shelter. In these episodes, institutionalized government is absent - the ordering of the moment takes place as engagement in immediate action through collective attention and negotiation (cf. Troeltsch, 1932:378). Each individual witnesses the course of others' actions, airs intentions, and acts within the context of ongoing events. 'Problems' arise within situations in which they can be acted upon, and participants work out solutions as they go along. Domination through the issuance of orders does not occur; if it exists in any sense, it is in the participants' continual discipline toward a form of acting together.

In this enterprise, the leader may be expected to point out errors and inadequacies, especially to those who are still 'green' recruits. But this function may equally fall to another participant, especially if he or she 'sees' an entrance to consciousness modification because of his or her own unique viewpoint. Indeed, the charisma of demonstration cannot survive on the acts of the leader alone. The fragile constructions of reality with which such powers are concerned can only be maintained through the active and attentive participation of others, whether seekers or those who, like the master, have tapped the source of ecstasy and power.

Such domination of a form only becomes apparent with the outsider's lack of understanding of it. Typically, the outsider looks for authority or assumes that there are rules and customary ways of doing things. Participants are then accosted for direction:

V: 'Should I season the asparagus?'
P: 'Do you want to season the asparagus?'
V: 'Well, I just wondered if it would be OK to sauté some garlic with it.'
P: 'Do you want it to be OK?'
V: 'Yeah, I do.'
P: 'Then it's OK.'

Once fears of censure are overcome, participants can act with self-reliance, or, in more broadly held concerns, broadcast intentions and acts which others can witness. Government then involves the confirmation of ideas and acts by others, in the course of daily life.

COMMUNAL GOVERNMENTS AND CRISES OF LEGITIMACY

I have already described (in chapter 2) examples of 'early failure' of communal groups. In such cases, participants never come to share a collective definition of situation which would enable them to produce a satisfactory group life. Groups where participants do develop a collective sense of relevance may come to face quite different problems. In the early phases of collective life, it may be that no particular definition of situation has gained credence; group life exists in a brief limbo between rejection of secular ideology and the grounding of utopia in actual life. Once, however, some shared viewpoint about the customs of life - the ways of doing and seeing things - has been achieved, the issues of political crisis become somewhat different. Those who, by whatever paths, emerge as the entrepreneurial virtuosi of a particular way of life come to be cast in the roles of ideologues who are expected to 'deliver the goods' and legitimate the process by which that occurs. Such entrepreneurs, whether they fancy themselves to be anarchists, mystics, patriarchs, promoters of rational administration, or charismatics, seek to sustain a collective definition of situation in the course of ongoing political and social life.

Certain stratagems of maintaining legitimacy may be employed regardless of the particular sources of legitimacy - traditional, bureaucratic or charismatic - or form of government and group life. All entrepreneurs develop a sense of how to head off crisis by identifying malcontents and troublemakers, 'cooling them out,' 'getting them to cop' (defer to the existing scheme of things), or 'easing them out' of the place. Indeed, greater group cohesion can sometimes be found by a majority of participants who identify a malcontent as the course of conflict and 'bad vibe' him or her out of the group.

In other cases, however, non-legitimated accounts are more widespread among participants, and the act of labelling protagonists merely brings more intransigent factionalization.

The course of political crisis involving a breakdown in the collective definition of situation derives in large part from the particular forms of life and legitimation which have previously been maintained. I therefore describe what from the current research seem to be the dynamics of crisis in groups politically based on constellations of interest, on rationalized bureaucracy, and on personal leadership. (I did not observe any crises in groups based on traditional legitimation.) Of concern in the comparative understanding of crises of legitimacy are three questions: first, what kinds of events open a group to crisis; second, how does the crisis occur; and third, what paths of resolution stem from the situation?

Crises of interest constellations

The collective life of natural synchronic groups is based on simple feelings of mutual solidarity, politically governed through constellations of interest rather than through promotion of any highly formulated ideology. Domination is accomplished through alliances, ad hoc and consensual collegial action, and the promulgation of customary rights and responsibilities. In such groups, a crisis of legitimacy is not experienced as a crisis of government, but as a more pervasive dissatisfaction with the entire web of social relations.

Collective crisis, under the conditions of natural administration, may be triggered by several kinds of occurrences. It may come from an (often uncommunicated) shift of interest and commitment, from an unsupported fait accompli, or from interpersonal feuds. In the fullblown crisis, such sources become connected in the minds of participants. Thus, one or more individuals may determine that feelings of solidarity are an illusion based on the simple fact of coexistence in a physical setting. They may also pinpoint material interests such as property ownership or other class position as the basis of division. In either event, those who withdraw commitment develop their own accounts of conditions.

> 'This place is no good. People are always laying mind trips on you. They say it has to be a work place, but they make it like worse than work. I need to spend a lot of time alone and I want to develop spiritually, but they don't seem to think both things can go on here. But I'm not going to stay if things don't change. I want to travel anyway, see what's going on in the rest of the world.'

While some people depart, others continue participating in the group as a matter of convenience, while failing to be involved in either the production of material or social life. Others may cultivate outside interests and 'personal trips' which similarly leave less time for involvement with group life. If such shifts go unnoticed or are tolerated by others because of their own predilections toward more individual interests, the process feeds upon itself.

The style of sociation shifts from that of commitment to alienation. Often, a series of disagreements come to be dimensioned by the participants in terms of one or two central themes, such as 'spirituality versus authority.' The participants come to label one another's positions and these in turn attain an independent symbolic existence; the disagreements become less and less face-to-face, and argument comes to be carried through in more and more obscure terms - through gossip and hearsay. The grapevine mediation of conflict comes to further heighten its problematic character for all participants, since the difference between fact and rumor cannot be discerned. The split feeds on retrenchment and grapevine amplification until people develop expectations about it (members of 'Country Collapse Farm'):

> K: (in woods) 'Want to get stoned?'
>
> N: 'Not when we have to go back so soon. I could dig it down here in the woods, but the "big one" might come down up there, and I don't want to be high when it happens.'
>
> J: 'What's the big one?'
>
> N: 'Well, Ed just laid into me again for not doing enough around here. But whenever I do something, they catch me for doing it wrong or taking over

> their trip. Like the garden's Mary's thing, and you can't do anything without her say-so. And Jim is always telling you how to do something, like ordering you, to make it more efficient. It's gotten to the point where I can't be around him or Linda or Mary. I just know the next time it happens is gonna be the last.'

In this example, anticipation of conflict comes to make all social interchange between factions problematic and, sooner or later, the 'big one' indeed takes place. If this course of collective life continues, personal ventures and withdrawal of commitment become widespread and the burden of production of group life falls more and more to a few entrepreneurial virtuosi who invoke the myth of solidarity and continue to act in good faith. With the falling away of synchronic sociation, the burden on virtuosi increases just as their numbers have decreased. Their feelings of solidarity and goodwill may be further strained. What begins in covert personal decisions and actions eventually becomes recognized and labelled by virtuosi, who may react themselves by withdrawing commitment and leaving, lapsing into cynicism, or venting hostility toward those who have been 'sleezing off.'

Self-righteousness and the presentation of non-negotiable demands in shouting matches become the order of the day in what collective discourse occurs, but as feelings of hostility spread, people come to avoid the collective social arena altogether.

> 'We can't even be in the same room together any more, much less have a meeting. Everybody gets too uptight, so we don't even have meetings any more. Now people just catch you alone and lay their trip on you. And I can't take it any more.... They won't budge an inch, and they're all so good with words, you can't argue with them. I battled Jim to a stalemate once, but usually he just bears me down. It's either their way or nothing. Take it or leave it.'

As perception of the crisis grows, virtuosi and those who have acted in good faith begin to lament the state of affairs.

> 'Sometimes it feels like an engine that's losing steam. I keep feeling like things are getting worse: we're further from community than when we started.'

If the crisis of a group based on constellations of interest is resolved in other than a passing of communal life, it occurs when people come to realign their social relations, interests, expectations and participatory roles. The direction of resolution is variable and dependent on specifics of situation. It may come simply in the voluntary or coerced departure of people who are dissatisfied or seen by others as the source of collective problems. A work strike by entrepreneurs may awaken others to renewed commitments. Alternatively, a small but determined group of allies may stage a coup of sorts, by asserting that everyone else has abdicated to the crisis. Such a faction may reach agreement quickly among themselves and, in acting in coordinated fashion, successfully hold the definition of situation against all challengers. They may follow the advice of a worldly utopian (member of The Farm):

> 'There are basically two ways to sort it - on a spiritual and on a material plane. If the people into spirit just start sorting it on a spiritual plane, the other people will catch it or go their own way.'

Indeed, any junta promoting a course of salvation will be persuasive in gaining support so long as the only alternatives are failure or a continuing morass of conflict.

The crisis of legitimacy in a natural synchronic group involves a breakdown in collective sociation from which a new set of viewpoints emerges among participants. If a revival is to take place, it is in negotiation in terms of these viewpoints that a new deal can be put forward, and the possibility of a reassertion of solidarity created.

The legal-rational crisis of legitimacy

Unlike natural synchronic groups, utopian groups operate under specific ideologies about the nature of the social world and legitimated ways of acting in it. Under such conditions, a crisis of legitimacy hinges on the specific utopian vision and its manifestations in group life.

The diachronic worldly utopia is more open to political crisis than other kinds of utopian communal groups. Since it is based on an egalitarian ethic, no organizing principle assures maintenance of ideological commitment; and since satisfaction of wants is based on diachronic and routinized forms of coordination, divergences in viewpoint and beliefs may occur without immediate consequences for ongoing social life.

At Twin Oaks, for example, there is no ideological test for membership. People who visit and decide they would like to join are 'polled': members are asked to rate the potential member as to desirability. While the scaling system is uniform, members may use any criteria they wish in determining the rating they give. Thus, one person may rate a potential member highly on the basis of skills, while another member could give a low rating on the basis of personal differences, divergence in ideology, or the like. A person may become a member on the basis of friendship, skills, or other factors having nothing to do with ideology. Yet the particular organization of social life at Twin Oaks is unequivocally ideological. The consequences of such a system of membership selection in an ideologically based group include a continuing divergence in ideological commitment. Many new members have been attracted to Twin Oaks on the basis of its reputation as an operating example of the 'Walden Two' formulation of a rational utopia. One member gives assurances that 'we're all behavioralists,' and another tells of her attraction to the place after reading 'Walden Two' for a psychology course in college. But other people join the group for diverse and unrelated reasons.

> 'When I got out [of the service] and didn't have any trip to do, my brother invited me here, and it seemed like a good thing, so I joined. Sure beats the rat race on the outside.'

And even one of the more committed members downplays the importance of behavioral ideology:

> 'It's a broad philosophy like empiricism, which is useful to some people who feel behavior is what they need to work on.'

Still others are totally unconcerned with idea legitimation:

> 'You can go ahead and play your games with that [i.e. the system] all you want; I'll just keep doing my job.'

According to one member, Twin Oaks is increasingly divided into two polar groups - proceduralists and persons of action. The proceduralists are said to want to be sure that everything is done properly, on the basis of authority, in accordance with precedents and policies, with clear mandates and with a sense of fairness to all. People of action are not particularly concerned with these issues. In an ethic which parallels that of The Farm in Tennessee, they would rather operate on good faith and the ability of people involved to work out solutions to problems as they go along. A number of such people generally ignore the labor credit system, nevertheless accruing substantial 'overages' of labor credits. Others have pushed for and obtained modifications of the labor credit system so that more synchronically integrated crews can organize and perform work in specific functional areas. Such concern with humanistic social relations has been felt in household life as well. One group of Twin Oaks members requested and received community permission to establish their own household to be taken care of outside the community labor credit system.

Tensions between the managerial ideologists and the debunkers of ideology at Twin Oaks have never reached the point of a total crisis of legitimacy. Nevertheless, on several occasions the divergence of opinion over issues has become quite apparent. In such situations, under an ethic of fairness, accommodations have been made to those who have wished to alter the character of work and household relations in the intentional community. Still, the rationalized satisfaction of wants remains the dominant institutional form, and neither faction's proponents feel their position to have won the day, so differences are subsumed under the ethic of pluralism.

For the ideologists, such a state of affairs can be difficult to accept. While there may be no return to the ideological purity of formation through use of an ideological test for membership, continued concessions to people indifferent to behaviorism and bureaucratic administration undermine a basic purpose of the group - that of demonstrating the viability of a behavioral utopia. If participants find that they can manage affairs without complicated bureaucratic procedures, the need for utopia may seem less pressing. Once precedent and policy are abandoned in favor of personalistic considerations, return is difficult. And so if the bureaucratic crisis of legitimacy is to be avoided, it is only with the gradualistic granting of concessions to those who oppose it.

Crises of charismatic legitimacy

In natural synchronic groups where politics is based on the free play of interests, legitimacy of group life turns on the maintenance of a form of sociation under which material, personal and social needs are met to the general satisfaction of participants. Legitimacy of a bureaucratically organized group such as Twin Oaks is bound up in the specific features of bureaucratic structure, as well as in the general notion that the institutional forms are equitable and humane ways of resolving the problematics of living communally. Charisma, on the other hand, is wholly based on the belief in special powers residing in certain individuals or the collectivity. The charismatic actor, in one way or another, creates a true belief on the part of others in the sanctity of a mission.

Those who oppose charismatic power characterize it as an ability to hypnotize or brainwash people; certainly people who accede to charismatic powers will tell you essentially the same thing: the power of personal presence can be felt in the eyes of the bearer of charisma. The mark of charisma is said to be noticeable in 'lightning,' 'electricity' or a serene and comprehending gaze of the charismatic individual.

The charismatic's subsuming of others' attention through eye contact bespeaks a more general phenomenon: the charismatic is able to focus other people's attention. Attention on the part of the believer is legitimated on the basis of self-evident rightness. People accede to charismatic direction not on the basis of any customs or rules, but simply because they believe it to be the 'way.'

The legitimacy of charismatic powers stands or falls on its social production in the course of episodes where its demonstration is expected by participants. A certain circularity obtains: people believe in the charisma because they witness it; while at the same time they are capable of witnessing it because they believe or want to believe in it, and therefore know to look for its demonstration. The charismatic leader who draws the attention and orientation of social action by others must therefore be capable of a continuous presentation of charismatic self for others; he can be no other than the person of power, at least for those engaged in true belief.

While the exact momentary sources of crisis in other kinds of groups may be difficult to point to, where solidarity is based on deference toward a charismatic leader, the crisis of legitimacy is often associated with a particular episode in which a lapse in the leader's ability to manifest special powers is witnessed by others. Defection by true believers marks the crisis.

In one communal group centering on a charismatic spiritual leader, several incidents reflect this relation of legitimacy to specific collective events. In one episode, members had gone to a nearby vacant farm to hold a festival featuring food, music and hallucinogenic drugs. One man who came was a wandering minstrel, a free spirit who had never allied himself with the group. He went in and among circles of people, playing his music. While this was going on, someone else 'laid a universalist rap' on the charismatic leader, a man quite committed to his particular sectarian viewpoint. One account is that the leader 'lost his power for a second,' long enough to 'scatter the energy' of his followers. In their momentary confusion, group members began 'looking for someone with authority,' and a number of people began to surround the minstrel.

R: 'He was creating confusion through difference. A lot of people do that, try to create confusion.

And we try to avoid it, because we are trying to all be one, and we are in agreement about a lot of things, and working to eliminate things we disagree about. But some people can't do that.'

J: 'Why do you think that is?'

R: 'They are afraid of giving up their individuality. They want to be different from other people and they hang on to that.'

Certain members became aggravated that the minstrel 'wasn't going along with the group consciousness,' and finally, two of the charismatic leader's personal staff escorted him out. Members of the group were later told that the minstrel was the devil.

In another series of episodes, several members of the same group defected to another group. Heaven apparently was not a satisfactory living situation. Successively, other members of higher and higher status were sent to convince the defectors to return, but each in turn became convinced of the higher powers of the other group's leader. Finally when some ten members of the group had defected, the charismatic leader himself went to convince his former followers to return. He was only successful with some people, and of these, several later left the group to start their own 'tribe' based on the personal leadership of a defector who had found new truths while at the other group.

In its pure form, as Weber (1968:1114-15) notes, charisma is ephemeral and unstable. In quests of transformation of charisma, which Weber (1968:1121-48) has described extensively, the person of acclaimed power, and more particularly those associated with that power, seek to institutionalize the unstable charismatic pneuma by way of arrangements which do not stand or fall on the continuously successful demonstrations of miracles, heroism and other supermundane acts.

In the above examples, the charismatic leader suffered a lapse in powers while in direct competition with alternative worldviews. No doubt because his charisma had already been institutionalized to some degree in the structure of a religious sect, these lapses did not result in a total collapse of his regime. Nevertheless, he lost face in situations where his command of presence was insufficient to deal with challenges to his authority.

The antecedents of such a crisis of charisma lie in the expectation by true believers that one individual, the leader, will manifest powers unfalteringly against all challenges. Groups where the sense of charisma is more broadly shared - what Weber (1968:243ff) has called charismatic communities - are not so susceptible to these crises.* In such groups, membership is based on the demonstration of a sense of charismatic action; those who form the community constitute the elect not simply as followers, but as charismatic virtuosi in their own rights. They do not maintain true belief on the basis of a single person's charismatic abilities, but instead perceive such powers in themselves and in each other. Charisma is demystified, at least to the extent that participants understand the ephemeral nature of its production and do not expect its continuous manifestation. Instead, it is understood that, as one person in such a group put it, 'people gotta be able to make mistakes and that be OK.' In the charismatic community, legitimacy does not depend on continuous demonstrations of powers but rather on the ability to 'come through when it counts.' Thus, certain incidents may require demonstration of charismatic abilities while others do not. Those true believers who are addicted to the authority of charisma without having personally experienced it become filled with doubt when they sense a lapse in charismatic production. But those who have experienced the phenomenon in themselves put no stake in such social productions of charisma.

SUMMARY

The establishment of a political community beyond the established order is predicated on the constitution of time and the mode of social enactment in a communal group. In natural synchronic groups, domination through constellations of interest establishes a relatively unstable collegial government where personal prerogatives and faits accomplis counter unified administration. A crisis of legitimacy is experienced in a broader crisis as the falling away of synchronic sociation. In produced social enactments, power stems not from a constellation of interests, but from a symbolically legitimated order of domination. In the diachronic worldly utopia, it assumes a legal-rational form of authority; a pluralist ethic opens the way to inclusion of participants who do not necessarily identify with legal-rational authority, and a

---

* They may have other problems of charisma, of succession, for example. Thus, after most members of the SLA's community of virtuosi had been killed, Bill Harris's claim of authority became a source of controversy among the Harrises, 'Tania' and the 'new team' support group (cf. Kohn and Weir, 1976; Harris and Harris, 1976).

crisis of legitimacy may take the form of a conflict between supporters of a legal-rational authority and various virtuosi of charismatic action as well as those who disdain irrational or unsentimental consequences of adherence to legal procedure. In the synchronic worldly utopia, a collegial administration obtains in various arenas where participants hold an interest; the emphasis is on maintenance of an unfactionalized collective consciousness through 'witnessing' and 'truth-speaking': intersubjective agreement rather than law serves as a binding force of order. Produced apocalyptic groups hold more specialized and sectarian missions of salvation than worldly utopian groups. In the warring sect, the ideological primary group shares a meaningful interpretation of political struggle which allows them to operate in moment-to-moment coordination as a charismatic community. Otherworldly sects of salvation, on the other hand, rely on theocratic authority for the administration of mundane affairs and hierocratic dispensation of spiritual grace. In such sects, the alternative forms of traditional and institutionalized charismatic legitimation frame emergences of priestly or ethically prophetic domination, and a crisis of legitimacy, where it occurs - takes the form of heresy. The transcendental formation does not depend on either a constellation of interests or legitimation of authority for power, and government has no institutionalized form. Instead, the problematics of group life are resolved in momentary association.

In decisive respects, the nature of government in communal groups is paralleled by a religious concept of the divine. It is noteworthy that Max Weber 'transferred the concept of the congregation or community ("Gemeinde") from the religious to the political sphere and came to define it as the typical charismatic association' (Roth, 1975: 151). In a similar fashion Weber (1968:54-6, 1158ff) only narrowly differentiated political from religious power when he recognized hierocratic domination through psychic coercion 'by distributing or denying religious benefits' as an alternative form to political domination ultimately based on physical coercion. In communal groups, distinctions between the 'religious' community and the 'political' community are for the most part blurred. All communal groups originate as charismatic rejections of the established order; the creation of utopian worlds derives from prophetic establishment of myth of one sort or another (see chapter 2). If religion is an illusion, as Marx would have it, then it is not just any illusion; rather, it is a politically tainted one. Taking Marx's formulation at its face value, Bryan Turner (1974:51) has suggested,

In broad terms, the language by which a society expresses human relationships of subordination and superordination may also become available for the description of status inequalities between men and their gods. In communal groups, it is as though the political and religious aspects of community and authority are bound in one. In an almost Durkheimian way, society is God; authority is religion. The politics of authority, legitimation and the processes of decision-making are held out as sacred or the communal group loses a crucial meaningful basis for existence.

In a transcendental formation, mystical engagement with the phenomenal world precludes conceptualization of a person-God relation; God is everywhere; authority is in the wind. In the warring sect, God is good, opposes evil and oppression; the person-God relation is played out as commitment to a Manichean struggle between forces of righteousness and those of oppression: identification with the forces of good provides a rejection of previous identity and a rebirth into the shared authority of those on the side of righteousness. Rebirth in other-worldly apocalyptic groups is to a 'heaven' where God is love or devotion, the manifestation of virtue or the act of piety: above all, God is not impersonal, and the most spiritually evolved member of the group exercises theocratic authority under God's direction, whether doctrinally or prophetically revealed. In the synchronic worldly utopian formation, God is especially the holy ghost (the living community of the saved), and authority stems from collectively witnessed truth. As opposed to these developments, both the diachronic worldly utopia and the natural synchronic formation seem more secular. A rational ethic of association substitutes for a spiritual idealization of authority in the diachronic worldly utopia, while a cult of individualism may easily emerge in natural synchronic groups unless collegial authority is strictly maintained. In both these latter formations, as Peter Berger (1967) has observed, religion loses its socially integrating function of providing a shared set of meanings. The problem of government then rests on the promotion and protection of 'natural rights' in a pluralistic world.

7 Conclusion

> The daughter of Babylon is like a threshing floor
> At the time when it is trodden;
> Yet a little while,
> And the time of her harvest will come.
>
> Jeremiah 51:33

Early in their lives, in 1846, Marx and Engels (1967:42ff) suggested that a transition from capitalism to socialism is achieved by people who abandon the fetters of their lives and act in union with others who have similarly freed themselves from the burdens of personal circumstance in class-conditioned society. In this formulation, revolution has perhaps a more voluntaristic character than in the Communist Manifesto. Marx's later and more scientific formulations provided a more deterministic model of social change based on the playing out of impersonal structural contradictions. Paralleling this emerging emphasis in the materialist theoretical perspective, radical politics drifted toward a party format; its association with 'scientific' socialism often came to be wed with evolutionary concepts of change and with a postponement of eschatological expectations concerning a great transformation (see Roth, 1963:159-92). Revolution, it was held, could only be achieved after a seizure of state power, through a dictatorship of the proletariat (or more exactly, a dictatorship of the representatives of the proletariat). Essentially, Marx's scientific socialism 'undermined revolutionary voluntarism in the name of an evolutionary and deterministic theory of history' (Roth, 1975:153; cf. Weber, 1968:873-4). Revolution, it was held, could only transpire as a response to objective conditions scientifically understood and prophetically revealed. The wavering masses were to await direction from that self-proclaimed radical intellectual elite which possessed an analytic understanding of historical necessities and revolutionary possibilities.

If contemporary American communalists have a legacy in Marx, it is to be found in the earlier, humanist Marx rather than in the later, more scientific one. For communalists radically reject their previous lives by taking on new lives, in new circumstances, with others who share a rejection of the dominant order. Communalists do not wait for a political upheaval; they do not wait for a crisis of capitalism. If they collectively share any idea of social change, it is that change stems from their own actions which transcend their own previous circumstances.

DOMINATION AND MEANING IN THE ESTABLISHED ORDER

For communalists, the established order represents a dead end. They perhaps feel the crisis of meaning to which Weber (1958:182) alluded; fully developed capitalism no longer depends on religious ethics for its ascetic discipline. The meaning of economic activity loses its ability to provide a sense of social unity. In the secular world of economic rationality, values become relativized and people are set adrift in a world of marketplace truth. As Turner (1974:156) has suggested, 'The result is an existential crisis in the meaning of life.'

Workers in the 'System' achieve integrated meaning not in a shared ethic, but instead by taking on needs and interests which may be resolved in institutionalized jobs and marketplace consumption. Power no longer rests solely in the exercise of authority or force. Instead, order is maintained as if in a magical way - through habituated discipline to the facticity of the extant world.

Weber defined hierocracy as a form of domination by priests, the Church, or a 'secular caesaropapist ruler.' The hierocratic organization, in Weber's (1968:54) view, 'enforces its order through psychic coercion by distributing or denying religious benefits.' In the 'age of bourgeois democracy,' the hierocratic organization seeks to promote family ties and defuse class consciousness by developing cultural associations and institutions of socialization such as workingmen's associations. Involvement of the faithful is maintained in controlled (i.e. bureaucratically produced) arenas of meaning (Weber, 1968: 1194-5).

While hierocracy itself thus draws upon the institutional forms of the era to promote its ends, its style of psychic coercion - through the production of objects of consciousness's attention - becomes more and more the vehicle of secular domination in mass society. In both the bureaucratic production of social institutions and the production of goods and ideas, power does not stem strictly from a relationship of authority. Mass habit supplants authority; order is maintained because people are dominated by the objects of attention - goods and ideas for which aesthetics and meanings have been designed, produced and distributed from elsewhere. In sports, in the modern television morality plays of work ethics, in mass music, as well as with the more obvious material things, consumers play spectator roles: they are to attend to the wholly other worlds presented to them; they are to draw meanings in the lifeworld from the appropriate consumption and use of mass-produced objects which fill that world, and most significantly, they are to spend a considerable portion of life immersed in realities 'piped in from beyond.' The secular order achieves a hierocratic character in the ability of organizers of production to focus the attention of masses of people. If as Heap and Roth (1973) suggest, ethnomethodology is to look at those events which provide for people the 'sense' of objective social structure, then it is in the identities of mass-produced culture that 'sense' may be found. In any of a variety of status-producing and anxiety-releasing ways, the individuals who consume in a mass-produced world place attention on the problem of 'keeping up' with the stream of experiences presented to them (Horkheimer and Adorno, 1972:126):

> The stunting of the mass-media consumer's power of imagination and spontaneity does not have to be traced back to any psychological mechanisms; he must ascribe the loss of those attributes to the objective nature of the products themselves, especially to the most characteristic of them, the sound film. They are so designated that quickness, powers of observation, and experience are undeniably needed to apprehend them at all; yet sustained thought is out of the question if the spectator is not to miss the relentless rush of facts.

In an era of concentrated capitalist production and of mass society, the hierocratic style of domination - that of producing and distributing events of consciousness - more and more becomes the province of the secular order. If, for Marx and Engels, the 'religious illusion' serves to mask the material relations of production, in contemporary society that illusion is a truly material one. It is contained in the illusion of free choice: consumers may select among prepackaged options those which reflect personally held but bureaucratically anticipated values (cf. Horkheimer and Adorno, 1972:124).

Religion itself becomes an object of consumption in a pluralistic world. According to Peter Berger (1967: 133-4), it loses its Durkheimian function of providing a unifying public sense of the sacred:

> Such private religiosity, however 'real' it may be to the individuals who adopt it, cannot any longer fulfill the classic task of religion, that of constructing a common world within which all of social life receives ultimate meaning binding on everybody.

The task of legitimation becomes a secular one. In a way, a caesaropapist order is approximated: the state guarantees religious freedoms, while the social order receives de facto sacred legitimation from a mass production of the objects of attention. The ritualistic 'reminding' process of religion - in which fundamental reality definitions are re-presented to consciousness (cf. Berger, 1967:40) - is appropriated by the entrepreneurs of a mediated, mass-produced society. Whether reminding serves to ground political, economic and social events in a context of mediated news or to cloak the objects of consumption in advertised status images and corporate symbols, the meaningful world is produced as a kind of secular religion through a mediated hierocratic domination of consciousness.

For its seeming pervasiveness, however, secular hierocratic domination has an ephemeral character. Since it is based on the ability to construct meaning and hold attention, in so far as people alter their attention, they break the bonds of domination. Such a choice can involve a holistic change in cognition, a charismatic metanoia. Individuals no longer see things as they have been trained to see them; they no longer care about those things which they have been told it is important to care about. Wholly other things, which had previously been no more than 'admirable but unrealistic sentiments,' may become crucial bases of action. Yet as Peter Berger (1967:39) has argued, counter-definitions of reality which reject an established production of meanings cannot easily be maintained by individuals in the absence of supportive social contexts. Communal groups, then, involve collective utopian deviance. Since value-based rejection of the established order is invoked in communal groups, in a broad sense, they may be considered religions. If hierocratic domination, in either its sacred or secular exercise, transpires as control over the objects of attention and their meanings, in communal groups, attention and meaning are modified away from activity in the domain of the established order and into some alternative domain.

Marx (1964:41) condemned religion as 'a reversed world-consciousness.' But he never sought to understand the connections between a given institution of religion, an established order, and what might metaphorically be called reversed reversed world-consciousness - that is, the utopian reflection of an alternative world. New historical possibility, whatever its basis in a new mode of production, becomes relevant only if people constitute it as such in consciousness. Different 'reflections' of the world have different consequences for action in the world. Some attend to and accept the world as presented in an established order; others reject it. Social change, Herbert Marcuse (1969:53) has argued, involves an initial rebellion of consciousness:

> Under total capitalist administration and introjection, the social determination of consciousness is all but complete and immediate: direct implantation of the latter into the former. Under these circumstances, radical change in consciousness is the beginning, the first step in changing social existence: emergence of the new Subject. Historically, it is again the period of enlightenment prior to material change - a period of education, but education which turns into praxis: demonstration, confrontation, rebellion.

Marcuse (1969:86) is still confronted with the thorny issue, 'What kind of life?' This concern is the primary one for those who engage in alternative communal ways of life. Praxis, while it may be directed on occasion to the strategies of direct political action, involves development of new awareness of 'the immediate issues which flow from *the phenomenology of everyday life*' (Gintis, 1972: 61; emphasis in original). In communal groups, consciousness does not exist solely in abstraction; it is grounded in situationally new conditions, in alternative arenas where people are immersed in encompassing lives with social others and material problems. Heretical religion as modification of attention and revolution as a change of the forms of social interaction obtain a congruence in communal attempts to move beyond routinely available possibilities in the established order. The courses of communal emergences are varied: some may lead to establishment of new institutionalized religions; others may surface as revolutionary struggles which are either successful or fade from the public eye; still others may provide an ethic of association which has a transforming effect on the character of life in a reconstructed social order.

COMMUNAL GROUPS: EMERGENCES AND IDEAL TYPES

Whatever their directions, communal groups are begun by circles of people who collectively legitimate myths of 'who we are as a group.' Such myths - whether they stem from friendship, prophecy and revelation, or utopian program - provide initial boundaries for enactment of collective life. In dealing with the tensions between a myth and the concerns of everyday life, communalists either are unable to develop a basis for resolving problematic issues and end in early failure or they come to enact situationally adequate ways of being together. These new ways of life may bear as little relation to one another as they do to the society-at-large left behind.

Differences between alternative communal worlds do not come down to various objective structures, institutions, norms or practices. In essence, communal worlds differ from one another because the participants in each one constitute time differently in their streams of consciousness and attend to events and action in the lifeworld according to different schemes of relevance. While any specific group has a totally unique ethos, we may come to grasp fundamental types of groups through a consideration of phenomenological possibilities of time and socially enacted meaning.

Though the stream of events of internal time consciousness may transpire in diverse ways, there are several archetypal possibilities. Individuals may attend solely to absolutely present events as they transpire in the internal stream of consciousness; they may become immersed in the social vivid present directed to intersubjective themes; they may engage in memory and anticipation; and they may act in terms of a diachronic schedule of events in which the here-and-now represents a finite moment in a stream of moments of equal physical duration.

Time grounds possibilities of cognized reality. A diachronic type of time consciousness provides a world with a history, with a past and its legacy of meanings, and with an anticipated future state of affairs which may be set up as a goal for the direction of present action. The present is meaningful, not in and of itself, but only in so far as it fulfills or fails to fulfill past expectations or contributes to realization of plans for the future. In synchronic time consciousness, on the other hand, the socially constituted vivid present serves as an organizing principle in and of itself. While reference may be made to past occurrences or plans for the future, by and large such references do not involve a linear sense of sequence or amounts of time; instead, they are relevant only as conditions for the execution of action situated in a vivid present. It is in the present itself that social coordination of activity transpires. Finally, the apocalyptic time construction posits a break between a diachronic time - in which the past and future dominate the present, and a new order of time - a synchronic time of freedom to create the present or a timeless eternity.

Just as the stream of consciousness may be experienced in various ways according to the locus of time in the present, in memory and in anticipation, so events of attention, cognition and interpretation may yield alternative modes of social enactment. In a natural enactment of the world, that which is attended to and interpreted as experience is taken-for-granted as valid and real. Though events may be subject to scrutiny, analysis and reinterpretation, no unifying philosophy or system of belief provides the rules for attention or interpretation of experience. On the other hand, in a produced enactment, the experiences of consciousness are framed according to a preordained scheme: attention is directed on the basis of already established relevances, and experience is interpreted according to perceptions of its congruence with the previously established relevances. The transcendental enactment is quite different: both taken-for-granted conceptions about how the world 'is' and preordained interpretations about how it 'should be' are bracketed or set aside (Husserl, 1931:s.31). Experiences are taken as valid and real, prior to any meaningful interpretation or belief.

The phenomenological distinctions described above are not simply abstractions; they differentiate among actual ways in which people constitute events in consciousness and in social relations. Distinctions among forms of time consciousness and modes of social enactment each provide useful ways of understanding social formations, but they are more meaningful when considered together, for the experience of time is modified according to how social life is enacted in time. Together, the archetypal possibilities of time and social enactment yield a two-dimensional typology which may be used to specify ideal types of communal groups.

Six ideal types of communal groups may be framed in terms of the analytic possibilities described (see Table 7.1). The commune represents a natural synchronic type. Two produced types involve what I have termed 'worldly utopian' operating models which participants claim as generalizable to all social life. They are the diachronic model of intentional association and the synchronic community. Produced apocalyptic groups, on the

TABLE 7.1 Typology of utopian communal groups. Ideal type of communal group according to mode of organizing time and mode of social enactment.

Mode of social enactment		Mode of organizing time: DIACHRONIC	SYNCHRONIC	APOCALYPTIC
	NATURAL		Commune	
	PRODUCED	Worldly utopian intentional association	Worldly utopian community	Sects: warring/ other-worldly
	TRANSCENDENTAL		Ecstatic association	

other hand, are boundaried sectarian associations, directed either, in the warring sect, to a final battle between the forces of good and evil, or, in the other-worldly sect, to salvation of the elect. Finally, the ecstatic association involves a transcendental mysticism.

In what follows, these types, though identified within a framework based on the mundane phenomenology of Alfred Schutz, are specified in both mundane phenomenological and interpretive terms. The a priori structures of the lifeworld which Schutz and Luckmann (1973) described are thus postulated as the limiting conditions of human and social existence, and empirical occurrences are understood to involve the selective emphasis (or de-emphasis) of a priori possibilities. In this sense, alternative cognitive orientations to the lifeworld are ways in which people, both individually and with one another, pay attention to (and thereby construct) one or another reality. On the other hand, Max Weber's comparative typifications of subjectively meaningful action are observers' typifications which may be applied to extant lifeworlds, where subjectively meaningful action unfolds in the vivid present. It thus becomes possible to articulate the connections between kinds of cognitive constructions of reality and the actions to which these constructions give context such that they are subjectively meaningful. Here, the implications of the present study are simple: bureaucracy, for example, is based on a particular consciousness of time; intersubjective reality involves a different kind of cognitive field and social ethic than that of individualism.

The types described below, like certain of Weber's, are intended as general socio-historical models (cf. Roth, 1971). Only seven cases have been presented in depth in the present study. They have been treated as approximating the analytic constructs of time and social enactment, while other cases have been drawn upon in so far as they permit the further specification and qualification of ideal-typical boundaries, or suggest transitional possibilities. In all, a total of twenty-eight cases have been considered. The set of ideal types derived from the present analysis must be regarded as one set of possibilities, predicated on a theoretical approach and methodological enterprise. Depending on the purpose, further research could indicate subtypes, hyphenated types and other transitional possibilities.

As Weber (1968:20) has remarked, even the characterization of a single empirical case is an enterprise filled with ambiguity, for the case may approximate more than one ideal type in various of its aspects: 'the same historical phenomenon may be in one aspect feudal, in another patrimonial, in another bureaucratic, and in still another charismatic.' The enterprise of formulating and using ideal types is thus not an easy one, nor, in contrast to the essences philosophical phenomenology has tried to establish, can sociological ideal types be treated as definitive. Moreover, ideal types are not empirical realities, and we cannot expect to predict empirical developments on the basis of such analysis. Nevertheless, using ideal types to distinguish the configurative features of communal groups provides a set of benchmarks which may be employed to trace empirical developments and clarify our understanding of their implications. On the basis of descriptive summaries of empirical cases approximating them, the ideal types listed above may be elaborated as alternative ways of life.

The commune

In the quasi-utopian commune, people live together in an association of convenience, friendship and mutual solidarity, surviving hard times and enjoying good times. In a natural approach to social enactment, no unifying beliefs provide a scheme of relevance, and eclectic possibilities of anarchism and individualistic interpretation enhance individual prerogatives and freedoms. The here-and-now of synchronic association thus involves the intersection of multiple viewpoints in pluralistically constructed episodes. Work is performed and wants are satisfied by way of customary (unproblematic), personal (collectively unlegitimated) and social (collectively legitimated) action, as well as through various forms of mutual aid and cooperation. If collective wants are provided according to diachronic scheduling devices, solidarity yields to convenience, in a transition to a purely cooperative (natural diachronic) household. Participants in the commune provide financial support according to collective agreement, usually through equitable individual contributions. If a collective basis for financial support is developed, synchronic work association may provide for greater solidarity. The commune is often founded on the basis of a charismatic mission, but if such mission is absent, or recedes as a collective enterprise, government may develop in one of several directions: in the free play of constellations of interest, it may hold to a direct democratic administration of collective affairs. But it may equally move in directions of consensual collegiality, of the domination of one or another person, or of backroom administration by an entrepreneurial, consensual minority. Because of its pluralistic and momentarily constituted character, the commune is often subjected to various utopian imageries and ethics of action. One or another of these may be adopted at various times by some participants. But the pluralistic nature of the commune leaves the mutual solidarity of friendship rather than unifying beliefs or ideology as the basis of commitment. Both shifting individual interests and ideological conflict are features of the commune which open the way to relatively high incidence of factionalization, membership turnover and failure. Yet if a commune survives its crises, freedom of association can move beyond more conventional social arrangements without being tied to assertions of ultimate truth.

In the worldly utopian production of collective life, the communal group serves especially as a demonstration, and potentially as a vehicle for the reconstruction of society-at-large. Communal life is thus enacted according to a utopian ideal of how the world should be. The group ostensibly demonstrates a way of life which is realizable for large numbers of people because it is realistic in dealing with all aspects of everyday life.

The intentional association

The diachronic worldly utopia involves intentional association on a rational basis by participants who, through bureaucratic organization, produce the conditions under which they live. A new system of managerial and work roles, specialized jobs, procedures, and legislated boundaries of personal and collective prerogatives is set up to operate through the successive moments of linear time; this system based on clock and calendar time is then subject to rational and universalistic administration and democratic planning. When irrational consequences of the system's operation are encountered, the features of the system may be progressively modified according to both technical criteria of efficiency and social criteria of justice and equality. Financial support and satisfaction of wants are achieved through collective organization, and work - both to provide income and for direct satisfaction of collective wants - is coordinated through diachronic allocation of units of labor time toward various tasks. Each participant contributes a rationally calculated fair share of clock-measured time toward work, optimally in personally preferred activities. Aside from the obligations of their work schedules, participants are on their own 'free time.' The ethics of the diachronically produced intentional association are enacted through legislation, rules, policies and technical rationalization 'from the outside.' Therefore, so long as participants behave 'legally,' the collectivity cannot infringe on 'natural rights' or personal prerogatives of belief and action. Pluralistic association is thus maintained within a legal frame of boundaries.

The community

The ethical enactment of the synchronically produced worldly utopia is based on an instantaneous and decisive 'inner' change of heart by the newcomer. Reformation of participant consciousness into a prophetically revealed revolutionary new world of the here-and-now is carried out in relations of communion in the here-and-now. The participant's conduct is subjected to the collective witnessing of peers, and a community of like-minded individuals is maintained. Under such conditions, communion occurs as an ongoing processional synchronicity: in households, function-centered work crews and other arenas of association, people walk through life together. Since daily life is treated as the context of communion, work is legitimated as an enjoyable form of rapport. Government is carried out largely as a collegial activity, both publicly and 'on the spot' through the process of witnessing and invocation of collective agreements and shared ethics. In the absence of either externalized rules and procedures or traditions, participants carry shared ethics in consciousness and forgo maintenance of socially unlegitimated worldviews. The integrity of the community is thus maintained by participants as an act of faith.

By contrast with worldly utopian communal groups, apocalyptic groups are sectarian in character. Rather than providing a way of life, course of salvation, or mission ostensibly open to all, such groups limit election to true believers who undergo a metanoia (change of cognition) typically associated with the development of a new persona, a new name, and a selfless adherence to collective mission. The 'monstrous' established order is seen as exerting its greedy oppression in every direction and at every turn; the sense of doom requires decisive action. Various types of apocalyptic groups may be distinguished according to whether the apocalypse is anticipated at some imminent point or regarded as having already transpired. In the former case, both the history of the diachronic order and plans directed to the future within that order become irrelevant; intense expectation focuses on strategic events of the present which lead to the apocalypse. On the other hand, if the apocalypse has transpired, the 'kingdom of heaven' is at hand. The pre-apocalyptic salvation sect exists as a logical possibility; yet so long as its enactment is a communal one, rather than a revivalist one of salvation before judgment day, it mirrors the other-worldly apocalyptic type.

The apocalyptic warring sect

If sectarian imagery is of an imminent and decisive Manichean battle between the forces of good and evil, the sectarian mission involves a struggle with opposing forces in historical time. A band of true believers, who become certified as charismatic warriors through a process of rebirth, act alone or in concert with a wider underground network of sympathizers and similar bands. These warriors engage in the moment-to-moment coordination of guerrilla-style action in pursuit of strategic, symbolic and terrorist missions. The members of the sect come out of the quiescent masses to act in historical significance far out of proportion to their actual numbers. The mundane concerns of everyday life are secondary to the events of missions, and the successful execution of actions related to missions and contingency plans depends on interpersonal trust, the development of high proficiency at various technical and strategic skills of war, and acts of commitment and bravery which place mission ahead of personal survival. No regimen or routinized satisfaction of wants can provide the resources necessary for the guerrilla warring mission, and the group operates in a hand-to-mouth communistic appropriation and distribution of spoils. Similarly, the strategic acts of warfare by an underground warring sect cannot depend on any traditional or rational authority, but instead rest on the ability of all participants to fend for themselves and count on others. At least initially, then, the warring sect operates as a charismatic community of virtuosi.

The apocalyptic other-worldly sect

The other-worldly sect engages in a withdrawal from 'this' world to a timeless heavenly plateau. The novice is either reborn into a community of the elect instantaneously or gradually achieves certification of grace through acts of piety. Indeed, the transition to an eternal union with the holy may take numerous directions, each having different implications for economic and other ethics of daily life. Similarly the tableau of the eternal may provide one or another metaphor of God. In each case, however, the sectarian beliefs - self-contained yet encompassing provinces of meaning - are invoked through a particular accent of reality in which attention is directed to selectively produced phenomena. The course of salvation, provided through the priestly or prophetic authority of those held to be nearest to God, is specified in acts of attention and schemes of interpretation for the acts of attention. Belief instigates a mission of demonstrating the reality of the way of salvation, and proselytization to the way is a crucial activity. Since activities of work cannot intrude on the demonstration of a heavenly tableau, wants are not satisfied through labor-intensive activity. Instead, the aesthetic and moral appeal of sacred activity may engender support by patrons and a flow of recruits. A community of goods or commercial capitalism, as well as devotion to a life of austere and direct satisfaction of wants, provide for the survival of the sect, while the material and spiritual needs of participants are met at the discretion of theocratic authority, the collegiality of elders or the democratic consensuality of the elect.

The ecstatic association

In a transcendental formation, the world is neither taken-for-granted as meaningful through the intentional interpretations of individuals nor produced according to a unified set of beliefs about its meaning. Instead, participants in ecstatic association engage attention freely in the absolute presentness of the phenomenal world 'before the word' and prior to symbolization. The synchronic now is thus neither episodically pluralistic (as in the commune) or socially constructed (as in the community). Instead, immersion in the direct and ecstatic experience of phenomena occurs as a relation between a teacher and disciples who collectively enter the shared duration of the vivid present. The ecstatic experience makes what is mundanely taken to be sense appear as socially perpetuated nonsense. A boundary is maintained between novices and the charismatic community of those who 'see.' Initiation is predicated on coming to the mystic consciousness of manifold reality in which 'people make their own relevances.' Neither satisfaction of wants nor government is routinized; nor does active proselytization serve to increase a community of goods. In lieu of continuous economic activity, financial support may be sustained through independent wealth, sinecures or tithes. Needs, especially those of a mystic character, are met through direct charismatic action which cannot depend on legitimation for its success. Any political order is regarded as a vehicle of domination, and, even when traditions are used as devices for the transmission of mystic consciousness, the power of charismatic action rather than 'authority' resolves problematic situations. While deference may be given the teacher, charisma of the community is unroutinized and may move collective attention among now one and then a wholly other experience of the vivid present.

COMMUNAL GROUPS AND UTOPIAN DIFFUSION

The socio-historical model of countercultural deviance sketched at the beginning of this study suggests that one or another of alternative groups - each of which critically rejects the established order - may become significant for society-at-large to the extent that diffusion of the group's vision and way of life occurs. In relation to communal groups, diffusion may be taken to be the proliferation of innovative cognitive modes, ethics, social forms of interaction and missions. Analytically, we may distinguish two aspects of diffusion: methods of propagation through communal groups themselves, and adoption of innovations beyond the utopian arenas, i.e. in sectors of the encompassing society. Though propagation may occur in diverse ways, certain processes of propagation seem especially associated with one or another type of communal group. Such processes bear particular relevance for the careers of utopian groups themselves. On the other hand, utopian innovations become especially important to societal development when they are adopted in sectors of the population beyond the communal groups.

Communal groups and propagation

Multiple tendencies of ecstatic association suggest that diffusion does not occur by any single or narrow process. In its pure form, ecstatic association is a world-rejecting 'cosmic' relationship, one which disdains the inevitable compromises of mundane life in favor of a separate reality. But ecstatic association may move in other directions as well. Charismatic education may produce certified warriors of the faith or spiritual seers who transform the ecstatic experience in directions of the warring sect, the other-worldly sect or the community - each of which may contain charismatic elements, as we have seen already. In quite another course, the carrier of an ecstatic perspective may act in 'the world' without engendering institutionalization of an associational form. Two possibilities may be noted. The mystic may temporize by partially setting aside the ecstatic perspective in order to participate in and influence occurrences in the world-at-large. Or such a person may play the part of the outsider who refuses to temporize, thus acting as the heretic, the deviant who denies the accent of reality which more situationally committed individuals share. This seems to have been the stratagem of the 'circumcelliones' of ancient Palestine, who lived neither as recluses nor in institutionalized monasteries, instead drifting from one spiritual enclave to another, wreaking havoc among pacified true believers (Cabrol, 1962:787). In either event, the bearer of transcendent consciousness acts in but is not 'of' the world.

Diffusion of transcendental mysticism, however, is a double-edged sword. It may arise in various arenas and equally serve the interests of ideology and those of utopia. The case of Rasputin in the Czarist courts points to the ambiguities. Whether his powers and motivations were bona fide is a moot point: in any event, Rasputin's ability to cure no-doubt 'hysterical' illnesses attracted widespread recognition while the Czarist regime was faltering in the face of both constitutional and revolutionary developments. At a time when other concerns were clearly more critical for aristocratic interests, Rasputin redirected attention of principal figures in the Russian courts to mystical possibilities. By the same token, in Germany during the 1920s, romantic mysticism, such as that conveyed in the writings of Hesse, may well have enhanced individuation of consciousness, thereby giving advantage to those who fomented social change through hierarchical charismatic organization.

Such cases do not suffice to conclude that mysticism is a purely apolitical force which segments individuals from social action. Ernst Troeltsch has sometimes been mistakenly identified with such a position. But in fact, he suggested (1932:378) that mysticism - though not a social institution - still involves social interaction. Aside from the face-to-face transmission of mystic consciousness, Troeltsch cited (1932:693), for example, the possibility of an 'invisible' church composed of believer-prophets who act independently yet in concert with one another. The more institutionalized derivative of such a form suggested to Troeltsch a third type of religious organization, one which has been largely ignored by scholars (e.g. Gustafson, 1967; Goode, 1967; Demerath, 1967; Eister, 1967; and those cited by them) concerned with the problems of differentiating sect from church. Troeltsch referred to this third type as a voluntary association of like-minded people who live together through a quasi-charismatic process. Such a form may be taken as akin to the community type of communal group described in the present study. Other directions of mysticism include the case of Thomas Münzer and other mystical anarchists described by Cohn (1970).

Propagation originating in ecstatic association may take diverse courses, arising both in more institutionalized communal groups and in society-at-large. For all their differences, these developments share a common theme: in all cases, attention of those exposed to transcendent consciousness is modified by the charismatic introduction of an alternative way of cognizing situation. Whatever the prevailing construction of time, it is, in a sense, interrupted by the introjection of a phenomenal experience constituted in the absolute vivid presentness of internal time consciousness, prior to any attribution of meaning. The effects of the transcendent vision are felt, if at all, as a seemingly magical, obvious yet inexplicable re-cognition. It is through alteration of the object of consciousness, not by any modification of structural or material conditions, that the diffusion of ecstatic association transpires.

By comparison, the propagation of cultural elements from other types of communal groups seems more straightforward than the diverse threads of ecstatic diffusion. Other-worldly sects which offer personal and collective salvation beyond the bounds of society-at-large depend on proselytization as a basis for survival. For such groups, adherence to a highly specified set of beliefs precludes compromise with alternative and competing formations. In the interests of protecting their right to a special point of view, other-worldly sects often adopt a position of tolerance toward alternative sects. But this toleration does not typically extend to the assertion of 'free conscience' held by the more voluntaristic associations that Weber (1968:1208-9) described. In each sect, the ultimate validity of their own understanding of the holy is maintained, and an attempt is made to subsume alternative religious formulations, both doctrinally and historically, under the newly revealed encompassing interpretation (cf. Berger and Luckmann, 1966:115). Believers hope to spread the faith by finding others to convert to the righteousness of their way. The devices for spreading the word range from seeking out the lonely and disillusioned on a personal basis, street preaching, and the staging of revivals to the institution of congregational religion. Various strategies of institutional replication may be employed through the establishment of missionary branches and efforts at conversion of other religious and communal groups. The tendencies toward institutionalization and, more particularly, toward hierarchy under such developments have been noted by Weber (1968:1205) and others (e.g. Harrison, 1959) as antithetical to congregational sovereignty. They thus seem likely to develop earlier and with more regularity among sects based on priestly authority (such as the contemporary American Krishna organization) rather than among groups where communion (even under a charismatic patriarch such as Love Israel) is emphasized. In either case, however, to the degree that propagation involves more than simple proselytization of novices into the fold, it is carried out under the auspices of those who have fully demonstrated the validity of their religious election.

The strategies of diffusion for the warring sect are of quite a different order. Guerrilla actions of such sects draw more widespread attention than pacifist enterprises of other-worldly salvation sects. But secrecy and absolutely selfless devotion to the revolutionary mission are required if the group is not to meet with extermination at the hands of police and military forces of the established order. Strategies of organization, such as that of the revolutionary cell, may be drawn upon, and various tests of membership and commitment may be employed in more far-flung networks. Still, the possibilities of infiltration and detection can never be fully eliminated. Any public action has its risks, even, on occasion, of death. But terrorist actions are a logical outgrowth of the propelling desire among warring sectarians to provide uncompromised and exemplary vanguard leadership to an incipient revolutionary struggle. The myth of revolution contained in the germs of revolutionary acts, it is hoped, will inspire the uncommitted, those who remain in the ranks of party politics, and the unorganized masses to rise up and join hands against bureaucratically organized forces of domination. It is this hope which sustains the faith of the warring sect. Its tactics are thus not directed to the gradual diffusion of an ethic for life under a new order. Instead, the attempt is to create a more immediate 'snowball' effect by inspiring people to redirect action beyond the contexts of their personal lives. The warring sect hopes to engender a world-historical struggle through the mediated propagation of a revolutionary outlaw ethic.

For worldly utopian groups, salvation of the world depends on the propagation of cognitive modes, ethics and social forms of new ways of life. Unlike ecstatic associations, warring sects and other-worldly sects, worldly utopian groups do not exist on the basis of esoteric beliefs or specialized missions. Their universally relevant ways of life are thus open to widespread diffusion. This may happen both through proliferation of the form of association itself and through the propagation of consciousness, ethics and forms of interaction in other social arenas. Though these procedures are employed by both the intentional association and the community, the proliferation of the form of association itself would seem especially to be the province of community diffusion.

In contrast to other-worldly sects, communities involve a kind of voluntaristic association based on the establishment of an intersubjective realm of consciousness devoid of doctrinal sectarian belief. In place of dispensation of grace through institutionalized spiritual authority, communion comes to provide rectitude in the ongoing praxis of collective activities. The interest in diffusion thus does not bear any attachment to dominance of an established group over newly initiated ones. Rather, the form itself is promoted as a basis of association for other groups and in the world at large. It is expected that newcomers to the faith will develop their own 'charismas of community' (Roth, 1975:155), however much they be inspired by precursor examples. To encourage this diffusion of ethically-based new associations of charisma, communities engage in various 'public relations' activities. They may support a tour of some members to cities, towns and universities to encourage people 'trapped' in the established order to start their own communities. Books and leaflets (e.g. Gaskin and The Farm, 1974; Gaskin, n.d.) may be published to describe the community, how it operates, and its teachings. And alliances may be made with other communities which seek the counsel of the more operational ones. Yet in so far as communities remain consistent with their anti-authoritarian underpinnings, the diffusion of the way of life is accomplished by propagation of ethics and forms of consciousness based on mutual witnessing rather than through any hierarchical extension of an ongoing group's direct sphere of influence.

Intentional associations may likewise encourage the instigation of similar communal groups, both through writings of publicists (e.g. Kinkade, 1973) and by provision of technical assistance to groups-in-formation. Yet the ethic of enactment in the intentional association is a normative behavioral one which depends on the existence of an autonomous 'system' of operations. The diffusion of the way of life demonstrated in intentional associations depends to a great degree on the modification of legislated and material conditions in terms of which people act. While it may be relevant to organization of large groups, small communal groups may for the most part conduct their affairs without drawing extensively on devices of bureaucratic organization. Diffusion of the intentional association thus becomes especially germane in new towns or old ones taken over by new majorities, or, on a broad scale, subsequent to attainment of political power through revolutionary seizure or legal party methods. Then, through bureaucratic reconstruction, the new system can be introduced on a large scale. Barring such an occurrence, propagation of technical and legislative advances in the rationalization of social relations is especially relevant within the ongoing society-at-large. While the synchronic community exists as a dialectical opposition to the established order, the radical rationality of the diachronic intentional association engenders a progressive tension with that order. In many respects, it does not move beyond previously existing bases for change, i.e. technological innovation, the liberal legislation of a more equitable and just social order, and normative diffusion. Though the intentional association engages in a planned socialist production, its features of progressive rationalization may be summarily co-opted within the established order. Successful diffusion as a socialist form of rationalized association then depends on either the effective competition of intentional associations and new town derivatives in the capitalist market (a somewhat difficult proposition in an era of multinational corporations) or evolutionary socialism through legislation.

The commune is based on the simple solidarity of friendship and common interest. But despite its lack of a unified utopian mission, it may serve as an arena for various kinds of utopian ethical and exemplary action. By its pluralistic openness, it may come to be the scene of efforts at propagation by more collectivized utopian groups and by proponents of all kinds of causes. The anarchist community at Home, Washington - established in the 1890s - apparently was spared no crank or philosopher who got the chance to visit. According to Bushue (1967: 12-14; cf. LeWarne, 1975:174ff), the haven for free thinkers and lovers saw social movements of its day running the gamut from promoters of vegetarianism and 'hatha' yoga to speakers on the evils of sex. While communards may grow weary of this kind of seemingly continual exposure to people out to save them, other entrances into a relatively unboundaried site may be more welcome: communes may serve as resources for various countercultural activities, and they may provide convenient and compatible homes for individuals who carry on activities in external public spheres. As Abrams and McCulloch (1976:188) have remarked, 'Their value is that they hover on the brink of constructing organic solidarity on the basis of an uncompromising assertion of the moral autonomy of the individual.' Thus, the commune as a type has dual tendencies of diffusion. It exists as a 'melting pot' of alternative utopias; in addition, and in contrast to more utopian and self-sufficient groups, it is enmeshed both in a wider counterculture and the institutions of society-at-large. This interface between the established world and the new ones, and between individualism and communalism may induce tensions and instabilities; but by the same token, communes exist at the eye of the storm of utopian alternatives; they may cast their members in various other directions of utopian action, and they may serve as arenas of mediation between utopian ways out, other people and their sensibilities, and the 'iron cage' of contemporary life.

Societal adoption of utopian innovations

The diffusion of utopian ways of life developed in communal groups depends on the existence of audiences for whom such ways of life bear relevance. From the point of view of people in communal groups, the intent of propagation is largely to achieve conversion. On the other hand, the adoption of utopian innovations within arenas in the encompassing society takes on the character of 'borrowing.' In what Everett Rogers (1971:9) has called 'selective contact change,' people in a society-at-large 'are exposed to external influences and adopt or reject a new idea from that source on the basis of their needs.' While the potential attention of individuals, status groups and members of various classes to utopian ways of life is a separate area of inquiry, something can be said about the sociology of situated knowledge involved: strategies, organizational forms and arenas of diffusion employed by utopian actors, as well as webs of affiliation and mediated communication, circumscribe audiences of potential adopters simply by the exposure to or ignorance of alternatives. A mutual selection process among people, their ideals, and material contexts would seem to operate. In what Weber referred to as an elective affinity, it is as though propagators of utopian ways learn whom to persuade and how to reach them, while, for their parts, people in society-at-large come to comprise audiences on the basis of one or another utopian wish. Confidence artists know their marks, and the marks often know they are being taken, but somehow they participate in the schuck nevertheless. In the propagation of utopian alternatives, the process is similar, though motives are usually not so opportunistic or cynical. Promoters of utopia simply try to 'separate the wheat from the chaff' and, finding 'religious seekers,' help them on their ways to a new world (cf. Lofland and Stark, 1965).

Yet the way an innovation spreads may be quite different if the process of diffusion is a less direct one of adoption rather than outright conversion. In such a situation, the utopian alternatives which have arisen in a communal context come to be detached from their original carriers, and modified and adopted by people in society-at-large who sustain certain material and ideal interests. This, of course, is the formulation made famous by Max Weber in his various analyses of the Protestant ethic and the spirit of capitalism (1958; 1946; 1968:1164-200, passim). The account is both wide-ranging and complex. But one aspect of it bears re-emphasis. Both the new, diachronic and rationalized process of production and the ethical discipline of asceticism originated in a monastic context beyond the pale of medieval feudalism, outside the existing secular order (Weber, 1968:1168, 1183; Duby, 1968:177). Together they comprised a new form of social interaction - in Marx and Engels's terms (1967:409), a new mode of life. While the innovations in organization - for example, specialization in production of commodities (Duby, 1968:178) - could diffuse as ideas easily replicable elsewhere, the staffing of new processes of production necessarily required a transmutation of work asceticism from monastic arenas to secular situations where a connection between godly devotion and productive activity was far less obvious than on the monastic side. In the absence of encompassing 'outer' manifestations of God's direction, an 'inner' meaningfulness of disciplined activity had to be maintained if it was to embody a certitude of religious grace. In later industrial developments, the assembly line came to define the rhythm and time discipline of work. But in medieval and early modern rationalized production, workers themselves had to inwardly maintain the discipline of diachronic time if efficient production was to be maintained as the heart of the spirit of capitalism (Thompson, 1967). It is in this context that the religious emphasis on time as commodity achieved economic significance. As Weber (1958:157) remarked, 'Waste of time is thus the first and in principle the deadliest of sins.'

Processes of diffusion may occur not only by conversion to a newly established way of life, but also, as I am suggesting they did in the emergence of capitalism, through the adoption of a new mode of production - a material process of production, a time-based form of social interaction, and an ethic of association. These elements may move in diverse ways beyond their original communal boundaries into interstitial arenas which are neither communal nor rigidly institutionalized under the old order. The emergence of capitalism with its diachronic and religiously sanctioned work ethic has been the historically decisive case. A similar process might, however, take place in the emergence of a new way of life. The new way of life would involve a historically new process of production, a new form of social interaction predicated on an alternative form of time-consciousness, and a new ethic of association. For example, in such a new way of life, work might be organized in terms of broadly specified projects rather than through the now prevalent division of labor according to specified tasks (cf. Weber, 1968:118ff). Specified work would be carried out by people in crews acting in synchronic association with an intersubjective ethic of work as communion. If it paralleled what I have suggested was the initial process in the emergence of capitalism, the new way of life would develop independently of the old order and initially spread in peripheral areas or reconstituted new towns, and at other sites where the predominance of the old order is at best ephemeral. In such an occurrence, the mode of production and forms of household association might comprise wholly separate arenas, where developments could obtain independently of one another.

Both Mannheim (1936; 1952) and Engels (1964b; 1964c) have suggested that in response to historically new conditions, one or another utopian alternative among many in competition with one another may come to be a decisive bearer of a historically new form of association which is realized in the emergence of a new order. Yet such a possibility is not realized simply as the flowering of an abstract ideal. The intricate but ultimately unworkable visions of people like Charles Fourier point to the difficulties. A utopian alternative is relevant to a larger society only in so far as it evidences a way of life. And the diffusion of that way of life depends on the existence of other people who believe their own ideal or material situations will be enhanced by adoption.

If an established order can no longer provide a viable life for its participants, if previous symbolic integrations prove irrelevant to new circumstances, widespread eschatological expectations and 'religious' anxieties may obtain. Historical 'accidents' and circumstances within a society-at-large often determine the viability of various alternative tracks of diffusion. Under certain situations, such as international war or an expanding economy, utopian visions remain inconsequential for anyone other than participants in carrier groups. The eschatological anxieties recede, and, as Weber (1968:1187) indicated, 'charismatic communism in all its forms declines and retreats into monastic circles, where it becomes the special concern of exemplary followers of God.' But if new circumstances persist beyond any short-term conditions, utopian alternatives become the focus of widespread attention. Then utopianists may come to provide - either in some concrete association or movement or through diffusion of their form of association - a viable basis of life in an emerging order.

SOME SPECULATIONS ON THE CONTEMPORARY SITUATION

I do not intend to carry on the misguided tradition of secular sociological prophecy initiated by Saint-Simon, Comte and Marx. The present study has been directed to an empirical analysis of communal groups. In an age of pluralism, it is unlikely that any single kind of utopian enactment will come to predominate. Certainly no utopian configuration represents an inevitable and necessary next evolutionary stage of social relations. Developments in society-at-large and in communal groups themselves may take diverse directions. The present study provides at best an interpretive framework for understanding radical alternatives; but future outcomes cannot be predicted on this basis.

Still, communal groups bear scrutiny especially because of their adversary relation to the contemporary social situation - a situation in which conflicts of interest are increasingly laid bare, a situation to which many people respond with despair and disillusionment for conflicting reasons, one for which the hard-nosed prophets (e.g. Heilbroner, 1974) see only bleak prospects, and one in which eschatological anxieties may all too easily find their release in unreflected and simplistic responses to unanticipated problems of existence. Two kinds of observations, however speculative, should be made. They are concerned with the societal context of communal emergences and with the implications of various types of communal emergences themselves.

Since the middle of the 1960s, many young people in the USA have sought and some have found new ideals; the conventional life has been abandoned by many who have been repulsed by the social, political and economic institutions of post-bourgeois capitalism and the ersatz culture of throw-away America. They have challenged the moral legitimacy of the established order. The forces of the established order have on one or another basis tried to reassert the legitimacy of domination where it has previously become problematic, either by 'delivering the goods' which defuse eschatological expectations, or through secular hierocratic domination and its mediated production of the objects of attention, or, in extreme situations, by maintaining order with brute force. But once legitimacy of the established order has been widely challenged, ideological justification of the status quo becomes another brand of utopia, while further attempts at domination may well feed the incipient critiques. This is especially so if eschatological anxieties are based on the failure of previous 'recipes' of participation in the social order under a new set of material circumstances.

If widespread anxieties, value-based rejections of 'the American way' and transcendent wishes persist even after the initial period of crisis and subsequent attempts at establishmentarian reconstruction, there is no assurance that the forces unleashed will lead to a better world, according to any standards. The struggles for domination and for social change may end in charismatic totalitarianism as well as in voluntaristic communism; they may be resolved in technological fascism as well as in planned socialism.

Some people hope to remain good citizens who can live out their lives without coming to terms with the new forces arising around them. Some simply seek religious sanctuary. Others cannot hope to reconcile their self-images with the new conditions under which they must live, yet passionately seek a reconstruction which both enables and legitimates personal survival and meaningful activity in the prevailing social order. Ideological 'fronts,' Mannheim (1936:194) suggested, produce 'situationally transcendent ideas which never succeed de facto in the realization of their projected contents.' The rhetoric is of change but the practices are ones of adjustment to a status quo. Especially in times of perceived crisis, social 'causes,' religions of salvation and ethics of adaptation to material, social and political conditions in an established order - however secular their forms in a secular age - come to the fore. The ideals of piety and ethical self-reliance may be reinvoked as ways for autonomous individuals to insure dignity amidst the uncertainties of a world filled with anomie and alienation. Ostensibly non-religious 'personal growth' movements such as EST (Erhard Seminar Training) and Re-Evaluation Co-Counseling may provide the basis for emotional adaptation to the 'proletarianization' of quasi-professional and service occupations (McKissick and Nigg, 1975). Members of certain strata may seek to certify their grace in an age beyond freedom or dignity by acting to 'save the future.' Such social movements, causes, religions of salvation, and new secular religions may be focused largely on organized activities of proselytization, public relations, the inculcation of ethics and practices, and planned production of future events. They either offer therapeutic adjustment to prevailing circumstances or hold out situationally transcendent objectives as wishes, fantasies or myths which serve as organizing principles; they appeal to individuals who bear one or another ideal of utopia; yet utopia is never realized as a concrete form of association. In such cases, 'religious' attention is typically directed to action unproblematic to the established order: to personal salvation, a sense of righteousness and charity, status honor, and career legitimation, rather than to the enactment of new and independent ways of life.

Communal groups, on the other hand, are places where 'the future is now.' Communalists encounter the problematic issues of everyday collective life, whereas such problems may be held in abeyance in other, more segmented social movements where change is to be expected only at some future point. Communal life involves an immediate modification in the character of social interaction itself. Social change is reconstituted as a change of the social.

With more and more certitude, chroniclers of the contemporary Western social situation argue that the established order has lost its ability to provide existentially meaningful bases for participation in economic and political life. It seems that the USA's era of abundance is at an end, not because of any short-term economic fluctuations, but because of the shifting role of the USA in international economic and political arenas. Both Robert Heilbroner and Daniel Bell predict that some sort of collectivist order is the likely replacement for an order based materially on mass consumption and morally on individual self-fulfillment. And in both their views (Bell, 1976:29), the vehicle of transformation (Heilbroner, 1976: 119),

> will be a new religious orientation, directed against the canons and precepts of our time, and oriented toward a wholly different conception of the meaning of life and a mode of social organization congenial to the encouragement of that life.

If the material conditions and cultural assumptions upon which an entire social order has been based are indeed changing, we may expect alternative ways of life, especially those involving sources and aesthetics of want satisfaction and new modes of production, to become increasingly important.

The contemporary political scene may increasingly become the battleground of class struggles and status group efforts at exclusions in the allocation of scarce resources. If an ongoing crisis focused on the social question ensues, some will seek out an other-worldly life. The various consequences of ecstatic association may be noticed, but they will probably not be understood, and they certainly will not be traced. The charismatic warriors who move to act in historical time may indeed precipitate political upheaval.

But I return to Marcuse's crucial question, 'What kind

of life?' If change to a more collectivist mode of life is a likely direction of societal development, it is those I have termed the worldly utopianists who especially confront the concrete issues of daily association in the new age. Just as Protestantism created an ethic for the culture of capitalism, contemporary utopianists search for an ethic of collectivism. Two worldly utopian possibilities - the diachronic intentional association and the synchronic community - would pose a critical choice, if such choice ever becomes relevant. The intentional association is purported to revolutionize the world by technical and legislated modification of the conditions under which people live. Its revolution initially involves a sudden transformation to a new 'system,' and this system is then subject to gradual, progressive and bureaucratically insured refinement. The synchronic community is based on a sudden and decisive change of participants' consciousnesses; the intentional association is derived from a previously extant philosophy of determinism which suggests that people act in pursuit of personal interests in an operating set of material and structural conditions. It is based on Rousseau's contractual attempt to defuse Hobbesian struggle through structural guarantees of an equitable social order. The synchronic community eschews this determinism and its linear and historicist conception of time in favor of an ethic of free will in the here-and-now. In the latter approach, people create their own circumstances, either through the bad faith of rote habit and conditioned responses to covertly held self-interest or by freely and publicly negotiating and enacting their collective will from moment to moment.

In its most positive frame, the new age of the intentional association would be one of increased rationality, justice and advances in the technical organization of production, all enhancing greater individual freedom and leisure. In the community, on the other hand, the world would be based on trust rather than institutionalized equity, communion rather than legislated individual freedom, and collective witnessing of truth rather than justice under codified law. The intentional association draws on the charisma of reason to make a religion out of bureaucratic collectivism, while the community represents a religious attempt to create a charismatic intersubjectivity based on a shared ethic and shared interests - of the many who act as one.

Ultimately these two alternatives involve differences in the way time is constituted in social relations: whether face-to-face synchronic sociation or the intersection of diachronic personal schedules is to be the organizing principle of social interaction. From these two alternatives flow wholly different ways of cognizing the world, ethics of association, work relations, and kinds of authority. Such choices remain largely theoretical within the bounds of an established order in which people are in many respects alienated from the production of their own lives. But utopian communalists evidence the possibilities of moving beyond habituated participation in established institutions. For people who have already begun to create new worlds and for those who join one or another of the utopian camps, the choice is not simply abstract - it is an immediate one.

Appendix 1
Some theoretical and methodological considerations

No simple test of hypotheses derived from theory will yield an understanding of alternative communal worlds. This is so for several reasons. Science, especially in its more positivist elaboration, entails certain assumptions - of causality, of transitivity, and of the progressive paradigmatic accumulation of valid objective knowledge. In a very real way, these assumptions may be called ideological, for they are beyond testability and still provide an epistemological backdrop for deterministic theorizing about why events occur.

In so far as people's actions are determined by external events, or as the more ecclesiastical among us would have it, through predestination, the scientific viewpoint as a paradigm of sociological explanation makes sense. Its statistical models succeed in explaining variance especially in so far as the social life subjected to study has become routinized. Even so, social science's abstract theories and statistical models interrelating sequences and quantities of causation fail to unmask the sources of routine behavior. In discounting a sociology of voluntaristic or willful action at the outset, the scientific enterprise cannot look to the organized mass production of both materials and ideas which underlies the statistically verifiable routine world. It is the statisticians of the not-so-hidden persuasion of Madison Avenue who, more than the sociologists, know wherein the determinism lies. Even to the degree that social relations occur in a way that is causally explicable, the scientific enterprise does not penetrate to the productions of meanings whereby statistical correlations obtain.

The epistemological problems of scientific sociology become especially pronounced in the study of new utopian social worlds. For the social scientist who proposes a causal or functional theory already subsumes multiple social realities under a single paradigm. In that act, value-free sociology becomes impossible; the researcher has already posited an abstract set of conceptual relations which mask the subjectively meaningful realities of participants' activities. When sociological concepts are reified as substitutions for the phenomena* they would describe, structuralist explanations necessarily replace more parsimonious explanations at a level of meaning (cf. Garfinkel, 1967:66-8).

For example, in Kanter's (1972) functional analysis of commitment mechanisms and success of nineteenth-century American communal organizations, use of longevity as a criterion variable provides an independent objective standard of 'success' which may not in all cases be meaningful to utopian actors, whose purposes may preclude institutional persistence. Communal groups which survive for long periods of time are not necessarily more likely than quixotic groups to induce broader social change, for routinization is hardly a vehicle of upheaval. Specifically, three considerations make longevity a questionable criterion. In the first place, groups which survive for a long period of time generally lose their original communal basis for endeavors and frequently modify the characters of their organizations. The communal group of the primitive Christian church flowered into a set of institutions which have maintained succession over nearly two millennia. The Amana colonies in Iowa began as a communal sect which gave way in the 1930s to a joint stock corporation. Presently, they manufacture and market a wide range of household appliances. 'Success' is a many-splendored thing, which need have nothing to do with the continuation of a communal form. Second, as a theorist of anarchy (Ward, 1966:382) suggests, the 'hardening of the arteries' involved in organizational persistence may be regarded by some people as an obstacle to be dealt with by dissolution

---

* Here and throughout, I treat 'phenomena' as events that occur. We know of such things through the experiences of individuals. I leave open the question of whether individuals' experiences of phenomena are constituted: 1 mundanely, in a 'natural attitude' (Schutz, 1967: 3ff) as objects external to consciousness, or 2 as acts of consciousness (Husserl, 1931:s.35). It would seem that phenomena could be constituted one way or the other by a person; the question is an empirical one. In either case, however, phenomena are available to analysis only on the basis of the experiences of individuals. I return to this problem below, but I do not treat it as a critical concern of this study.

and reformation. Especially given the readiness of many former members of dissolved communal groups to start or join other communal groups, it becomes obvious that communalism as a form of social organization may persist independently of the survival of one or another group. Third, many secular utopian experiments are touted as models of the way in which the entire social world could be organized; for their founders, they may be little more than grist for an intellectual debate. Subsuming divergent motives under a single criterion of success implies a basic problem of Kanter's functional analysis: its thesis of commitment mechanisms does not differentiate types of utopian alternatives and their own paradigms of action.

Kanter has argued that 'successful' nineteenth-century American groups (those lasting over twenty-five years) differed from unsuccessful ones in their development of various 'commitment mechanisms' which reinforce attainment of three systemic needs: retention of members, group cohesiveness, and social control (1972:64-74). Six broad processes of commitment are proposed: sacrifice in order to belong, investment (gaining a stake in the group), renunciation of the outside world, communion among members, mortification (submitting to a group derived identity), and transcendence of personal interest. Whatever the results of such commitment-building mechanisms, those groups in Kanter's analysis which most <u>employed</u> them were sects which continued after the deaths of their founders. All the groups in the 'successful' category claimed some sort of religious belief and, of these successful ones, those which lasted longest were sects, mostly of immigrants (e.g. Mother Ann's Shakers and George Rapp's Harmonists), while the shorter-lived ones were those of charismatic leaders such as John Humphrey Noyes (Oneida) and Dr Keil (Aurora and Bethel), native Americans who failed to develop their communities on a basis other than personal rulership. Of Kanter's 'unsuccessful' groups, only two were immigrant sects, both founded in the middle of the nineteenth century when religious persecution in Europe was well on the wane. The rest of the unsuccessful groups included Owenists, Fourierists, several anarchist colonies, Mormon ventures prior to the settlement of Utah, and a potpourri of other experiments (1972:246-8).

Such an array of group longevities, in which institutionalized sects last longest and religious groups with charismatic leaders make up the remainder of 'successful' groups, suggests that commitment mechanisms are one facet of the routinization of charisma. Charismatic authority, according to Weber (1968:1121-8), 'cannot remain stable, but either becomes traditionalized or routinized, or a combination of both.' Thus, those groups which lasted longest were able to do so because charisma became routinized (through any of a variety of devices), while others of Kanter's successful groups died off with their initial leaders. For the rest, the unsuccessful ones, routinization never became an issue: charismatics failed to provide for their following, theoretical utopias failed to provide a practical basis for group life, or broader historical events swept away the meaning and utility of group life.

Science's causal or functional explanations have little to offer by way of penetrating to an understanding of social realities as they are constituted by the people involved. Especially in communal groups where the scientific enterprise is already widely disdained, causal and functional research represent a worldview which cannot hope to encompass the worlds it would claim to understand; its account is inevitably partial, for participants act in terms of paradigms which transcend the assumptions and ideology of science.

In a poetic way, Bob Dylan poses the problem: 'Something's going on, but you don't know what it is, do you, Mr Jones?' Though Dylan is describing a man of bourgeois rationality attending a strange party, the predicament of the social scientist in a strange communal world is much the same: the 'objective' measurement of structures of collective life, of socio-economic background of participants or of similar quantified variables does not necessarily penetrate to the aspects of collective life that form a meaningful basis of action for participants. A scientific sociology cannot subsume the relativity of myriad alternative enactments of the 'way the world is'; instead, it must resort to an objectified causality wherein all cases are taken to be 'the same,' differing only in the degree of presence of one or another attribute. An epiphenomenal set of data is inevitably created as a product of such a research enterprise. What passes as empiricism is in fact non-empirical, for the experience on which it is based is not of the phenomena being studied, but of standardized measurements about a theoretical model - selected and juxtaposed by the researcher in order to test the hypotheses derived from a theory. While Alfred Schutz has been faulted by Hindess (1972) for relegating the sociological enterprise to 'a special kind of storytelling,' the positivist scientists create stories not about social phenomena, but about data they have created themselves.

The statistical profile - disjointed from the empirical world - has all-too-often become the sole province of sociological knowledge. But the problem of the meaning of the world for the participants must be the essential concern of any sociology of alternative communal groups. In such groups, people abandon previous patterns of living and adopt new, collective ways of living and making ends meet. Such changes, at least at the outset, involve modifications of life situations from some previous household situation to a communal situation, and from a previous to a new range of associations and concerns. These changes differ from rites of passage and steps in the pursuit of career or status. Especially for those who initiate communal living sites, the world does not come prefabricated, and the various ways in which groups of people construct communal worlds seemingly bear little relation to one another. Those who emulate utopia are not always in agreement with each other about the nature of utopia, and often devote considerable efforts to debunking alternative views, both within and beyond their own groups. Others live communally without giving credence to the notion of utopian possibility. The existence of divergent orientations toward living communally suggests that the understanding of communal life is bound up in discovering the ways people construe it, as well as in discerning more obvious economic and organizational strategies.

The understanding of any one communal group thus entails an 'emic' (Pike, 1967:37) immersion into the constitutions of world that participants themselves evoke, both in ongoing ways and on special occasions. The concerns of the participants become those of the observer, who tries to understand the world as they understand it, by moving with them through the courses of life activities. On the other hand, since different communal worlds represent alternative ways of life opposed to the prevailing order, it is also important to have a comparative basis for understanding these alternatives. For the most part, participants in a given social world are not alienated from it, at least in the sense that they experience it as the world, not as one possibility out of a range of possibilities. Participants themselves, then, are only obliquely concerned with comparison; such a concern typically involves a more 'etic' (Pike, 1967:37) viewpoint of an outsider who has been exposed to a variety of social worlds, and can thus establish the distinctive as well as the widely shared features of each world.

These two concerns - understanding social worlds as the constituted realities of participants, and comparing such alternative worlds on some independently meaningful basis - set the boundaries for providing a sociology of communal groups. However divergent these concerns might seem, they are the methodological basis of Max Weber's sociological legacy. Weber sought to provide ideal types derived from an interpretation of action in terms of its subjective meaning (1968:4,8). Ideal types were taken by Weber to be 'pure' in that they represent theoretical constructs devoid of the ambiguities present in any empirical situation. Nevertheless, in so far as ideal types represent models of meaning drawn from the meanings and actions of persons involved in social relationships, they have a subjective basis. Thus, Weber argued (1968:7) that even objects of consciousness which have existences independently of any single attribution of meaning (e.g. birth, an eclipse, a gun) are sociologically intelligible only when their subjective meanings for persons interacting with them come to be understood. It is the same with such 'commonsense' concepts of collective entities such as church, family and class. While these and other phenomena could be studied in a purely objective and functional fashion, such an approach, Weber felt (1968:15), involves an illegitimate reification. Interpretative understanding of subjective action, difficult though it may be to attain and tentative as its results may be, is the only epistemologically valid basis for the study of human action, and is therefore 'the specific character of sociological knowledge' (1968:15).

Writing in 1932, about a decade after Weber's death, Alfred Schutz (1967) sought to penetrate further into the problem of subjective meaning, which he felt Weber had resolved too casually. For Schutz, a reinterpretation of the constitution of meaning provided the basis for describing the a priori structures of the lifeworld from a phenomenologically derived perspective (Schutz and Luckmann, 1973).

Essentially, Schutz scrutinized Weber's claims for the possibility of understanding ('Verstehen'). For Schutz, Weber had chosen to treat the outward manifestations of meaning as relatively unambiguously discernible to the observer. In Schutz's view, Weber moved from a sociology of subjectively meaningful action to the formulation of a sociology of observed meanings. Schutz, for his part, praised Weber's achievement in interpretive sociology; he criticized Weber's discussion of subjective meaning only to 'give to interpretive sociology the philosophical foundation it has hitherto lacked' (1967:43). For these purposes, Schutz looked beneath interpretations of meanings and ideal types of observed meanings: he looked to the situational constitution of meaning through the 'operating intentionality of an Ego-consciousness' (1967:37). In this situated and non-anonymous context, Schutz found subjective meaning in a social setting to be 'nothing more than the referral of constituted objectivities ("Gegenständlichkeiten") to the consciousness of others' (1967:38). In this sense, 'meaning harks back to the internal time-consciousness, to the durée in which it was constituted originally and in its most generic sense' (1967:40). For Schutz, then, subjective meaning comes into being as a momentary event in the unfolding stream of inner time of an Ego-consciousness. It is the constitution of phenomena in the individual's stream of consciousness in a specific lifeworld which distinguishes subjective meaning from the observer's account of meaning, itself an analogue abstracted ex post facto from situation. For Schutz, subjective meaning is available, if at all, through its momentary referral by an Ego-consciousness toward others in a vivid present situation. It is not the meaning attributed to the actor through interpretation by the observer. Weber's typologies represent observers' interpretations and typifications, while subjective meaning itself is always a situated meaning. Schutz therefore sought to provide an account of the general structures of the lifeworld in which subjective meaning and action occur. In order to do this, he grounded his analysis in the phenomenology of Edmund Husserl.

Husserl (1931:106) had suggested that in a general thesis of the natural standpoint,

> 'the' world is as fact-world always there; at the most it is at odd points 'other' than I supposed, this or that under such names as 'illusion,' 'hallucination,' and the like, must be struck out of it, so to speak; but the 'it' remains ever, in the sense of the general thesis, a world that has its being out there.

Husserl countered this possibility with one of 'phenomenological reduction' or 'bracketing': here the general thesis of the natural standpoint - of the world 'out there' - is suspended or held in abeyance. This act does not necessarily suspend consciousness of the world 'out there,' but it does suspend any judgment or interpretation concerning spatio-temporal existence. Neither the world 'out there' experienced as real 'free from all theory' nor theories, explanations or sciences have any validity in the phenomenological reduction (Husserl, 1931:111). What is left, according to Husserl (1931:113), is a 'phenomenological residuum' consisting of 'pure' consciousness of a Transcendental Ego.

Schutz made no claim to provide a strictly Husserlian phenomenological sociology. Instead, Schutz argued that the problem of intersubjectivity - that is, of sociality in the vivid present - cannot be solved on the transcendental plane of the phenomenological reduction. He therefore employed the reduction - suspending belief in the outer world - 'only in so far as this is necessary for acquiring a clear understanding of the internal time-consciousness' (1967:43). This internal time consciousness (the subjectively constituted stream of events in consciousness) represents a primordial transcendental feature of the individual acting in the everyday world which must be comprehended in order to understand the character of subjectively meaningful action, but the life-world, subjective meaning and others are themselves constituted in the mundane 'natural attitude' of the 'world-given-to-me-as-being-there' (1967:43). It is this mundane world for which Schutz (and Luckmann, 1973) sought to describe the a priori structure (but not its contents or 'facts').

Elsewhere (Hall, 1977), I have considered at greater length the objections of various critics to Schutz's mundane phenomenology. The details of this controversy need not concern us here. At the crux of the matter is the issue of whether people constitute meaning and intersubjectivity in a way which makes them available as essences through phenomenological bracketing (cf. Peritore, 1975). This problem may be resolved, if at all, only through a purely phenomenological investigation. Until the implications of such an investigation have been described, empirical research must proceed on the level of mundane phenomena, while remaining open to various constitutions of meaning and intersubjectivity among social actors who in one way or another themselves transcend the mundane world of the natural attitude. Under a mundane phenomenological approach, Schutz's description of the lifeworld derived from a partial phenomenological bracketing may be assessed in terms of its utility for specifying alternative constitutions of social worlds. The issue becomes one of whether the ideal-typical concepts of subjectively meaningful action (e.g. in Weber's work) have referents in situated occasions which are describable in terms of a mundane phenomenology.

The contribution of a mundane phenomenology lies in typification of social phenomena and their occasional boundaries, rather than in carrying out any philosophical phenomenological program of discovering the essence of objects of sociologically analytic consciousness (e.g. 'the' family). In an enterprise of mundane phenomenological sociology, it is possible, at least in theory, to specify alternative ways in which internal time consciousness and the objects of that intentional consciousness are constituted in various lifeworlds. Schutz opened the way to this enterprise by formulating the a priori limits of the lifeworld, but his efforts at typification had a markedly naive character, as Hindess (1972:19) is quick to point out. Still, there is no inherent reason why the lifeworldly constitution of, say, feudal or capitalist phenomena could not be made available to sociological investigation. Such an approach entails a shift from Schutz's purely epistemological critique of Max Weber's 'verstehende Soziologie' to an exploration of substantive relationships between the structure of the lifeworld and the character of subjectively meaningful social action. For these purposes, it is important to understand the epistemological status of Weber's substantive inquiries in relation to his theory of 'Verstehen.'

For Weber, the inference of meaning and identification of consequences of intentional action, though tentative, are all anyone has to go on in historical researches, and not such problematic matters as to have required a halt to his empirical endeavors. Weber's difficulties with an interpretive sociology of subjectively meaningful action thus stemmed as much from his sources of information as from any methodological inconsistency. For while Weber asserted the methodological importance of subjective meaning, he necessarily relied in his historical researches on secondary accounts which were already, in Schutz's terms, objective meanings torn from their situated and occasional constitutions. Much of Weber's 'Economy and Society' consists of typifications and distinctions drawn on the basis of segmented and partial descriptions of diverse phenomena (such as medieval monasticism) which form the horizons of lifeworlds. The use of these kinds of accounts is not devoid of implications in Weber's empirical work. Recently, for example, Bryan Turner (1974:19,56,70-1) has shown that Weber and other comparative social analysts confused categories derived from objective interpretation with subjective meaning for actors. Thus, Weber subsumed Christian sainthood and Islamic 'sainthood' (maraboutism) under a typification as charisma which obscured the fundamentally divergent character of non-institutionalized spirituality in the two cultures. In the end, Turner finds this confusion inconsequential for Weber's understanding of barriers to capitalist development in Islamic society. Nevertheless, it belies the complex and occasionally erratic relation of Weber's diverse empirical and comparative studies to his methodological program.

The difficulties inherent in the use of historical sources providing trans-lifeworld accounts do not ipso facto invalidate the distinctions which Weber made.

Rather, they simply imply that, as Weber well understood, 'Economy and Society' is what its subtitle suggests - 'an outline of interpretive sociology.' Weber's units of analysis necessarily were often whole complexes of events, rather than the subjective meanings constituted in non-anonymous vivid present social situations. The subjective meanings of any given phenomenon would therefore require far more detailed in situ analysis. Weber maintained, in the interests of historical researches, that he did not 'have to have been Caesar in order to understand Caesar' (1968:5). Yet his exploration of the lifeworldly meanings of the Protestant ethic in American sects (1946) suggests that he regarded subjective meaning - in Schutz's sense of its situated constitution - as the ultimate basis for his inferences of interpretation in the analysis of broader complexes of phenomena.

Weber sacrified methodological strictness in favor of analysis and typification based on historical and life-worldly researches. Schutz took quite an opposite tack. He sought to provide an ideal-typical formulation of the lifeworldly context of Ego-consciousness. The result is a comprehensive yet abstract mundane phenomenology of the Ego-consciousness, time, others, themes and relevances. Only in the most incidental way, for example in his essay on citizenship (1964), did Schutz try to apply this phenomenology to extant worlds of social life. Even these attempts represent only phenomenological models of social actors in the world (e.g. the technical expert, the man on the street). Schutz himself did not apply the phenomenological perspective to the explication of any given life-world, wherein he claimed subjective meaning is situated. Weber relaxed certain methodological requirements in order to offer a comparative sociology. Schutz, on the other hand, sought to maintain a high degree of philosophic and methodological consistency while failing to demonstrate the relevance of his perspective to understanding diverse social formations where meanings are constituted.

The present study of communal groups is an attempt, in its theoretical and methodological approach, to reconcile Weber's interpretive typifications of subjective meanings with Schutz's mundane phenomenology of the life-world. If it has any sociological utility, Schutz's phenomenology should be capable of discerning among quite different subjective constitutions of the social world. By the same token, if Weber's typifications of subjective meanings derived from an observer's viewpoint reflect subjective meanings for actors, they should be compatible with Schutz's phenomenological perspective. If this is the case, it should be possible to delineate, for example, a phenomenological sociology of charisma or of bureaucracy. Such a sociology would describe lifeworldly constitutions of these phenomena as kinds of internal time consciousness and ways of invoking various themes and relevances. A given phenomenon could be examined in the contexts of alternative situations (or horizons), and the playing out of the phenomenon in these contexts could be specified.*

In the problem at hand - the study of communal groups - we may seek for phenomenology to be relevant to differentiation of alternative realities, while Weber's interpretive sociology may be expected to have a grounding in lifeworldly subjective meanings. The relevance of Schutz's phenomenology and Weber's comparative sociology to the understanding of communal groups can in no way be

---

* The approach employed here bears comparison to ethnomethodology, e.g. in the works of Garfinkel (1967), Cicourel (1973), and Mehan and Wood (1975). In each case, 'objective' reality is taken to be a product of situated activities of people. This similarity is not simply fortuitous, since Harold Garfinkel (1967, passim) frequently draws on the works of Alfred Schutz; and Heap and Roth (1973) describe ethnomethodology as one of four types of 'phenomenological' sociology. Among their types (which seem more like aspects of an overall approach), Heap and Roth identify 1 the 'interpretive paradigm' (with Weber as one exemplar), 2 the phenomenologically founded sociology of Alfred Schutz (which 'elucidates the a priori structure of the world in which sociological phenomena are apprehended'), 3 reflexive sociology which recognizes that 'sociology is in and about the very life-world that it studies,' and 4 ethnomethodology, in which 'the foundational nexus of meaning in the social world is the immediately present, directly observable social situation' (1973:362-4). The present study is particularly concerned with exploring substantive relationships between Weber's interpretive categories and Schutz's a priori structures, but this program involves the 'type 3' recognition that there is 'no absolute observer.' Moreover, the arenas studied are just those 'directly observable social situation[s]' of interest to people who take on the label of 'ethnomethodologist.' In comparison to what is usually called ethnomethodological research, the present study is distinctive in its use of an explicit comparative framework for analysis of situated constructions of reality.

proven at the outset; the present study draws on these two approaches by way of argument and brings to bear evidence by way of illustration. I propose a phenomenologically derived typology for the comparison of alternative communal lifeworlds, and proceed to describe communal groups both in terms of their situated lifeworldly constitutions and in terms of Weber's interpretive categories. In the end, I propose six ideal types of communal groups set in the comparative phenomenological typology and described both in terms of the lifeworldly constitutions of subjective meaning and the observational categories of Weber's sociology. Though the categories used in the analysis may at times differ from those of actors themselves, the illustration of such categories as sociologically meaningful referents is based on events constituted in vivid present situations at various communal groups.

The present empirical study is not the place to analyze the complicated problem of intersubjective understanding in any detail; still, for methodological clarity, it should be noted that in Schutz's (incomplete) formulation (1967:97-138), intersubjectivity is possible when two or more Ego-consciousnesses share the same vivid present. Under such conditions, a 'participant-observer,' i.e. one who attends to a vivid present, does not start with an outcome of action and seek to reconstruct the genesis and meaning of that action a posteriori; instead the participant-observer is present as 'the other person's action unfolds step by step before his eyes.' A participant-observer thus stands a chance of 'keeping pace' with the objects of attention (1967:115). Still, there are limits, for if one person could know the other person's every thought, they would be the same person (1967:106). While the participant-observer has available a stream of events and intersubjectively constituted acts (but not necessarily the acts of a Husserlian phenomenological reduction) in a vivid present, some meanings are inaccessible. As Weber (1968:4) points out, some action is covert; some consists of ambiguous acquiescence. A sociology adequate at the level of subjective meaning is achieved, if at all, by use of examples derived from a sociology of arcane knowledge: the participant-observers (i.e. the Ego-consciousnesses in a given vivid present) 'show each other the world.' No one gets the whole story; there is always more that can be brought into relevance in relation to a given theme. A strategy of searching out further interpretive relevances (interviewing), however, breaks the previously established accent of reality and the ongoing streams of cognitions and acts. On the other hand, free attention to the moment at hand provides access to shifts among various themes, relevances and acts as they transpire in an uninterrupted situation. On the one hand, the interviewer constitutes a reality apart from the ongoing one as the information base. On the other hand, the participant-observer attends to events as they are constituted by others in an ongoing stream of life activities. While the participant-observer, like anyone else, does not have access to all of the multiple realities which are the horizons of an episode, participation in the vivid present intersubjective world permits exposure to events as they occur in the course of peoples' daily lives. The participant-observer may later summarize lifeworldly constitutions of events, establish boundaries of constitution of such phenomena with negative evidence and, on this basis, explore the utility of sociological concepts for explaining empirical realities. A correspondence between phenomena of the lifeworld and sociological categories of subjective meanings can be established by such a procedure. The phenomenological sociologist moves between 1 sociological categories (concepts) concerning the structure of the lifeworld, 2 ideal types (models) of the constitution and boundaries of various kinds of phenomena, and 3 summary descriptions of lifeworldly constitutions of meaning and action (cases), themselves based on vivid present participant-observation. These three possibilities, based on intersubjective meaning, provide counterpoint in a comparative sociology of lifeworlds to Weber's use in interpretive sociology of 1 formal concepts of action and meaning, 2 ideal types or 'socio-historical models' (e.g. of patrimonial domination) which elucidate configurational aspects of repetitive social forms, and 3 'secular theories' which describe and explain particular historical phenomena (Roth, 1971, 1975). The difference in the two approaches is predicated on the opposition between the phenomenological concern with characterizing the lifeworld and Weber's interest in historical explanation. Phenomenological sociology, in the sense proposed here, parallels the logic of Weber's interpretive sociology, but depends for its analysis on the lifeworldly constitutions of events rather than the interpretation of historical events. These differences of methodology are thus based on differences in sources of data, but the broadly shared epistemological presuppositions of the two approaches should permit cross-validation of analyses and concepts, since the two approaches ultimately share a theoretical perspective which focuses the sociological enterprise on the actions of human beings in worlds they constitute as meaningful.

Appendix 2

Descriptions of communal groups included in the study

The present study is particularly based on information gathered on twenty-eight communal groups. For one group - the Symbionese Liberation Army - I have relied solely on the available documents created by members (e.g. Symbionese Liberation Army, 1974; Tania, 1974; Yolanda, 1974) and secondary accounts. For each other case included in the study, I conducted field research at the communal site. The groups which comprise the non-random sample of the study are briefly described below. Unless otherwise noted, my relation to a given group was primarily that of a sociological researcher. Here and throughout the study, real names are used for well-known groups; quotation marks indicate the use of consistent pseudonyms of other groups, for which protection of isolation or anonymity was a consideration. In the alphabetical list of groups below, asterisks (*) mark the seven groups which are the principal cases of analysis in the study.

BROTHERHOOD OF THE SPIRIT, Northfield, Massachusetts: A community of over eighty people centered on the leadership of Michael Metelica, charismatic rock star and acclaimed man of God. The group supports itself through extensive gardening, rock group record sales, outside work and donations. Work is organized ad hoc by 'elders' who are part of Metelica's personal bureaucracy. The group has been a haven for dropouts, street people and those who have wished to escape their previous lives. I visited the group for two days in the summer of 1972.

*'THE CABIN,' Colorado: A small group started in the mountains in the summer of 1970 by three friends whose ideological analysis and spiritual visions led them to seek a radical alternative to their previous lives. A wide variety of people visited the group, coming away with

quite divergent accounts of what was happening there. The group has had strong mystical and charismatic features, and has never had a stable basis of financial support. Interpersonal conflict and career callings unrealizable in a mountain setting led to the group's demise in its broadly emerging original form, though a household directly descendant from it continues today. I have been involved with 'The Cabin' as a participant since its inception.

'COLORADO PLAINS FARM,' Colorado: A small farm owned by a young woman, who lives there with her child and up to six other residents, several of them students at a nearby university. Individuals make house payments to the woman and share in the work of raising animals and vegetables, meanwhile pursuing their own careers. I visited friends in the group at various times from 1971 to 1974.

'COOPERATIVE HOUSEHOLD,' Massachusetts: An urban household of eight people associated originally through friendship and the leadership of a young woman. Expenses and household work are shared by the group of students and jobholders. Departure of all the original members has left the group in a situation which the participants find ambiguous, fearing their group life is becoming that of a boardinghouse. I visited the group for a day in the summer of 1972.

'CORNELL HOUSE,' Western mountain state: A group of some eight to ten friends who came to know each other through circles of acquaintance that centered in the 'State Project' (q.v.). After getting to know each other through 'State Project' and other community activities, ten people located a house and began to live communally. Several members of the group wanted to leave 'Western mountain state' in search of arable land in a better climate. They convinced the majority of other 'Cornell House' participants to leave with them, but in subsequent travels they were unable to locate land which met with all participants' satisfaction. They decided to go their separate ways for a time, but still remain in contact with one another. I have known a number of the participants as friends since 1971.

'COUNTRY COLLAPSE FARM,' Eastern border state: Started in the summer of 1972 by a group of disaffected academicians who obtained a grant to study the communal movement. Other, younger people were recruited as members, and the group supported itself from the grant and by outside work of those not on the grant. Since the completion of the grant, the group has started a cottage industry which is still struggling for survival. Collective life has undergone several phases of factionalization and membership turnover; each time, the group has emerged with a somewhat different political balance between anarchism and collegiality. I have visited the group on several occasions, originally to discuss research on communes, later to visit friends.

*THE FARM, Summertown, Tennessee: Over eleven hundred people (in 1976) living communally on 1700 acres of land under the spiritual leadership of Stephen Gaskin, who says he is 'out to save the world.' The wisdom of all religious vision is entertained, but emphasis is on social relations and acts rather than doctrine or piety. A special language is used by participants to witness social relations and organize work. Participants in the 'small town' are attempting self-sufficiency through intensive and technologically sophisticated farming, but outside work is still a necessity. The group maintains a free communal food store, dry goods store, laundromat, telephone system, kitchen and school. I visited The Farm for six days in 1973.

'FREE UNION,' East central coastal state: An experiment in 'open land' set up by a nearby landowner who decided to provide forty acres to anyone who cared to live on it. Under a minimum of ground rules and land use constraints, the land has been occupied for typically short periods of time by innumerable groups and individuals from the street population and commune circuits. In the present study, the site is treated as a baseline for understanding non-familial household situations obtaining under a minimum of social organization and commitment. I visited 'Free Union' for four days in 1973.

'HANS' PLACE,' Colorado: A nuclear family and associated non-family participants headed by a self-styled charismatic patriarch. 'Hans' and his family have befriended a great many young people. The group is supported by 'Hans's' full-time job and from various short-term and on-going odd jobs organized out of the household. The group is controversial for its post-liberal politics (e.g. openness to longhaired freaks) and necessary to other members of the mountain community for the skills its members can provide. In the present study, I have gained a sensitivity to parallels between familial and communal association by knowing the people in this group. I have visited the household on numerous occasions since 1970.

'HILLBILLY HOLLOW RANCH,' East central coastal state: A group of people who surrounded a secular charismatic figure. The participants, including members of the leader's nuclear family, pooled financial resources and personal skills to engage in 'creative capitalism' or 'beating the capitalists at their own game.' Strong talk, insight and initiative supplant ideology in efforts to get the edge on the real estate market through speculation involving property acquisition, renovation, rentals and sales. I visited the group's ranch site for two days in 1973.

KARMU, Cambridge, Massachusetts: An old black shaman and medicinal healer cared for by his mistress and surrounded by his followers. Karmu holds forth nightly, using massage, ointments and mysterious liquids, as well as a clear mind and a sharp tongue in his 'treatment' intended to make 'good citizens' out of those who come to him. He supports himself by driving a taxicab as well as from the donations of those who believe in his healing powers. I visited Karmu on several occasions during the summer of 1972.

KRISHNA TEMPLE, Evanston, Illinois: A temple of the International Society for Krishna Consciousness (ISKCON). Devotees of the religion follow the teachings of Krishna, a Hindu god, as interpreted by the contemporary spiritual master and ISKCON director, A.C. Bhaktivedanta Swami Prabhupada. Participants in the group, following traditional priestly authority and strict 'regulative principles,' seek elimination of karma through chanting of the Krishna mantra and other glorification of God. As part of ISKCON, the temple is supported through sale of religious literature, distribution of incense and 'hip' cosmetic goods, street begging, and donations from patrons. I visited the temple for a day in 1973.

'LEAPING STAR RANCH,' Colorado: An abortive effort by a small group of college students and recent college graduates to create a place where they could escape the awesome and dismal demands of 'society.' Land was loaned to the group by 'Hans' (q.v.), but a hippie work ethic, lack of material skills, interpersonal conflict over values, lack of preparation for a hard winter, and migratory lifestyles led to the failure of the group. I knew the people involved in this venture as friends over several summers.

*THE LOVE FAMILY, Washington and Alaska: A group of over 125 people living in houses in Seattle and on farms in Washington, Hawaii and Alaska. The group is led by a charismatic patriarch who calls himself Love Israel. Love was a used-car salesman when he started having religious visions and began gathering his family together. What began as a crash pad became a primitive Christian group of true believers who see themselves as creating heaven on earth. The group supports itself by receiving all personal possessions of those who join, by engaging in barter and trade of goods and services and, more recently, by working in crews for money. I have visited the group's various sites on numerous occasions.

THE LYMAN FAMILY (FORT HILL COMMUNITY), Boston, Massachusetts and branches elsewhere: A group including over forty participants at the Boston site surrounding Mel Lyman, self-styled second coming of Christ. Lyman and his group try to force people to be 'real,' to give up all pretense. They hold great disdain for moralists, liberals, radicals and hippies, as well as the established order. The family has been a center of controversy for acts - including physical assault and bank robbery - allegedly perpetrated by its members on the outside world. 'Rolling Stone' (Felton, 1972) has published articles on the group which label it as 'acid fascism.' I visited the group on several occasions before I began the present research.

*NEW VRINDABAN, Moundsville, West Virginia: A part of ISKCON. This group is similar in character to other Krishna temples (q.v.), but the possession of farm land permits emphasis on the creation of an ideal Vedic community by emulation of the culture, technology and social forms thought to exist in the ancient form. Hence the group has a hand pump, woodburning stoves, a herd of dairy cows and a team of work horses. The temple and farm are run by the temple president and his staff, and financial support is obtained through incense distribution, street sale of books, and donations. I visited the farm and temple on two occasions, once for a day in the summer of 1972 and again for four days in the spring of 1973.

NORTH MOUNTAIN COMMUNITY, Lexington, Virginia: A behavioral community formed in 1972 as an outgrowth of a Twin Oaks (q.v.) conference on community. The group of ten adults and their children emulates Twin Oaks in ideology and organization. The group bears comparison with similarly sized groups less committed to a utopian organizational structure, as well as with the larger but similarly organized Twin Oaks. I visited the group for two days in 1973.

PRIMAL SCREAM RADICAL MINISTRY, Brookline, Massachusetts: A group of three young professional couples with training in psychotherapy and the ministry. Participants provide group therapy to outsiders for support. Some of the members are admirers of Karmu (q.v.). I visited the group for a day in 1972.

'RED SEA,' Washington: An urban egalitarian radical political collective. Participants shared the collective material and political work while they held outside jobs to meet expenses. The group dispersed as its members moved to other places and activities. I visited informally on several occasions.

'SALAMANDER RUN FARM,' Upper New England state: A rural anarchist 'family' group of several couples of dropouts from professional careers and some young people who put their combined resources into purchasing a piece of land. The participants are now slowly developing the land while minimizing outside consumption. Present support comes from book royalties, outside work by those who can get it, and maple sugaring. I visited the group for four days in the summer of 1972.

'SALT OF THE EARTH COOPERATIVE,' Washington: An urban commune begun in 1970 by a dropout economist and others interested in creating a radical economic and social alternative. A restaurant was operated by the group for two years, but during this time the communal household broke up because of interpersonal conflict. While the communal group was failing, several members began a wholesale food operation which presently serves local food cooperatives. Several of my friends had participated in the group during its early phases. I sometimes visited them at the communal household before it disintegrated.

'SLUG BOTTOM,' Washington: A small farm run by a man to whose patriarchical authority all others submitted. The group, now disbanded, obtained much of their food from gardening and animal husbandry. Financial support came from crafts and other activities of commerce and barter, as well as from welfare and donations. As a friend of the 'patriarch,' I visited the group frequently between 1972 and 1974.

'SPIRIT SOUNDS,' Colorado: A group of five folk musicians, their manager, and their women. The group plays 'mountain' music, presenting itself as a fixture of the regional mountain and hip community. People in the area support the group by providing gigs, patronage and short-term employment in non-musical work. For the most part, I have had only an outsider's view of the group as performing musicians.

'THE STATE PROJECT,' Western mountain state: A radical political group originally composed of people from the East Coast who had come to live in a college town in the state. The people worked to induce political change in the state. The group was associative rather than communal, and various participants organized community enterprises such as a food cooperative, a bookstore, a newspaper and a restaurant. Initially people supported themselves as best they could and lived as they wished, shying away from communal living. Instead, energies were directed at influencing the community-at-large through social service and political organizing work. Later a subset of the circle of friends and others formed a communal group, the 'Cornell House' (q.v.).

*THE SYMBIONESE LIBERATION ARMY, California: A guerrilla-style band of people whose members assassinated the superintendent of schools in Oakland in November of 1973. In February of 1974 the group kidnapped Patricia Hearst, daughter of newspaper executive Randolph Hearst. The Symbionese Liberation Army (1974) published a revolutionary program for armed overthrow of the 'forces of fascism and reaction.' They demanded a food program for the poor as a condition for Ms Hearst's return. On April 3, 1974, Ms Hearst announced in a taped message that she had joined the SLA and taken the name 'Tania.' On April 15 'Tania' participated in a bank holdup with other SLA members. On May 17 police finally located an SLA hideout and precipitated a shootout which left the six inhabitants of the house dead. After a sixteen-month intensive search for the survivors, the FBI finally captured 'Tania' and Bill and Emily Harris. Hearst subsequently denied that she had been a willing convert to the SLA, though this was disputed by the Harrises.

*TWIN OAKS, Louisa, Virginia: A forty-member community (in 1973) based in large part on B.F. Skinner's utopian novel 'Walden Two.' The group holds to an ideology of egalitarian relations and justice, as well as belief in progress and the use of effective management and technology to increase efficiency. Work is organized under a 'labor credit' system, while membership rights and responsibilities are the subject of an emerging set of policies. Twin Oaks is highly dependent on the external market economy for the sale of rope hammocks produced by members. I visited the intentional community for a week in 1973.

'UNCLE JOHN'S BAND,' Colorado: A shortlived group of rock musicians and their women who had emigrated from Louisiana to Colorado in hopes of 'making it' there as a regional group. The band fell apart after a summer owing to a lack of gigs and conflicts among virtuosi. I lived near the group during their stay in Colorado.

*'URON AND URONEARTH FARM,' Washington: A group started in the spring of 1971 as an outgrowth of political activities. Though it was originally based on a radical and anarchist ideology, after its inception, it included people who were not specifically concerned with political analysis and action. Presently, 'URON' is a leaderless, family-style household supported by equal monthly payments of participants, who obtain money in whatever way they can. The group also owns a twenty-acre farm which has been worked under various arrangements. 'URON' and 'Uronearth Farm' were my home between 1971 and 1975.

Appendix 3
Methods of research

I obtained the information for the present study in large part by participating in daily life at twenty-seven communal groups; for one group which I did not visit - the Symbionese Liberation Army - I relied on documents created by participants and secondary sources. Appendix 2 provides brief descriptions of the groups taken into account in the study, their specific relevances to the analysis, and the length and nature of my association with them. The principal analysis of the study is based on seven of the twenty-eight groups. The other groups are drawn upon to clarify unique and generalizable features of the principal seven cases, transitional possibilities, and effects of site, size of group, and other situational features.

I selected the sample of groups for the study on a non-random basis. I visited some groups simply because the opportunity presented itself. For the most part, however, a group was chosen either because I had not encountered similar ones or because it was widely known among communalists for being particularly successful. I specifically decided not to include several kinds of groups where - for one reason or another - I would have been too much of an outsider to gain an adequate understanding of the character of group life. Thus, I did not conduct research on any women's, homosexuals' or ethnic communal groups. In no way do I discount the wider movements such groups represent; nor do I suggest that such groups are inconsequential for their participants. But I could not do them justice in the present research; they are therefore not included in the analysis. Aside from these groups, the ones I have visited represent the diversity of groups with which I have become familiar by word of mouth, through inspection of various listings of communal groups, and by reading letters to magazines such as 'Communities' written by communalists interested in attracting new members. The sample of the study includes urban cooperatives, several subsistence farming groups, an anarchist experiment in 'open land,' a primitive Christian group, a priestly Hindu sect, a Buddhist-inspired 'congregational' community, groups formed around a shaman, a mystic and a patriarch, two 'behavioralist' intentional communities, several communes of political activists, a revolutionary action cell, and several groups of musicians. The groups range in size from three to over eight hundred people. The sample includes groups supported by participants' involvement in mainstream economic life, others based in large part on subsistence agriculture, and others supported by communal production for exchange. Similarly, practically no basis of authority or form of government is unrepresented. In short, though the sample of communal living groups is non-random, a diverse set of groups is included.

The research for the study was initiated in July of 1970; the most intensive gathering of information took place between June of 1971 and August of 1973. From then through July of 1976, I gathered information only on a happenstance or follow-up basis. During the initial phases of my life as a communalist, beginning in July of 1970, I had no intention of studying alternative kinds of communal groups. I became involved in two groups - 'The Cabin' and 'URON' - as a personally committed participant with my own concerns, relations to others and orientation to collective living. As I had done on previous occasions, I kept a journal as part of my daily life. Beginning in 1971, I became increasingly interested in understanding ways of life at different communal groups. My journal entries became more detailed, but they still dealt solely with my experiences in groups where I had a direct personal involvement. Because I have taken part in what has been loosely called 'the counterculture,' I sometimes became privy to information in situations where my presence did not stem from intentional research activities. I have decided that it is not intellectually honest to ignore information I came upon, however accidentally. On the other hand, I do not regard the ethics of sociological research to permit extended and intentional study of social action without knowledge of participants. Though certain accidental information is included in the present study, I have maintained the anonymity of persons involved, and in any event, I have avoided use of such information as a central basis of the analysis.

Beginning in 1972, I visited communal groups specifically for the purposes of research. During the summer, I wandered by truck from Boston, Massachusetts, to Seattle, Washington, visiting communal groups. From March through

August of 1973, I undertook a similar journey beginning and ending in Seattle. On both trips, I found myself on an established circuit: 'on the road' and at places I visited, I found people who could direct me to one or another communal group. I specifically tried to visit groups which were either notably successful or different from ones I had already visited. In general, I contacted a group before arriving to explain my research interest and ask permission to visit; on some occasions the logistics of travel without a fixed home made correspondence impossible; in such cases, I would simply appear at a group without forewarning, explain that I was conducting a sociological study of communes and ask permission to visit. Whether I wrote first or not, in all cases people were willing to have me visit with them. Because I had been living in a commune myself, they may have been more open to my presence; in many cases they were pleased to 'talk shop' with someone who had visited a variety of other communal groups. Though I did not usually describe my research concerns in great detail, I remained open to doing so if others so wanted it. At most groups, my status as a researcher did not receive any extensive attention. I was typically one of many people who came to experience communal life; if a status distinction was invoked, it turned on the difference between a visitor and a member. At only one group, The Farm in Tennessee, did people repeatedly inquire about my motives in writing a book on communal groups. I respect their concern, for they did not take my presence for granted; instead they felt free to relate to me on an equal basis of open communication. However willing people at other groups were to have me present, they may have felt intimidated without openly voicing their feelings. At The Farm, a number of people told me they felt my research was 'a conceptual trip.' People were, as they say, 'on my case.' I responded that I felt it was important for someone to write about new communal groups. One man told me he did not think I could understand very much about The Farm, but another person told him I deserved more credit than that. The recurrent theme was that I should be 'digging this not to write about it, but for your own head.' I dug it - I did not try to maintain an impervious status as a researcher; at The Farm and elsewhere, I went through 'changes' as a person.

The research techniques I employed for the study were largely those of participant-observation. At times, I conducted unstandardized, in-depth interviews at communal groups; on other occasions, I interviewed people who had departed from communal groups, some of which I had also visited. In addition, the study draws on documents produced by communal participants, as well as some secondary source material. At two groups, 'The Cabin' and 'URON,' I was a totally equal participant with the other people involved. At other groups, I was a visitor - a special kind of stranger who had no specific personal interest to pursue, who simply sought to participate in the momentary unfolding of collective life. I thus came to experience communal life in a number of different roles; even at any given place, I shared moments with various individuals who held quite divergent orientations to communal living. The events I witnessed and episodes in which I participated were variegated and unique.

Field research and subsequent analysis did not involve a search for latent or structural 'causes' of phenomena; I simply sought to provide an account, in each case, of phenomena constituted at the moment at hand. Whether I was a participating member or a visitor at a group, I engaged in what I will call a mundane phenomenological method of 'free attention.' Rather than establishing my own scheme of relevance by asking questions, I usually held in abeyance any concern with theory or working hypotheses. I simply attended to the events of the day and the concerns of other participants as they invoked them. I became involved in the routines and activities of daily life at each place I visited. In countercultural parlance, I 'hung out' with other people. We shared work, meals, meetings, play, sleeping quarters, sometimes worship and chanting, other activities of the day, and each other's company. I participated in group life in much the same ways as did other people.

I did not conduct 'field experiments'; I did not intentionally 'set up' situations to elucidate the character of social action. On one occasion, my symbolic action extended beyond the bounds which a communalist found acceptable: at a Krishna temple I became involved in a heated discussion about scriptural authority and a devotee forcibly asked me to leave. Other devotees, more secure in their belief, sought me out and apologized for the action; we subsequently discussed the same issues of authority at length.

In general, rather than seeking to learn from ambiguity by precipitating it, I paid special attention to the occurrence of ambiguity and its resolution by participants in situ. Though much social interaction at any communal group, as elsewhere, is relatively straightforward, certain interactions turned out to be crucial ones: conflict took place over a particular issue; authority was invoked on a special basis; an ethic was invoked to provide a course of action; a 'conspiracy' was formed; and so forth. The character of these 'crucial interactions' differed markedly from group to group, but the incidence of such events could easily be discerned by participants' attention to them. I took special note of such interactions and frequently asked participants questions about them on later occasions.

Much of daily life was 'taken for granted' by participants: there was nothing problematic at Twin Oaks about moving from one job to another on the basis of a schedule; rarely did Krishna devotees question the meaning of their devotional activities; seldom did people at The Farm come into conflict about performance of chores. 'Taken-for-granted' activities - those for which participants could give accounts without encountering disagreement from peers - were as enlightening as crucial interactions. In the course of taken-for-granted daily life, I did not openly evidence disbelief or invoke any judgment. On the other hand, I suspended belief in any preordained nature of the world. In this way I sought to learn the social construction of both the world-taken-for-granted and more problematic crucial interactions.

During the course of each day, I gave the fullest possible attention to the events that occurred. I kept a running set of rough notes which I used to aid my memory at other times when I wrote more detailed accounts. In the course of the research, I accumulated some nine hundred pages of field notes on communal groups. Aside from descriptions of location, site development, economic enterprises and other apparent features of groups, these notes dealt with episodes of social interaction in the course of daily life. The field notes as well as interviews and some secondary source material form the information base of the study.

After I completed the greater part of the field work, I selected seven groups for the principal analysis of the study. Seven groups represented 'early failures' (discussed in chapter 2) excluded from consideration as principal cases. Two other cases (The Lyman Family, Brotherhood of the Spirit) were excluded for lack of sufficient information. The majority of the remaining groups - just, I suspect, as is the case in the general population of contemporary communal groups - embodied a natural mode of social enactment: they lacked a unifying system of belief or shared transcendental engagement in the phenomenal world. Of these groups, I selected the one with which I was most familiar ('URON' and its farm, 'Uronearth Farm') as the principal case and drew on others by way of comparison. For the rest, several groups (the Krishna

Temple and New Vrindaban; North Mountain and Twin Oaks; Karmu and 'The Cabin') were paired; they represented similar ways of life. Among these I either selected the more established one (Twin Oaks) or the one with which I had greatest familiarity (New Vrindaban and 'The Cabin'), while remaining sensitive to the others throughout the analysis.

In order to have ready access to information, I catalogued field, interview and secondary source materials according to relevance to various subjects - beginnings, time, social enactment, want satisfaction and government. In analyzing any given aspect of communal life, I retrieved all information for a given case relevant to the question at hand. In general, analysis involved two steps. First, I sought to characterize the essence of a phenomenon in conceptual terms; for example, I brought to bear information relating to the diachronic constitution of time by participants in a specific group. I then purposely sought out negative evidence - information which indicated spatial, temporal or social boundaries of the phenomenon. Together these two vectors of analysis permitted a descriptive summary of the constitution of a phenomenon in a communal group. In subsequent analysis (see chapter 7), such summary descriptions were drawn upon for the formulation of ideal types of communal groups.

From a scientific sociological stance, it could be argued that the information I obtained through field work has inherent and multiply skewed biases. My information does not derive from standardized interactional situations; therefore, it might be argued, my perspective in one situation, for example, as a stranger, could not produce information commensurate with that derived from a completely different perspective (e.g. as an insider) at another group. By the same token, however, I was not limited to any single role; I could learn about communal life from many different points of view. I could develop an empathy for people in a situation I experienced as an outsider simply because I had 'walked the other side of the street' in participating in a similar situation as an insider. Anyone who seeks to understand social life as it transpires is faced with a dilemma: either the researcher employs a consistent method of interaction which is intentionally insensitive to nuances of specific situations beyond dimensions of measurement, or, on the other hand, such a person employs a flexible method which yields a situationally circumscribed subjectivity. In the former approach, commensurability of information is assured, but there is no guarantee that the information reflects the relevant aspects of the situation for either the participants or the sociological theorist. In the more flexible approach, information is inevitably embedded in unique intersubjective constitutions of meaning in a situation, but there is no assurance that the arcane knowledge obtained bears any comparison to other situations.

In the present study, I have sought to discern how participants in communal groups constituted meaningful shared social worlds; to temper the inherent subjective biases of this approach, I maximized the number of biased perspectives I experienced in a given group. I tried to understand how collective life was played out, given the multiple subjective perspectives of participants. The basis of comparison between different communal groups is therefore not derived from standardized measurement, but rather, from the elucidation of alternative ways in which social action was constituted as meaningful.

The problems of research based on participant observation are especially bound up in the issue of validity. 'How,' the researcher asks, 'do I know whether what I experienced is what actually happened? How can I be sure that the experience is real, instead of just a production for my benefit?' As a member of a communal group myself, I can know at the outset that communalists, like the proverbial South Sea islanders visited by an anthropologist, possess the ability to weave a reality around outsiders simply by selectively revealing aspects of their world. Visitors can as easily come to certain conclusions on the basis of their own selective attention, even when no attempt at deception is being made by others. I can remember several occasions when I and others living together shared our amusement at an outsider's view of who we were and how we lived together. Sometimes we could reconstruct the events which produced a certain impression. I was thus aware of the possibility that I was being 'put on' during my visits to other communal groups; I therefore put little stake in events which seemed to involve impression management on others' parts. If I was successfully duped, the reader will have to bear the consequences with me, for we will never know for sure.

In participant-observation research, validity of information depends in large part on rapport established between the visitor and participants. Because I have lived in a commune myself, I have had a consuming interest in issues of collective living which seem to recur in the most disparate situations. Though I was a total outsider at many groups I visited, I often felt an immediate empathy with situations I encountered. More than once people made statements to the effect that 'there's no point in trying to hide anything from you; you can see what's going on anyway.' We thus generally avoided the charade of pretense: people trusted me enough for my discretion and motives to be willing to 'open up' in my presence. Communalists, it seems to me, do not mind someone trying to learn about their ways of life so long as they believe the effort to be a sincere and sympathetic one. In general I think relations of rapport were sustained. Though I and others did not always 'see things the same way,' I rarely sensed any miscommunication. And in so far as I was able to follow the themes of concern invoked by others, the information I obtained bears a validity stemming not from its isomorphic correspondence with (representation of) something else, but quite simply as a record of what happened in any given episode.

The present study may suffer from ambiguities of validity bound up in a humanistic method of research, but I cannot identify any biases stemming from this approach. Still, the reader should be aware that I did not seek to construct a special research identity. In the end, I believe that the approach may have been more of an asset than a detriment to the study.

Bibliography

ABRAMS, PHILIP and McCULLOCH, ANDREW (1976) 'Communes, Sociology and Society.' Cambridge University Press.
ALLEGRO, JOHN (1970) 'The Sacred Mushroom and the Cross.' Garden City, NY: Doubleday.
BELL, DANIEL (1976) 'The Cultural Contradictions of Capitalism.' NY: Basic Books.
BENDIX, REINHARD (1970) 'Embattled Reason.' NY: Oxford University Press.
BENDIX, REINHARD (1974) Inequality and Social Structure: a Comparison of Marx and Weber. 'American Sociological Review' 39 (April):149-61.
BENEDICTUS, ST [c.525?] (1975) 'The Rule of Saint Benedict.' NY: Doubleday Image.
BENNETT, H. STITH (1972) Other People's Music. Doctoral dissertation. Evanston, Ill.: Northwestern University.
BERGER, BENNETT, HACKETT, BRUCE and MILLER, R. MERVYN (1973) Supporting the Communal Family. Pp.245-8 in Rosabeth Moss Kanter (ed.), 'Communes; Creating and Managing the Collective Life.' NY: Harper & Row.
BERGER, PETER (1967) 'The Sacred Canopy.' NY: Doubleday.
BERGER, PETER and LUCKMANN, THOMAS (1966) 'The Social Construction of Reality.' NY: Doubleday.
BERGSON, HENRI [1910] (1960) 'Time and Free Will.' NY: Harper Torchbooks.
BESTOR, ARTHUR E., JR [1950] (1970) 'Backwoods Utopias: the Sectarian Origins and the Owenite Phase of Communitarian Socialism in America, 1663-1829.' 2nd edn. Philadelphia: University of Pennsylvania Press.
BHAKTIVEDANTA, A.C. (1972) 'The Bhagavad Gita: As It Is. Translated with extensive purports.' NY: Collier.
BUSHUE, PAUL B. (1967) Dr. Herman F. Titus and Socialism in Washington State. Master's thesis. Seattle: University of Washington.

CABROL, F. (1962) Monasticism. Pp.781-97 in 'Encyclopedia of Religion and Ethics,' vol.8. NY: Scribner's.
CAHILL, TIM (1973) Infiltrating the Jesus Army. 'Rolling Stone' no.136 (June 7):1, 42-50; no.137 (June 21):50-60.
CASTANEDA, CARLOS (1972) 'Journey to Ixtlan.' NY: Simon & Schuster.
CHURCH OF ARMAGEDDON (1971) 'Charter.' Seattle: Church of Armageddon.
CICOUREL, AARON (1973) 'Cognitive Sociology.' NY: Free Press.
COHN, NORMAN [1957] (1970) 'The Pursuit of the Millenium.' NY: Oxford University Press.
CSIKSZENTMIHALYI, MIHALY and BENNETT, H. STITH (1971) An exploratory model of play. 'American Anthropologist' 73 (Feb.):45-58.
DEMERATH III, N.J. (1967) In a sow's ear: a reply to Goode. 'Journal for the Scientific Study of Religion' 6 (Spring):77-84.
DIAMOND, STEPHEN (1971) 'What the Trees Said.' NY: Delta.
DUBY, GEORGES [1962] (1968) 'Rural Economy and Country Life in the Medieval West.' Columbia, SC: University of South Carolina Press.
DUPONT-SOMMER, A. (1954) 'The Jewish Sect of Qumran and the Essenes; New Studies on the Dead Sea Scrolls.' London: Valentine & Mitchell.
EDGERTON, FRANKLIN (trans.) (1972) 'The Bhagavad Gita.' Cambridge, Mass.: Harvard University Press.
EISTER, ALAN W. (1967) Toward a Radical Critique of Church-Sect Typologizing. 'Journal for the Scientific Study of Religion' 6 (Spring):85-90.
ELIADE, MIRCEA (1959) 'Cosmos and History.' NY: Harper & Row.
ELLWOOD, ROBERT S., JR (1973) 'One way; the Jesus Movement and its Meaning.' Englewood Cliffs, NJ: Prentice-Hall.
ENGELS, FREDERICK [1850] (1964a) The Peasant War in Germany. Chapter II, pp.97-118 in Reinhold Niebuhr (ed.), 'Karl Marx and Frederick Engels on Religion.' NY: Schocken.
ENGELS, FREDERICK [1883] (1964b) The Book of Revelation. Pp.205-12 in Reinhold Niebuhr (ed.), 'Karl Marx and Frederick Engels on Religion.' NY: Schocken.
ENGELS, FREDERICK [1882] (1964c) Bruno Bauer and Early Christianity. Pp.194-204 in Reinhold Niebuhr (ed.), 'Karl Marx and Frederick Engels on Religion.' NY: Schocken.
FAIRFIELD, RICHARD (1972) 'Communes Europe.' San Francisco: Alternatives Foundation.

FANON, FRANZ [1961] (1968) 'The Wretched of the Earth.' NY: Grove Press.
FELTON, DAVID (1972) The Lyman Family's Holy Siege of America. Pp.146-324 in David Felton (ed.), 'Mindfuckers.' San Francisco: Straight Arrow.
FESTINGER, LEON, RIECKEN, HENRY W. and SCHAIFER, STANLEY [1956](1964) 'When Prophecy Fails.' NY: Harper & Row.
GARDNER, JOYCE (1970) Cold Mountain Farm: an Attempt at Community. Mimeo.
GARFINKEL, HAROLD (1967) 'Studies in Ethnomethodology.' Englewood Cliffs, NJ: Prentice-Hall.
(GASKIN), STEPHEN (1970) 'Monday Night Class.' Summertown, Tennessee: Book Publishing Co.
GASKIN, STEPHEN [1976] (n.d.) '...This Season's People.' Summertown, Tennessee: Book Publishing Co.
(GASKIN), STEPHEN and THE FARM (1974) 'Hey Beatnik! This is the Farm Book.' Summertown, Tennessee: Book Publishing Co.
GEHLEN, ARNOLD (1963) 'Studien zur Anthropologie und Soziologie.' Berlin: Luchterhand.
GINTIS, HERBERT (1972) Activism and Counterculture: the Dialectics of Consciousness in the Corporate State. 'Telos' 12 (Summer):42-62.
GLAZER, BARNEY and STRAUSS, ANSELM (1971) 'Status Passage.' Chicago: Aldine.
GOFFMAN, Erving (1969) 'Strategic Interaction.' Philadelphia: University of Pennsylvania Press.
GOODE, Erick (1967) Some Critical Observations on the Church-Sect Dimension. 'Journal for the Scientific Study of Religion' 6 (Spring):69-77.
GOODY, JACK (1966) Time: Social Organization. 'International Encyclopedia of the Social Sciences' 16:30-2.
GUSTAFSON, PAUL (1967) UO-US-PS-PO: a Restatement of Troeltsch's Church-Sect Typology. 'Journal for the Scientific Study of Religion' 6 (Spring):64-8.
HALL, JOHN R. (1977) Alfred Schutz, his Critics, and Applied Phenomenology. 'Cultural Hermeneutics' 4, no.3 (Summer): forthcoming.
HARRIS, BILL and HARRIS, EMILY (1976) Twenty Months with Patty/Tania. 'New Times' 6, no.5 (March 5):18-36.
HARRIS, BILL, HARRIS, EMILY, LITTLE, RUSSELL and REMIRO, JOSEPH (as told to Susan Lyne and Robert Scheer) (1976) The Story of the SLA. 'New Times' 6, no.8 (April 16): 26-36.
HARRISON, PAUL (1959) 'Authority and Power in the Free Church Tradition.' Princeton University Press.
HEAP, J.L. and ROTH, P.A. (1973) On Phenomenological Sociology. 'American Sociological Review' 38 (June): 354-67.

HEILBRONER, ROBERT L. (1974) 'An Inquiry into the Human Prospect.' NY: Norton.
HEILBRONER, ROBERT L. (1976) 'Business Civilization in Decline.' NY: Norton.
HERRIGEL, EUGEN (1953) 'Zen and the Art of Archery.' NY: Pantheon.
HEUSLER, ANDREAS (1886) 'Institutionen des deutschen Privatrechts.' Leipzig.
HINDESS, BARRY (1972) The 'Phenomenological' Sociology of Alfred Schutz. 'Economy and Society' 1 (Feb.):1-27.
HOLQUIST, MICHAEL (1968) How to play utopia. 'Yale French Studies' 41:106-23.
HORKHEIMER, MAX and ADORNO, THEODOR [1944] (1972) 'Dialectic of Enlightenment.' NY: Herder & Herder.
HOURIET, ROBERT (1971) 'Getting Back Together.' NY: Coward, McCann & Geoghegan.
HUSSERL, EDMUND [1913] (1931) Ideas: General Introduction to Pure Phenomenology. NY: Macmillan.
HUSSERL, EDMUND [1928] (1964) 'The Phenomenology of Internal Time Consciousness.' Bloomington: Indiana University Press.
ISKCON (International Society for Krishna Consciousness, Inc.) (1973) Easy Journey to Other Planets. Chicago: ISKCON, Inc.
JAMES, WILLIAM (1890) 'Principles of Psychology.' NY: Holt.
JENKINS, BRIAN (1975) 'International Terrorism; a New Mode of Conflict.' Los Angeles: Crescent Publications.
KANTER, ROSABETH MOSS (1972) 'Commitment and Community; Communes and Utopias in Sociological Perspective.' Cambridge, Mass.: Harvard University Press.
KAUTSKY, KARL [1897] (1966) 'Communism in Central Europe at the Time of the Reformation.' NY: August Kelly.
KINKADE, KATHLEEN (1973) 'A Walden Two Experiment.' NY: Morrow.
KNOX, RONALD A. (1956) 'Enthusiasm; a Chapter in the History of Religion.' Oxford University Press.
KOHN, HOWARD and WEIR, DAVID (1975) The Inside Story: Tania's World; an Insider's Account of Patty Hearst on the Run. Installments I and II. 'Rolling Stone' no.198 (October 23):1,40-6, 76-8; no.200 (November 20):1,32-40, 78-84.
KOHN, HOWARD and WEIR, DAVID (1976) The Last Year of the SLA. 'Rolling Stone' no.211 (April 22):32-7, 68-72.
KROPOTKIN, PETR (1914) 'Mutual Aid.' Boston: Extending Horizon.
LAO TZU (1961) 'Tao Teh Ching.' NY: St John's University Press.
LAQUER, WALTER (1962) 'Young Germany; a History of the

German Youth Movement.' London: Routledge & Kegan Paul.
LENIN, V.I. [1908] (1947) 'What is to be Done?' Moscow: Foreign Languages Publishing House.
LeWARNE, CHARLES P. (1975) 'Utopias on Puget Sound, 1885-1915.' Seattle: University of Washington Press.
LOFLAND, JOHN (1966) 'Doomsday Cult.' Englewood Cliffs, NJ: Prentice-Hall.
LOFLAND, JOHN and STARK, RODNEY (1965) Becoming a World-Saver: a Theory of Conversion to a Deviant Perspective. 'American Sociological Review' 30 (Dec.):862-75.
MANNHEIM, KARL (1934) 'Rational and Irrational Elements in Contemporary Society.' London: Oxford University Press.
MANNHEIM, KARL (1936) 'Ideology and Utopia.' NY: Harcourt, Brace & World.
MANNHEIM, KARL [1927] (1952) The Problem of Generations. Pp.276-322 in Karl Mannheim, 'Essays on the Sociology of Knowledge.' NY: Oxford University Press.
MARCUSE, HERBERT [1955] (1962) 'Eros and Civilization.' NY: Vintage.
MARCUSE, HERBERT (1969) 'An Essay on Liberation.' Boston: Beacon Press.
MARX, KARL [1844] (1964) Contribution to the Critique of Hegel's Philosophy of Right. Introduction, pp.41-58 in Reinhold Niebuhr (ed.), 'Karl Marx and Frederick Engels on Religion.' NY: Schocken.
MARX, KARL and ENGELS, FREDERICK [1848] (1959) The Manifesto of the Communist Party. Pp.6-41 in Lewis S. Feuer (ed.), 'Marx and Engels: Basic Writings on Politics and Philosophy.' Garden City, NY: Doubleday.
MARX, KARL and ENGELS, FREDERICK [1846] (1967) The German Ideology. Pp.403-73 in Loyd D. Easton and Kurt H. Guddat (eds), 'Writings of the Young Marx on Philosophy and Society.' Garden City, NY: Doubleday.
McKISSICK, DOROTHY L. and NIGG, JOANNE M. (1975) 'Social Change via the Mind: the Growth Movement as an Adaptation for Proletarianized Professionals.' Paper presented at the Pacific Sociological Association meetings, Victoria, British Columbia, April 18.
MEHAN, HUGH and WOOD, HOUSTON (1975) 'The Reality of Ethnomethodology.' NY: Wiley-Interscience.
MOORE, WILBERT (1963) 'Man, Time and Society.' NY: Wiley.
MULLER, MAX (ed.) (1897) The Rig-Veda. 'Sacred Books of the East,' vol.46. Oxford: Clarendon Press.
MUNGO, RAY (1970) 'Total Loss Farm.' NY: Bantam.
NEARING, HELEN and NEARING, SCOTT (1970) 'Living the Good Life.' NY: Schocken.
NEEDHAM, JOSEPH (1965) 'Time and Eastern Man.' London:

Royal Anthropological Institute of Great Britain and Ireland.
NEW VRINDABAN [1973] (n.d.) 'Now, a Chance to Become a Member of the Most Potent Spiritual Community in the West Today.' Moundsville, W. Va: New Vrindaban Community.
OGILVY, JAY and OGILVY, HEATHER (1972) Communes and the Reconstruction of Reality. Pp.83-99 in Sallie TeSelle (ed.), 'The Family, Communes and Utopian Societies.' NY: Harper Torchbooks.
PERITORE, N. PATRICK (1975) Some Problems in Alfred Schutz's Phenomenological Methodology. 'American Political Science Review' 69 (March):132-40.
PIKE, KENNETH (1967) 'Language in Relation to a Unified Theory of Human Behavior.' The Hague: Mouton.
PITTS, JESSE (1973) On Communes. 'Contemporary Sociology' 2 (July):351-9.
RABBIT, PETER (1971) 'Drop City.' NY: Olympia.
REICH, WILHELM [1942] (1970) 'The Mass Psychology of Fascism.' NY: Farrar, Strauss & Giroux.
REPS, PAUL (1957) 'Zen Flesh, Zen Bones.' Rutland, Vt: Tuttle.
RIGBY, ANDREW (1974) 'Alternative Realities: a Study of Communes and their Members.' London: Routledge & Kegan Paul.
RODALE, ROBERT (ed.) (1971) 'The Basic Book of Organic Gardening.' NY: Organic Gardening/Ballantine.
ROGERS, EVERETT M. (1971) 'Communication of Innovations.' NY: Free Press.
ROSZAK, THEODORE (1969) 'The Making of a Counterculture.' Garden City, NY: Doubleday.
ROTH, GUENTHER (1963) 'The Social Democrats in Imperial Germany.' Totowa, NJ: Bedminster Press.
ROTH, GUENTHER (1971) Sociological Typology and Historical Explanation. Pp.109-28 in Reinhard Bendix and Guenther Roth, 'Scholarship and Partisanship: Essays on Max Weber.' Berkeley: University of California Press.
ROTH, GUENTHER (1975) Socio-Historical Model and Developmental Theory: Charismatic Community, Charisma of Reason and the Counterculture. 'American Sociological Review' 40 (April):148-57.
SCHLUCHTER, WOLFGANG (1972) 'Aspekte Bürokratischer Herrschaft.' Munich: List.
SCHMALENBACH, HERMAN [1922] (1961) The sociological category of communion. Free and abridged translation, pp. 331-47 in Talcott Parsons et al. (eds), 'Theories of Society,' vol.I. NY: Free Press.
SCHUTZ, ALFRED (1964) 'Collected Papers II: Studies in Social Theory.' The Hague: Martinus Nijhoff.
SCHUTZ, ALFRED [1932] (1967) 'The Phenomenology of the

Social World.' Evanston, Ill.: Northwestern University Press.
SCHUTZ, ALFRED (1970) 'Reflections on the Problem of Relevance.' New Haven: Yale University Press.
SCHUTZ, ALFRED (1973) 'Collected Papers I: The Problem of Social Reality.' The Hague: Martinus Nijhoff.
SCHUTZ, ALFRED and LUCKMANN, THOMAS (1973) 'The Structures of the Lifeworld.' Evanston, Ill.: Northwestern University Press.
SELZNICK, PHILLIP (1960) 'The Organizational Weapon.' Chicago: Free Press.
SHILS, EDWARD A. (1966) The Concept and Function of Ideology. 'International Encyclopedia of the Social Sciences' 7:66-76.
SIMMEL, GEORG [1908, 1912] (1950) 'The Sociology of Georg Simmel.' NY: Free Press.
SIMMEL, GEORG [1900] (1963) Money and Freedom. Trans. of pp.371-2, Philosophie des Geldes. Berlin: Duncker & Humboldt. Pp.552-3 in Robert E. Park and Ernest W. Burgess, 'Introduction to the Science of Society,' 3rd edn. University of Chicago Press.
SKINNER, B(URRHUS) F. (1948) 'Walden Two.' NY: Macmillan.
SOREL, GEORGES [1921] (1961) 'Reflections on Violence.' NY: Collier.
SPECK, ROSS V. (1972) 'The New Families: Youth, Communes and the Politics of Drugs.' NY: Basic Books.
SUZUKI, DAISETZ T. (1965) 'The Training of the Zen Buddhist Monk.' NY: University Books.
SYMBIONESE LIBERATION ARMY (1974) Statement. Reprinted pp.A16-17, 'Seattle Post-Intelligencer,' Feb. 13.
TANIA (PATRICIA HEARST) (1974) Taped Statement. Received by radio station KPFK, Los Angeles. Reprinted, p.4, 'San Francisco Chronicle,' June 8.
THOMPSON, E.P. (1967) Time, Work-Discipline and Industrial Capitalism. 'Past and Present' 38:56-97.
TROELTSCH, ERNST (1932) 'The Social Teachings of the Christian Churches,' vols I and II. NY: Macmillan.
TURNER, BRYAN S. (1974) 'Weber and Islam.' London: Routledge & Kegan Paul.
WARD, COLIN (1966) Anarchism as a Theory of Organization. Pp.386-96 in Leonard I. Krimerman and Lewis Perry (eds), 'Patterns of Anarchy.' Garden City, NY: Doubleday.
WASSON, GORDON (1971) 'Soma, the Divine Mushroom of Immortality.' NY: Harcourt Brace Jovanovich.
WAX, MURRAY (1960) Ancient Judaism and the Protestant Ethic. 'American Journal of Sociology' 65 (April):449-55.
WEBER, MAX [1905] (1946) The Protestant Sects and the Spirit of Capitalism. Pp.302-22 in H.H. Gerth and

C. Wright Mills (eds), 'From Max Weber: Essays in Sociology.' NY: Oxford University Press.
WEBER, MAX [1905] (1958) 'The Protestant Ethic and the Spirit of Capitalism.' NY: Scribner's.
WEBER, MAX [1922] (1968) 'Economy and Society.' NY: Bedminster Press.
WHITROW, C.J. (1961) 'The Natural Philosophy of Time.' London: Nelson.
WOLFE, TOM (1968) 'The Electric Kool Aid Acid Test.' NY: Farrar, Strauss & Giroux.
YABLONSKY, LEWIS (1968) 'The Hippie Trip.' NY: Pegasus.
YOLANDA (EMILY HARRIS) (1974) Taped Statement. Received by radio station KPFK, Los Angeles. Reprinted, p.4, 'San Francisco Chronicle,' June 8.
ZABLOCKI, BENJAMIN (1971) 'The Joyful Community; an Account of the Bruderhof, a Communal Movement Now in Its Third Generation.' Baltimore: Penguin.

Index

Abrams, Philip, 3n, 8-9, 214
action, 47, 47n
Adorno, Theodor, 197-8
agriculture, communal, 29, 122, 124-5, 136, 141-2, 148, 153, 159
Allegro, John, 113n
Amana Colony, 224
anarchism: discussed, 5, 25, 214, 224; communal groups, 25, 87, 90; want satisfaction, 125-7, 130, 153
apocalyptic time, 52-3, 62, 66, 68-79, 81, 102-13, 127, 131-3, 167, 206-7; see also other-worldly sect; warring sect
asceticism, 5, 41, 153, 216
attention: communal groups, 44-9 passim, 83-6 passim; established order, 196-8; see also phenomenology
Aurora, 225
authority: legitimation, 30, 32-3, 164-8 passim, 179, 180-1, 187-92; theocratic, 79, 102-3, 151-2, 167-8, 179-81, 211; work, 146, 148, 151-3; patriarchal, 153, 165, 179; basis of domination, 164; pluralism, 164-5, 169-70; legal, 165, 173-4, 187-9; collegial, 166, 169, 171-2, 174-6; charismatic, 168, 181-3, 189-92; see also charisma; domination; legitimacy; politics

Bakunin, Michael, 25
Baxter, R., 42
Bear Tribe, 23
Bell, Daniel, 220
Bendix, Reinhard, 43, 142n
Benedict, St, 3n, 40
Benjamin, Walter, 43
Bennett, H. Stith, 124, 149
Berger, Bennett, 122
Berger, Peter, 1, 9, 20, 194, 198, 211
Bergson, Henri, 11, 43-5, 62
Bestor, Arthur, 4
Bethel, 225
'Bhagavad Gita,' 26, 32-3, 72-3, 103
Bhaktivedanta, A.C., 26, 27, 32-3, 72-5, 103, 178, 180-1, 239
Blavatsky, Madame Helen, 32
'brainwashing,' see consciousness, shift of
Brotherhood of the Spirit, 79n, 236
Buddhism, 27, 76, 113, 168,

182
bureaucracy, 55, 144-5, 197-8, 213
Bushue, Paul, 213

'Cabin, The,' 67-8, 114-17, 182-3, 236-7; see also ecstatic association
Cabrol, F., 209
Cahill, Tim, 104n
capitalism: social change, 5, 195-6, 215-16, 231; time, 41-2, 79-80; communal, 121-2, 129, 133, 158-9
Castaneda, Carlos, 76, 114, 116, 134, 181
charisma: social change, 1, 24, 164-5, 166, 193, 198, 209, 213; Love Family, 26, 167, 180-1; The Farm, 27, 32, 166; want satisfaction, 132-6 passim, 158; routinization, 158, 166, 175, 192, 192n; legitimation, 165, 168, 189-92; Symbionese Liberation Army, 177-8, 193; as domination, 182-3; Troeltsch on, 210; nineteenth-century communal groups, 225-6; see also authority, charismatic
Children of God, 104n
chiliasm, 12, 117
China, 41, 161
Christian church: primitive, 4-6, 113n, 224; of middle ages, 4-6, 40-1, 168, 231; Love Family and primitive, 77, 167, 180; see also Protestantism
Church of Armageddon, see Love Family
Cicourel, Aaron, 233n
Cinque, see DeFreeze, Donald
class, social: conflict, 5-6, 69-70, 195-6; communal groups, 129, 167
Cohn, Norman, 4-5, 7, 210
commitment, 225
Common Market of Denver, 141
communal group: social change, 1, 4, 8-9, 122, 217, 220; defined, 3, 3n; failure, 34-8, 91n, 224-6; past cases, 4, 224-6; formation, 19-22, 28-30; rural and urban, 122, 128, 146; phenomenology, 200-2; typology, 201-8; see also communal group myth; communal group, participants
communal group myth, 22-7, 28, 32-4, 59-60, 187-8, 200, 212
communal group, participants: joining, 21, 33, 187; novices, 63-4, 79, 114, 117, 179, 182; visitors, 100-1, 115, 129, 134, 183; virtuosi, 153, 172-3, 175, 178, 183, 186-7, 192; members, 163-4, 165; see also individual, communal
communal movement, 1, 3-4, 122, 217
commune (type of communal group), 15, 23-4, 58-61, 87-91, 194, 203-4, 214; want satisfaction, 128-9, 152-3, 158-9; politics, 164-5, 169-72, 184-7; see also natural enactment; synchronic time; 'URON'
communion, 62, 64-6, 109n, 124, 124n, 154-5
communism, 69, 125-6, 130, 132-4, 195

'Communities,' 244
community (type of communal group), 15, 194, 205, 212-13, 221-2; see also Farm, The; produced enactment; synchronic time; utopianism, worldly
conflict, communal, 7, 36-8, 88, 93-4, 169-72, 177, 184-7, 189
congregation, 157, 193, 211
consciousness: stream of, 44-9, 76, 210; shift of, 68-9, 104n, 177; social change, 199, 210, 213; collective, see intersubjectivity
consumption: capitalism, 121-4 passim, 197; communal groups, 134-5, 137-8; cooperative, 140-1
Cooperating Community of Seattle, 141
cost of living, 138, 158, 160
cottage industry, 122, 144
counterculture, 2-7 passim, 208-9
'Country Collapse Farm,' 185-6, 237-8
Csikszentmihalyi, Mihaly, 149
culture, 123, 197

DeFreeze, Donald, 71-2, 112, 177
Demerath III, N.J., 210
deviance: utopian, 1-2, 4-7, 20, 198; intra-communal, 29-30, 184
diachronic time: defined, 11, 53; established order, 17, 39-42, 79-80, 215-16, 221-2; communal groups, 54-8, 60, 80, 92-5, 130, 144-5, 166, 173-4, 187-9, 204-5; see also intentional association
Diamond, Stephen, 4
domination: communal groups, 164-5, 169-72, 175-6, 184-7, 193-4; established order, 196-9; see also authority
drugs, 23-4, 67, 103, 103n, 124, 124n, 134
Duby, Georgs, 40, 216
Dupont-Sommer, A., 40
Durkheim, Emile, 194, 198

ecology, human, 80, 125, 128, 130, 159, 180
economics, communal, 35-6, 140-2, 142n; see also wants, satisfaction of
ecstatic association (type of communal group), 16, 156, 168, 181-3, 194, 208, 209-11; see also 'Cabin, The'; synchronic time; transcendental enactment
Edgerton, Franklin, 26
Eister, Alan W., 210
Eliade, Mircea, 40
Ellwood Jr, Robert S., 4, 26
enactment, social, 12-13, 58, 83-119 passim, 266; see also natural enactment; produced enactment; transcendental enactment
Engels, Frederick, 1, 4, 5-6, 7, 41-2, 69, 195-6, 197, 216, 217
Essenes, 40
established order, 5, 7, 40-2, 51-2, 55, 112-13, 196-8, 218, 220
ethics: countercultural conduct, 1, 4, 17; worldly utopian, 98, 116, 176, 188-9, 213;

pluralist, 23, 34, 60, 171; work, 41-2, 153-6, 160-1, 216-17; time, 41-2, 60, 80; self-sufficiency, 122, 134-5, 153; politics, 166, 171, 176, 249; see also Protestantism
ethnomethodology, 197, 233n

Fairfield, Richard, 2
Fanon, Franz, 113
Farm, The, 27, 32, 61-6, 78, 95-101, 165, 166, 174-6, 187, 238, 246; want satisfaction, 131, 154-5, 160-1; see also community
Felton, David, 240
Festinger, Leon, 91n
feudalism, 40, 126
food, 29, 76, 137, 138, 141, 143
Foster, Marcus, 71, 110
Fourier, Charles, 27, 225
'Free Union,' 30-1, 147, 153
Fuller, Buckminster, 122

Gardner, Joyce, 37
Garfinkel, Harold, 224, 233n
Gaskin, Stephen, 27, 32, 61-3, 63n, 96, 99, 100, 124n, 155, 166, 174-5, 176, 178, 213, 238
Gehlen, Arnold, 42n
Germany, 4, 210
Gintis, Herbert, 199
Glazer, Barney, 21, 43
Goffman, Erving, 110-11
Goode, Erick, 210
Goody, Jack, 40
Gustafson, Paul, 210

Harris, Bill, 25, 32, 70-1, 149, 177, 192n, 242
Harris, Emily, 71, 71n, 110, 149, 177, 192n, 236, 242
Harrison, George, 133, 211
Heap, J.L., 197, 233n
Hearst, Patricia, 70-2, 71n, 110-12, 112n, 149, 177, 192n, 236, 242
Hearst, Randolph and Catherine, 110
Heilbroner, Robert L., 218, 220
heresy, 1-2, 5, 168, 209
Herrigel, Eugen, 113, 182
Heusler, Andreas, 1
hierocracy, 163, 178, 193, 196-8; see also religion; theocracy
Hindess, Barry, 226, 231
Hinduism, 113n; see also Krishna Society
history, 42-3, 42n, 69, 71
Holquist, Michael, 18
Home (Washington) anarchist community, 19, 214
Horkheimer, Max, 197
Houriet, Robert, 4, 23
household association, cooperative, 22, 142, 164
Husserl, Edmund, 11, 13n, 15, 43-5, 86, 201, 224n, 229

ideology, 51-2, 80, 87, 135, 141-2
income, 121; communal want satisfaction, 3, 123, 124, 128, 129, 143, 149, 159-60; patronage, 128, 133, 133n, 134, 158; production for exchange, 128, 139, 143, 159; see also wants, satisfaction of
individual, communal: time, 48-9, 55-7, 65-6, 75, 78, 81; Twin Oaks, 55-7, 92, 93-4, 130, 145, 187-8; The Farm, 65-6, 96, 175; other-worldly sects, 78,

78n, 108, 127; communes, 58-60, 81, 87, 169-72, 185, 214; enactment, 87, 92, 93-4, 96-7, 108; want satisfaction, 125-7, 130, 145; politics, 169-72, 175, 185, 187-8; see also communal group, participants; individualism
individualism, 18, 30, 37-8
innovation, 6, 122, 209-17
intentional association (type of communal group), 15, 194, 204-5, 213-14, 221-2; see also diachronic time; produced enactment; Twin Oaks; utopianism, worldly
International Society for Krishna Consciousness, see Krishna Society
intersubjectivity, 47-9, 62-6, 81, 95-6, 98-9, 175-6, 230, 234
ISKCON, Inc., see Krishna Society
Islam, 231
Israel, Love, 26, 27, 32, 78, 108, 151, 155-6, 167, 180-1, 211, 240
Israel, Serious, 180

James, William, 44
Jenkins, Brian, 109
Jesus, 26, 53, 77-8
Judaism, 40

Kanter, Rosabeth Moss, 24, 91n, 224-6
Kautsky, Karl, 1
karma, 72-4, 136, 239
Keil, Dr William, 225
Kesey, Ken, 21-2
kidnapping, 70-1, 104n, 110-11, 242
Kinkade, Kathleen, 4, 26, 33, 213
Knox, Ronald, 2
Kohn, Howard, 111, 149, 177, 192n
Krishna Society (ISKCON), 26, 32, 72-7, 102-3, 104-8, 167, 178-81, 211, 239, 247; chanting, 73, 75-7, 104-6; want satisfaction, 133, 137, 149-52, 155, 157; see also New Vrindaban; other-worldly sect
Kropotkin, Petr, 1, 139

Lao Tzu, 113, 116-17, 182
Laquer, Walter, 4
'Leaping Star Ranch,' 35-6, 239
Lee, Mother Ann, 225
legitimacy: communal crises, 183-92; established order, 198, 218; see also authority
Lenin, V.I., 25, 27, 69-70
LeWarne, Charles P., 214
lifeworld: epistemology, 9-10, 228-35; communal, 44, 84, 110, 116; see also phenomenology
Little, Russell, 110
Lofland, John, 91n, 215
Love Family, 26, 32, 77-9, 102, 103-5, 108, 240; want satisfaction, 132-3, 137, 139, 149-52, 155-7; politics, 167, 178, 179-81; see also other-worldly sect
Luckmann, Thomas, 1, 9, 20, 28, 38, 43-6, 50, 60, 65, 84-5, 101, 106, 202, 211
Lyman, Mel, 240

McCulloch, Andrew, 3n, 8-9, 214

McKissick, Dorothy, 219
Mannheim, Karl, 4, 6-7, 10-12, 13n, 18, 39, 52, 117, 146, 217, 219
Marcuse, Herbert, 43, 199
Marx, Karl, 41-2, 69, 193, 195-6, 197, 199, 216
Marxism, 25, 69-70, 195-6
meaning, 8, 66-7, 83-6, 113, 118-19, 194; apocalyptic sects, 102, 103, 105, 107-8, 109; epistemology, 227-35; see also phenomenology
Mehan, Hugh, 233n
Merion (branch of Twin Oaks), 145
metanoia, see consciousness, shift of
Metelica, Michael, 79n, 236
methodology, 8-10, 15, 244-5, 248-51; participant-observation, 15, 234-5, 245-8, 250-1; phenomenology and, 15, 231-5, 247; see also typology
monasticism, 5, 24, 40-1, 114, 131n, 168, 209
Moore, Wilbert, 54n
Mormons, 225
Muller, Max, 103n
Mungo, Ray, 4
Münzer, Thomas, 5, 210
mysticism, 4-5, 17, 67, 67n, 113, 113n, 209-10; see also religion; shamanism; transcendental enactment
myth, see communal group myth

natural enactment: defined, 12, 85; time, 58-61, 80-1; communal groups, 87-91, 126-7, 128-9, 158-9, 164, 169-72, 184-7, 203-4; see also commune
Nearing, Helen and Scott, 123
Needham, Joseph, 41
New Vrindaban, 73-5, 105, 133n; see also Krishna Society; other-worldly sect
Nigg, Joanne M., 219
norms, 88, 93-4, 102
now, here-and-, see synchronic time
Noyes, John Humphrey, 225

Ogilvy, Jay and Heather, 8, 24, 89
Oneida, 225
other-worldly sect (type of communal group), 68-9, 102, 131-2, 155-6, 178-9, 194, 207, 211; see also apocalyptic time; Krishna Society; Love Family; produced enactment; utopianism, other-worldly
Owen, Robert, 225

patriarchy, see authority, patriarchal
Patrick, Ted, 104n
Paul, St, 155
Peritore, N. Patrick, 230
phenomenology, 9-10, 13n, 15, 43-51, 83-6, 200-2, 224n, 233n; see also attention; lifeworld; meaning; relevance
Pike, Kenneth, 227
Pitts, Jesse, 3n
pluralism, communal, 24, 33-4, 58-61, 87-9, 126-7, 165, 169-72, 184-7, 249
politics, 163-4, 169-83, 209-10; see also authority
privacy, 21, 30, 87, 93,

96-7, 101
produced enactment, 16-17, 54-8, 61-6, 68-79, 85, 91-113, 164, 165-7, 172-81, 204-8; see also community; intentional association; other-worldly sect; warring sect
production, mode of: time, 18, 41-2, 130-1, 159-60; industrial, 121, 122, 137, 160-1, 215-17; see also wants, satisfaction of
property, 3, 78, 125, 126, 136, 139
prophecy, 20, 26-7, 77-8, 167, 178
proselytization, 103-5, 132-3, 149-51, 211
Protestantism, 5, 10, 18, 41, 51, 161, 215-16, 221, 232; see also Christian church

Rabbit, Peter, 4
Rainbow Family, 23
Rapp, George, 225
Rasputin, G.E., 209-10
rationality, 92, 131, 137, 145-6
rationalization, 42, 52, 54-6, 58, 79-80, 131, 160-1
rebirth, see consciousness, shift of
Reich, Wilheim, 146
relevance, 28-34, 85, 89-91, 94, 95, 106, 117; see also phenomenology
religion, 1, 5-6, 167, 193-4, 197-9, 219-20; transcendental, 13n, 113-14, 113n; other-worldly sectarian, 102, 105, 211; see also hierocracy; salvation; sects; theocracy
Remiro, Joseph, 112, 177-8
Reps, Paul, 113
revolution, 24-5, 42-3, 69-70, 81, 167, 195-6, 199, 212; see also Marxism
Rigby, Andrew, 2, 10
Rodale, Robert, 124-5
Rogers, Everett M., 215
Roszak, Theodore, 4
Roth, Guenther, 4, 193, 195, 203, 213, 235
Roth, P.A., 197, 233n
Russia, 43, 54n, 209-10

'Salt of the Earth Co-operative,' 36, 241
salvation, 20, 61-2, 72-8, 181, 211; see also religion
Schluchter, Wolfgang, 42n
Schmalenbach, Herman, 109
Schutz, Alfred, 11-14, 28, 38, 106, 224n, 226; and Weber, 9-10, 228-35, 233n; phenomenology of time, 39, 43-8, 50, 60; lifeworld, 65, 83-5, 89, 101, 202
sects, 6, 10, 68-9, 109n, 131n, 191, 210, 225; see also other-worldly sect; religion; warring sect
Selznick, Phillip, 69
sexual stratification, 62, 78, 93, 101, 149, 151-3, 155, 177, 178
Shakers, 225
shamanism, 113, 134; see also mysticism
Shils, Edward A., 109
Simmel, Georg, 22, 25-6, 130, 156
Skinner, B.F., 26, 33, 242
'Slug Bottom,' 24, 241
social change, 5, 7-8, 21,

166, 195-6, 199
socialism: nineteenth-century sects, 6; economic, 36, 126, 127, 130; party, 70, 195, 213
society-at-large, 2-3, 7-8, 34, 215-20
socio-historical model, see typology
sociology, 8-11 passim, 223-35
solidarity, communal, 24, 36-8, 131, 139-40, 141, 152, 159, 184
Sorel, Georges, 23, 27
Speck, Ross V., 23
Stalin, Joseph, 69
Stark, Rodney, 215
status, 142n, 167, 193-4
Stephen, see Gaskin, Stephen
Strauss, Anselm, 21, 43
Suzuki, D.T., 114, 168
Symbionese Liberation Army, 25, 32, 70-2, 78, 110-13, 112n, 236, 242, 244; want satisfaction, 132, 149, 166-7; politics, 176-8, 192n; see also warring sect
synchronic time, 11, 47-9, 53, 58; at Twin Oaks, 54, 58; in natural enactment, 24, 58-61, 87-91, 186, 203-4; in produced enactment, 61-6, 72, 77, 80-1, 95-101, 166, 174-6, 205, 221-2; in transcendental enactment, 66-8, 208; organization of work, 130-1, 145-9, 160; see also commune; community; ecstatic association

Tania, see Hearst, Patricia
Taoism, 113, 182
Taylor, Frederick W., 43
terrorism, 25, 32, 70-2, 108-13 passim
theocracy, 167, 178-81; see also hierocracy; religion
Theosophical Society, International, 32
Thompson, E.P., 42, 216
time: Protestantism, 10, 41-2, 216; types of, 11-12, 43-51; social change, 10-11, 17-18, 221-2; communal groups, 54-79, 83, 143, 200-1; epistemology, 229-30; see also apocalyptic time; diachronic time; synchronic time
transcendental enactment: defined, 13, 86; time, 66-8, 81; communal groups, 113-17, 127, 133-4, 156, 157-8, 168, 181-3, 208; see also ecstatic association; mysticism
Troeltsch, Ernst, 182, 210
Turner, Bryan S., 193, 196, 231
Twin Oaks, 26, 33, 54-8, 92-5, 240, 242-3; want satisfaction, 130, 144-6, 153-4, 159-60, 166; politics, 172, 173-4, 187-9; see also intentional association
typology: socio-historical model, 4-5, 7, 203; approach to research, 13-14, 16n, 228, 229, 235, 249; of communal groups, 201-8; see also methodology

understanding, 9-10, 227-35 passim
United States, 2, 4, 10, 218, 220
'URON,' 22, 33, 58-61,

87-90, 146-7, 153, 243; see also commune; pluralism
utopianism: communal groups, 1, 2, 10-11, 17-18, 80, 91, 198-9, 292-3; mentalities of, 10-11, 14n, 20, 52, 219-20; see also utopianism, other-worldly; utopianism, worldly
utopianism, other-worldly, 102, 108; see also other-worldly sect
utopianism, worldly: typology, 15-16, 204-6; social change, 17-18, 212-14, 221-2; communal groups, 54-8, 61-6, 80-1, 91-102, 129-31, 131n, 144-6, 148-9, 153-5, 159-61, 165-6, 173-6; see also community; intentional association

value-rationality, 2-3, 7-8, 17, 196
'verstehen,' see understanding

wants, 28-9, 36, 123-5, 131-3, 135; see also wants, satisfaction of
wants, satisfaction of, 35, 125, 127-8, 134-5, 138-40, 159, 179-80; efficiency of, 130, 131, 156-61; see also economics, communal; income; production, mode of; work, organization of
Ward, Colin, 224
warring sect (type of communal group), 16, 131-2, 149, 163, 176-8, 194, 206-7, 211-12; politics, 163, 176-8; see also apocalyptic time; produced enactment; Symbionese Liberation Army
Wasson, Gordon, 103n, 113n
Wax, Murray, 40
Weather Underground, 110
Weber, Max: value-rational action, 2-3, 196; religion, 5-6, 7, 24, 67n, 68, 122, 193, 211; and Schutz, 9-10, 202-3, 228, 230-4, 233n; mysticism, 17, 113; charisma, 24, 133-4, 158, 191, 217; action, 34, 47n; Protestant ethic, 41, 154, 215-16; want satisfaction, 121, 125, 127-8, 130, 131, 131n, 133-4, 139, 158; work legitimation, 152, 153n, 154, 155; domination, 163-4, 166, 172, 191, 193; social change, 166, 195, 215-16, 217
Weir, David, 111, 149, 177, 192n
Whitrow, C.J., 40
witnessing, 96-9, 175, 176, 182
Wolfe, Tom, 22
Wolfe, William, 177
Wood, Houston, 233n
work, organization of: medieval, 5, 40-1; time, 54-5, 130-1; communal groups, 54-5, 129, 142-52, 159-61; crew, 144-5, 148-9, 159-61; legitimation of, 152-6; see also wants, satisfaction of
worldly utopianism, see utopianism, worldly

Yablonsky, Lewis, 23

Yolanda, see Harris, Emily
youth, 2, 162, 218
Zablocki, Benjamin, 4
Zappa, Frank, 117n

Routledge Social Science Series

Routledge & Kegan Paul London, Henley and Boston

39 Store Street, London WC1E 7DD
Broadway House, Newtown Road, Henley-on-Thames, Oxon RG9 1EN
9 Park Street, Boston, Mass. 02108

Contents

International Library of Sociology 3
General Sociology 3
Foreign Classics of Sociology 4
Social Structure 4
Sociology and Politics 5
Criminology 5
Social Psychology 6
Sociology of the Family 6
Social Services 7
Sociology of Education 8
Sociology of Culture 8
Sociology of Religion 9
Sociology of Art and Literature 9
Sociology of Knowledge 9
Urban Sociology 10
Rural Sociology 10
Sociology of Industry and Distribution 10
Anthropology 11
Sociology and Philosophy 12
International Library of Anthropology 12
International Library of Social Policy 13
International Library of Welfare and Philosophy 13
Primary Socialization, Language and Education 14
Reports of the Institute of Community Studies 14
Reports of the Institute for Social Studies in Medical Care 15
Medicine, Illness and Society 15
Monographs in Social Theory 15
Routledge Social Science Journals 16
Social and Psychological Aspects of Medical Practice 16

Authors wishing to submit manuscripts for any series in this catalogue should send them to the Social Science Editor, Routledge & Kegan Paul Ltd, 39 Store Street, London WC1E 7DD

● *Books so marked are available in paperback*
All books are in Metric Demy 8vo format (216 × 138mm approx.)

International Library of Sociology

General Editor John Rex

GENERAL SOCIOLOGY

Barnsley, J. H. The Social Reality of Ethics. *464 pp.*
Belshaw, Cyril. The Conditions of Social Performance. *An Exploratory Theory. 144 pp.*
Brown, Robert. Explanation in Social Science. *208 pp.*
● Rules and Laws in Sociology. *192 pp.*
Bruford, W. H. Chekhov and His Russia. *A Sociological Study. 244 pp.*
Cain, Maureen E. Society and the Policeman's Role. *326 pp.*
●**Fletcher, Colin.** Beneath the Surface. *An Account of Three Styles of Sociological Research. 221 pp.*
Gibson, Quentin. The Logic of Social Enquiry. *240 pp.*
Glucksmann, M. Structuralist Analysis in Contemporary Social Thought. *212 pp.*
Gurvitch, Georges. Sociology of Law. *Preface by Roscoe Pound. 264 pp.*
Hodge, H. A. Wilhelm Dilthey. *An Introduction. 184 pp.*
Homans, George C. Sentiments and Activities. *336 pp.*
Johnson, Harry M. Sociology: *a Systematic Introduction. Foreword by Robert K. Merton. 710 pp.*
●**Keat, Russell,** and **Urry, John.** Social Theory as Science. *278 pp.*
Mannheim, Karl. Essays on Sociology and Social Psychology. *Edited by Paul Keckskemeti. With Editorial Note by Adolph Lowe. 344 pp.*
Systematic Sociology: *An Introduction to the Study of Society. Edited by J. S. Erös and Professor W. A. C. Stewart. 220 pp.*
Martindale, Don. The Nature and Types of Sociological Theory. *292 pp.*
●**Maus, Heinz.** A Short History of Sociology. *234 pp.*
Mey, Harald. Field-Theory. *A Study of its Application in the Social Sciences. 352 pp.*
Myrdal, Gunnar. Value in Social Theory: *A Collection of Essays on Methodology. Edited by Paul Streeten. 332 pp.*
Ogburn, William F., and **Nimkoff, Meyer F.** A Handbook of Sociology. *Preface by Karl Mannheim. 656 pp. 46 figures. 35 tables.*
Parsons, Talcott, and **Smelser, Neil J.** Economy and Society: *A Study in the Integration of Economic and Social Theory. 362 pp.*
Podgórecki, Adam. Practical Social Sciences. *About 200 pp.*
●**Rex, John.** Key Problems of Sociological Theory. *220 pp.*
Sociology and the Demystification of the Modern World. *282 pp.*
●**Rex, John** (Ed.) Approaches to Sociology. *Contributions by Peter Abell, Frank Bechhofer, Basil Bernstein, Ronald Fletcher, David Frisby, Miriam Glucksmann, Peter Lassman, Herminio Martins, John Rex, Roland Robertson, John Westergaard and Jock Young. 302 pp.*
Rigby, A. Alternative Realities. *352 pp.*
Roche, M. Phenomenology, Language and the Social Sciences. *374 pp.*

Sahay, A. Sociological Analysis. *220 pp.*

Simirenko, Alex (Ed.) Soviet Sociology. *Historical Antecedents and Current Appraisals. Introduction by Alex Simirenko. 376 pp.*

Strasser, Hermann. The Normative Structure of Sociology. *Conservative and Emancipatory Themes in Social Thought. About 340 pp.*

Urry, John. Reference Groups and the Theory of Revolution. *244 pp.*

Weinberg, E. Development of Sociology in the Soviet Union. *173 pp.*

FOREIGN CLASSICS OF SOCIOLOGY

●**Durkheim, Emile.** Suicide. *A Study in Sociology. Edited and with an Introduction by George Simpson. 404 pp.*

●**Gerth, H. H.,** and **Mills, C. Wright.** From Max Weber: *Essays in Sociology. 502 pp.*

●**Tönnies, Ferdinand.** Community and Association. (*Gemeinschaft und Gesellschaft.*) *Translated and Supplemented by Charles P. Loomis. Foreword by Pitirim A. Sorokin. 334 pp.*

SOCIAL STRUCTURE

Andreski, Stanislav. Military Organization and Society. *Foreword by Professor A. R. Radcliffe-Brown. 226 pp. 1 folder.*

Carlton, Eric. Ideology and Social Order. *Preface by Professor Philip Abrahams. About 320 pp.*

Coontz, Sydney H. Population Theories and the Economic Interpretation. *202 pp.*

Coser, Lewis. The Functions of Social Conflict. *204 pp.*

Dickie-Clark, H. F. Marginal Situation: *A Sociological Study of a Coloured Group. 240 pp. 11 tables.*

Glaser, Barney, and **Strauss, Anselm L.** Status Passage. *A Formal Theory. 208 pp.*

Glass, D. V. (Ed.) Social Mobility in Britain. *Contributions by J. Berent, T. Bottomore, R. C. Chambers, J. Floud, D. V. Glass, J. R. Hall, H. T. Himmelweit, R. K. Kelsall, F. M. Martin, C. A. Moser, R. Mukherjee, and W. Ziegel. 420 pp.*

Johnstone, Frederick A. Class, Race and Gold. *A Study of Class Relations and Racial Discrimination in South Africa. 312 pp.*

Jones, Garth N. Planned Organizational Change: *An Exploratory Study Using an Empirical Approach. 268 pp.*

Kelsall, R. K. Higher Civil Servants in Britain: *From 1870 to the Present Day. 268 pp. 31 tables.*

König, René. The Community. *232 pp. Illustrated.*

●**Lawton, Denis.** Social Class, Language and Education. *192 pp.*

McLeish, John. The Theory of Social Change: *Four Views Considered. 128 pp.*

Marsh, David C. The Changing Social Structure of England and Wales, 1871-1961. *288 pp.*

Menzies, Ken. Talcott Parsons and the Social Image of Man. *About 208 pp.*

● **Mouzelis, Nicos.** Organization and Bureaucracy. *An Analysis of Modern Theories. 240 pp.*

Mulkay, M. J. Functionalism, Exchange and Theoretical Strategy. *272 pp.*

Ossowski, Stanislaw. Class Structure in the Social Consciousness. *210 pp.*

● **Podgórecki, Adam.** Law and Society. *302 pp.*

Renner, Karl. Institutions of Private Law and Their Social Functions. *Edited, with an Introduction and Notes, by O. Kahn-Freud. Translated by Agnes Schwarzschild. 316 pp.*

SOCIOLOGY AND POLITICS

Acton, T. A. Gypsy Politics and Social Change. *316 pp.*

Clegg, Stuart. Power, Rule and Domination. *A Critical and Empirical Understanding of Power in Sociological Theory and Organisational Life. About 300 pp.*

Hechter, Michael. Internal Colonialism. *The Celtic Fringe in British National Development, 1536–1966. 361 pp.*

Hertz, Frederick. Nationality in History and Politics: *A Psychology and Sociology of National Sentiment and Nationalism. 432 pp.*

Kornhauser, William. The Politics of Mass Society. *272 pp. 20 tables.*

● **Kroes, R.** Soldiers and Students. *A Study of Right- and Left-wing Students. 174 pp.*

Laidler, Harry W. History of Socialism. *Social-Economic Movements: An Historical and Comparative Survey of Socialism, Communism, Co-operation, Utopianism; and other Systems of Reform and Reconstruction. 992 pp.*

Lasswell, H. D. Analysis of Political Behaviour. *324 pp.*

Martin, David A. Pacifism: *an Historical and Sociological Study. 262 pp.*

Martin, Roderick. Sociology of Power. *About 272 pp.*

Myrdal, Gunnar. The Political Element in the Development of Economic Theory. *Translated from the German by Paul Streeten. 282 pp.*

Wilson, H. T. The American Ideology. *Science, Technology and Organization of Modes of Rationality. About 280 pp.*

Wootton, Graham. Workers, Unions and the State. *188 pp.*

CRIMINOLOGY

Ancel, Marc. Social Defence: *A Modern Approach to Criminal Problems. Foreword by Leon Radzinowicz. 240 pp.*

Cain, Maureen E. Society and the Policeman's Role. *326 pp.*

Cloward, Richard A., and **Ohlin, Lloyd E.** Delinquency and Opportunity: *A Theory of Delinquent Gangs. 248 pp.*

Downes, David M. The Delinquent Solution. *A Study in Subcultural Theory. 296 pp.*

Dunlop, A. B., and **McCabe, S.** Young Men in Detention Centres. *192 pp.*

Friedlander, Kate. The Psycho-Analytical Approach to Juvenile Delinquency: *Theory, Case Studies, Treatment. 320 pp.*

Glueck, Sheldon, and **Eleanor.** Family Environment and Delinquency. *With the statistical assistance of Rose W. Kneznek. 340 pp.*

Lopez-Rey, Manuel. Crime. *An Analytical Appraisal. 288 pp.*

Mannheim, Hermann. Comparative Criminology: *a Text Book. Two volumes. 442 pp. and 380 pp.*

Morris, Terence. The Criminal Area: *A Study in Social Ecology. Foreword by Hermann Mannheim. 232 pp. 25 tables. 4 maps.*

Rock, Paul. Making People Pay. *338 pp.*

●**Taylor, Ian, Walton, Paul,** and **Young, Jock.** The New Criminology. *For a Social Theory of Deviance. 325 pp.*

●**Taylor, Ian, Walton, Paul,** and **Young, Jock** (Eds). Critical Criminology. *268 pp.*

SOCIAL PSYCHOLOGY

Bagley, Christopher. The Social Psychology of the Epileptic Child. *320 pp.*

Barbu, Zevedei. Problems of Historical Psychology. *248 pp.*

Blackburn, Julian. Psychology and the Social Pattern. *184 pp.*

●**Brittan, Arthur.** Meanings and Situations. *224 pp.*

Carroll, J. Break-Out from the Crystal Palace. *200 pp.*

●**Fleming, C. M.** Adolescence: Its Social Psychology. *With an Introduction to recent findings from the fields of Anthropology, Physiology, Medicine, Psychometrics and Sociometry. 288 pp.*

● The Social Psychology of Education: *An Introduction and Guide to Its Study. 136 pp.*

●**Homans, George C.** The Human Group. *Foreword by Bernard DeVoto. Introduction by Robert K. Merton. 526 pp.*

● Social Behaviour: *its Elementary Forms. 416 pp.*

●**Klein, Josephine.** The Study of Groups. *226 pp. 31 figures. 5 tables.*

Linton, Ralph. The Cultural Background of Personality. *132 pp.*

●**Mayo, Elton.** The Social Problems of an Industrial Civilization. *With an appendix on the Political Problem. 180 pp.*

Ottaway, A. K. C. Learning Through Group Experience. *176 pp.*

Plummer, Ken. Sexual Stigma. *An Interactionist Account. 254 pp.*

●**Rose, Arnold M.** (Ed.) Human Behaviour and Social Processes: *an Interactionist Approach. Contributions by Arnold M. Rose, Ralph H. Turner, Anselm Strauss, Everett C. Hughes, E. Franklin Frazier, Howard S. Becker, et al. 696 pp.*

Smelser, Neil J. Theory of Collective Behaviour. *448 pp.*

Stephenson, Geoffrey M. The Development of Conscience. *128 pp.*

Young, Kimball. Handbook of Social Psychology. *658 pp. 16 figures. 10 tables.*

SOCIOLOGY OF THE FAMILY

Banks, J. A. Prosperity and Parenthood: *A Study of Family Planning among The Victorian Middle Classes. 262 pp.*

Bell, Colin R. Middle Class Families: *Social and Geographical Mobility. 224 pp.*

Burton, Lindy. Vulnerable Children. *272 pp.*

Gavron, Hannah. The Captive Wife: *Conflicts of Household Mothers. 190 pp.*

George, Victor, and **Wilding, Paul.** Motherless Families. *248 pp.*

Klein, Josephine. Samples from English Cultures.

1. Three Preliminary Studies and Aspects of Adult Life in England. *447 pp.*
2. Child-Rearing Practices and Index. *247 pp.*

Klein, Viola. The Feminine Character. *History of an Ideology. 244 pp.*

McWhinnie, Alexina M. Adopted Children. *How They Grow Up. 304 pp.*

● **Morgan, D. H. J.** Social Theory and the Family. *About 320 pp.*

● **Myrdal, Alva,** and **Klein, Viola.** Women's Two Roles: *Home and Work. 238 pp. 27 tables.*

Parsons, Talcott, and **Bales, Robert F.** Family: Socialization and Interaction Process. *In collaboration with James Olds, Morris Zelditch and Philip E. Slater. 456 pp. 50 figures and tables.*

SOCIAL SERVICES

Bastide, Roger. The Sociology of Mental Disorder. *Translated from the French by Jean McNeil. 260 pp.*

Carlebach, Julius. Caring For Children in Trouble. *266 pp.*

George, Victor. Foster Care. *Theory and Practice. 234 pp.*

Social Security: *Beveridge and After. 258 pp.*

George, V., and **Wilding, P.** Motherless Families. *248 pp.*

● **Goetschius, George W.** Working with Community Groups. *256 pp.*

Goetschius, George W., and **Tash, Joan.** Working with Unattached Youth. *416 pp.*

Hall, M. P., and **Howes, I. V.** The Church in Social Work. *A Study of Moral Welfare Work undertaken by the Church of England. 320 pp.*

Heywood, Jean S. Children in Care: *the Development of the Service for the Deprived Child. 264 pp.*

Hoenig, J., and **Hamilton, Marian W.** The De-Segregation of the Mentally Ill. *284 pp.*

Jones, Kathleen. Mental Health and Social Policy, 1845-1959. *264 pp.*

King, Roy D., Raynes, Norma V., and **Tizard, Jack.** Patterns of Residential Care. *356 pp.*

Leigh, John. Young People and Leisure. *256 pp.*

● **Mays, John.** (Ed.) Penelope Hall's Social Services of England and Wales. *About 324 pp.*

Morris, Mary. Voluntary Work and the Welfare State. *300 pp.*

Nokes, P. L. The Professional Task in Welfare Practice. *152 pp.*

Timms, Noel. Psychiatric Social Work in Great Britain (1939-1962). *280 pp.*

● Social Casework: *Principles and Practice. 256 pp.*

Young, A. F. Social Services in British Industry. *272 pp.*

SOCIOLOGY OF EDUCATION

Banks, Olive. Parity and Prestige in English Secondary Education: a Study in Educational Sociology. *272 pp.*

Bentwich, Joseph. Education in Israel. *224 pp. 8 pp. plates.*

●**Blyth, W. A. L.** English Primary Education. *A Sociological Description.*
1. Schools. *232 pp.*
2. Background. *168 pp.*

Collier, K. G. The Social Purposes of Education: *Personal and Social Values in Education. 268 pp.*

Dale, R. R., and **Griffith, S.** Down Stream: *Failure in the Grammar School. 108 pp.*

Evans, K. M. Sociometry and Education. *158 pp.*

●**Ford, Julienne.** Social Class and the Comprehensive School. *192 pp.*

Foster, P. J. Education and Social Change in Ghana. *336 pp. 3 maps.*

Fraser, W. R. Education and Society in Modern France. *150 pp.*

Grace, Gerald R. Role Conflict and the Teacher. *150 pp.*

Hans, Nicholas. New Trends in Education in the Eighteenth Century. *278 pp. 19 tables.*

● Comparative Education: *A Study of Educational Factors and Traditions. 360 pp.*

●**Hargreaves, David.** Interpersonal Relations and Education. *432 pp.*

● Social Relations in a Secondary School. *240 pp.*

Holmes, Brian. Problems in Education. *A Comparative Approach. 336 pp.*

King, Ronald. Values and Involvement in a Grammar School. *164 pp.*

School Organization and Pupil Involvement. *A Study of Secondary Schools.*

●**Mannheim, Karl,** and **Stewart, W. A. C.** An Introduction to the Sociology of Education. *206 pp.*

Morris, Raymond N. The Sixth Form and College Entrance. *231 pp.*

●**Musgrove, F.** Youth and the Social Order. *176 pp.*

●**Ottaway, A. K. C.** Education and Society: An Introduction to the Sociology of Education. *With an Introduction by W. O. Lester Smith. 212 pp.*

Peers, Robert. Adult Education: *A Comparative Study. 398 pp.*

Pritchard, D. G. Education and the Handicapped: *1760 to 1960. 258 pp.*

Stratta, Erica. The Education of Borstal Boys. *A Study of their Educational Experiences prior to, and during, Borstal Training. 256 pp.*

Taylor, P. H., Reid, W. A., and **Holley, B. J.** The English Sixth Form. *A Case Study in Curriculum Research. 200 pp.*

SOCIOLOGY OF CULTURE

Eppel, E. M., and **M.** Adolescents and Morality: *A Study of some Moral Values and Dilemmas of Working Adolescents in the Context of a changing Climate of Opinion. Foreword by W. J. H. Sprott. 268 pp. 39 tables.*

●**Fromm, Erich.** The Fear of Freedom. *286 pp.*

● The Sane Society. *400 pp.*

Mannheim, Karl. Essays on the Sociology of Culture. *Edited by Ernst Mannheim in co-operation with Paul Kecskemeti. Editorial Note by Adolph Lowe. 280 pp.*

Weber, Alfred. Farewell to European History: *or The Conquest of Nihilism. Translated from the German by R. F. C. Hull. 224 pp.*

SOCIOLOGY OF RELIGION

Argyle, Michael and **Beit-Hallahmi, Benjamin.** The Social Psychology of Religion. *About 256 pp.*

Glasner, Peter E. The Sociology of Secularisation. *A Critique of a Concept. About 180 pp.*

Nelson, G. K. Spiritualism and Society. *313 pp.*

Stark, Werner. The Sociology of Religion. *A Study of Christendom.*

Volume I. *Established Religion. 248 pp.*

Volume II. *Sectarian Religion. 368 pp.*

Volume III. *The Universal Church. 464 pp.*

Volume IV. *Types of Religious Man. 352 pp.*

Volume V. *Types of Religious Culture. 464 pp.*

Turner, B. S. Weber and Islam. *216 pp.*

Watt, W. Montgomery. Islam and the Integration of Society. *320 pp.*

SOCIOLOGY OF ART AND LITERATURE

Jarvie, Ian C. Towards a Sociology of the Cinema. *A Comparative Essay on the Structure and Functioning of a Major Entertainment Industry. 405 pp.*

Rust, Frances S. Dance in Society. *An Analysis of the Relationships between the Social Dance and Society in England from the Middle Ages to the Present Day. 256 pp. 8 pp. of plates.*

Schücking, L. L. The Sociology of Literary Taste. *112 pp.*

Wolff, Janet. Hermeneutic Philosophy and the Sociology of Art. *150 pp.*

SOCIOLOGY OF KNOWLEDGE

Diesing, P. Patterns of Discovery in the Social Sciences. *262 pp.*

● **Douglas, J. D.** (Ed.) Understanding Everyday Life. *370 pp.*

● **Hamilton, P.** Knowledge and Social Structure. *174 pp.*

Jarvie, I. C. Concepts and Society. *232 pp.*

Mannheim, Karl. Essays on the Sociology of Knowledge. *Edited by Paul Kecskemeti. Editorial Note by Adolph Lowe. 353 pp.*

Remmling, Gunter W. The Sociology of Karl Mannheim. *With a Bibliographical Guide to the Sociology of Knowledge, Ideological Analysis, and Social Planning. 255 pp.*

Remmling, Gunter W. (Ed.) Towards the Sociology of Knowledge. *Origin and Development of a Sociological Thought Style. 463 pp.*

Stark, Werner. The Sociology of Knowledge: *An Essay in Aid of a Deeper Understanding of the History of Ideas. 384 pp.*

URBAN SOCIOLOGY

Ashworth, William. The Genesis of Modern British Town Planning: *A Study in Economic and Social History of the Nineteenth and Twentieth Centuries. 288 pp.*

Cullingworth, J. B. Housing Needs and Planning Policy: *A Restatement of the Problems of Housing Need and 'Overspill' in England and Wales. 232 pp. 44 tables. 8 maps.*

Dickinson, Robert E. City and Region: *A Geographical Interpretation 608 pp. 125 figures.*

The West European City: *A Geographical Interpretation. 600 pp. 129 maps. 29 plates.*

● The City Region in Western Europe. *320 pp. Maps.*

Humphreys, Alexander J. New Dubliners: *Urbanization and the Irish Family. Foreword by George C. Homans. 304 pp.*

Jackson, Brian. Working Class Community: *Some General Notions raised by a Series of Studies in Northern England. 192 pp.*

Jennings, Hilda. Societies in the Making: *a Study of Development and Redevelopment within a County Borough. Foreword by D. A. Clark. 286 pp.*

●**Mann, P. H.** An Approach to Urban Sociology. *240 pp.*

Morris, R. N., and **Mogey, J.** The Sociology of Housing. *Studies at Berinsfield. 232 pp. 4 pp. plates.*

Rosser, C., and **Harris, C.** The Family and Social Change. *A Study of Family and Kinship in a South Wales Town. 352 pp. 8 maps.*

●**Stacey, Margaret, Batsone, Eric, Bell, Colin,** and **Thurcott, Anne.** Power, Persistence and Change. *A Second Study of Banbury. 196 pp.*

RURAL SOCIOLOGY

Haswell, M. R. The Economics of Development in Village India. *120 pp.*

Littlejohn, James. Westrigg: *the Sociology of a Cheviot Parish. 172 pp. 5 figures.*

Mayer, Adrian C. Peasants in the Pacific. *A Study of Fiji Indian Rural Society. 248 pp. 20 plates.*

Williams, W. M. The Sociology of an English Village: *Gosforth. 272 pp. 12 figures. 13 tables.*

SOCIOLOGY OF INDUSTRY AND DISTRIBUTION

Anderson, Nels. Work and Leisure. *280 pp.*

●**Blau, Peter M.,** and **Scott, W. Richard.** Formal Organizations: *a Comparative approach. Introduction and Additional Bibliography by J. H. Smith. 326 pp.*

Dunkerley, David. The Foreman. *Aspects of Task and Structure. 192 pp.*

Eldridge, J. E. T. Industrial Disputes. *Essays in the Sociology of Industrial Relations. 288 pp.*

Hetzler, Stanley. Applied Measures for Promoting Technological Growth. *352 pp.*

Technological Growth and Social Change. *Achieving Modernization. 269 pp.*

Hollowell, Peter G. The Lorry Driver. *272 pp.*

●**Oxaal, I., Barnett, T.,** and **Booth, D.** (Eds). Beyond the Sociology of Development. *Economy and Society in Latin America and Africa. 295 pp.*

Smelser, Neil J. Social Change in the Industrial Revolution: *An Application of Theory to the Lancashire Cotton Industry, 1770–1840. 468 pp. 12 figures. 14 tables.*

ANTHROPOLOGY

Ammar, Hamed. Growing up in an Egyptian Village: *Silwa, Province of Aswan. 336 pp.*

Brandel-Syrier, Mia. Reeftown Elite. *A Study of Social Mobility in a Modern African Community on the Reef. 376 pp.*

Dickie-Clark, H. F. The Marginal Situation. *A Sociological Study of a Coloured Group. 236 pp.*

Dube, S. C. Indian Village. *Foreword by Morris Edward Opler. 276 pp. 4 plates.*

India's Changing Villages: *Human Factors in Community Development. 260 pp. 8 plates. 1 map.*

Firth, Raymond. Malay Fishermen. *Their Peasant Economy. 420 pp. 17 pp. plates.*

Gulliver, P. H. Social Control in an African Society: a Study of the Arusha, Agricultural Masai of Northern Tanganyika. *320 pp. 8 plates. 10 figures.*

Family Herds. *288 pp.*

Ishwaran, K. Tradition and Economy in Village India: *An Interactionist Approach.*

Foreword by Conrad Arensburg. 176 pp.

Jarvie, Ian C. The Revolution in Anthropology. *268 pp.*

Little, Kenneth L. Mende of Sierra Leone. *308 pp. and folder.*

Negroes in Britain. *With a New Introduction and Contemporary Study by Leonard Bloom. 320 pp.*

Lowie, Robert H. Social Organization. *494 pp.*

Mayer, A. C. Peasants in the Pacific. *A Study of Fiji Indian Rural Society. 248 pp.*

Meer, Fatima. Race and Suicide in South Africa. *325 pp.*

Smith, Raymond T. The Negro Family in British Guiana: *Family Structure and Social Status in the Villages. With a Foreword by Meyer Fortes. 314 pp. 8 plates. 1 figure. 4 maps.*

Smooha, Sammy. Israel: Pluralism and Conflict. *About 320 pp.*

SOCIOLOGY AND PHILOSOPHY

Barnsley, John H. The Social Reality of Ethics. *A Comparative Analysis of Moral Codes. 448 pp.*

Diesing, Paul. Patterns of Discovery in the Social Sciences. *362 pp.*

●**Douglas, Jack D.** (Ed.) Understanding Everyday Life. *Toward the Reconstruction of Sociological Knowledge. Contributions by Alan F. Blum. Aaron W. Cicourel, Norman K. Denzin, Jack D. Douglas, John Heeren, Peter McHugh, Peter K. Manning, Melvin Power, Matthew Speier, Roy Turner, D. Lawrence Wieder, Thomas P. Wilson and Don H. Zimmerman. 370 pp.*

Gorman, Robert A. The Dual Vision. *Alfred Schutz and the Myth of Phenomenological Social Science. About 300 pp.*

Jarvie, Ian C. Concepts and Society. *216 pp.*

●**Pelz, Werner.** The Scope of Understanding in Sociology. *Towards a more radical reorientation in the social humanistic sciences. 283 pp.*

Roche, Maurice. Phenomenology, Language and the Social Sciences. *371 pp.*

Sahay, Arun. Sociological Analysis. *212 pp.*

Sklair, Leslie. The Sociology of Progress. *320 pp.*

Slater, P. Origin and Significance of the Frankfurt School. *A Marxist Perspective. About 192 pp.*

Smart, Barry. Sociology, Phenomenology and Marxian Analysis. *A Critical Discussion of the Theory and Practice of a Science of Society. 220 pp.*

International Library of Anthropology

General Editor Adam Kuper

Ahmed, A. S. Millenium and Charisma Among Pathans. *A Critical Essay in Social Anthropology. 192 pp.*

Brown, Paula. The Chimbu. *A Study of Change in the New Guinea Highlands. 151 pp.*

Gudeman, Stephen. Relationships, Residence and the Individual. *A Rural Panamanian Community. 288 pp. 11 Plates, 5 Figures, 2 Maps, 10 Tables.*

Hamnett, Ian. Chieftainship and Legitimacy. *An Anthropological Study of Executive Law in Lesotho. 163 pp.*

Hanson, F. Allan. Meaning in Culture. *127 pp.*

Lloyd, P. C. Power and Independence. *Urban Africans' Perception of Social Inequality. 264 pp.*

Pettigrew, Joyce. Robber Noblemen. *A Study of the Political System of the Sikh Jats. 284 pp.*

Street, Brian V. The Savage in Literature. *Representations of 'Primitive' Society in English Fiction, 1858–1920. 207 pp.*

Van Den Berghe, Pierre L. Power and Privilege at an African University. *278 pp.*

International Library of Social Policy

General Editor Kathleen Jones

Bayley, M. Mental Handicap and Community Care. *426 pp.*

Bottoms, A. E., and **McClean, J. D.** Defendants in the Criminal Process. *284 pp.*

Butler, J. R. Family Doctors and Public Policy. *208 pp.*

Davies, Martin. Prisoners of Society. *Attitudes and Aftercare. 204 pp.*

Gittus, Elizabeth. Flats, Families and the Under-Fives. *285 pp.*

Holman, Robert. Trading in Children. *A Study of Private Fostering. 355 pp.*

Jones, Howard, and **Cornes, Paul.** Open Prisons. *About 248 pp.*

Jones, Kathleen. History of the Mental Health Service. *428 pp.*

Jones, Kathleen, with **Brown, John, Cunningham, W. J., Roberts, Julian,** and **Williams, Peter.** Opening the Door. *A Study of New Policies for the Mentally Handicapped. 278 pp.*

Karn, Valerie. Retiring to the Seaside. *About 280 pp. 2 maps. Numerous tables.*

Thomas, J. E. The English Prison Officer since 1850: *A Study in Conflict. 258 pp.*

Walton, R. G. Women in Social Work. *303 pp.*

Woodward, J. To Do the Sick No Harm. *A Study of the British Voluntary Hospital System to 1875. 221 pp.*

International Library of Welfare and Philosophy

General Editors Noel Timms and David Watson

- **Plant, Raymond.** Community and Ideology. *104 pp.*

- **McDermott, F. E.** (Ed.) Self-Determination in Social Work. *A Collection of Essays on Self-determination and Related Concepts by Philosophers and Social Work Theorists. Contributors: F. P. Biestek, S. Bernstein, A. Keith-Lucas, D. Sayer, H. H. Perelman, C. Whittington, R. F. Stalley, F. E. McDermott, I. Berlin, H. J. McCloskey, H. L. A. Hart, J. Wilson, A. I. Melden, S. I. Benn. 254 pp.*

Ragg, Nicholas M. People Not Cases. *A Philosophical Approach to Social Work. About 250 pp.*

● **Timms, Noel,** and **Watson, David** (Eds). Talking About Welfare. *Readings in Philosophy and Social Policy. Contributors: T. H. Marshall, R. B. Brandt, G. H. von Wright, K. Nielsen, M. Cranston, R. M. Titmuss, R. S. Downie, E. Telfer, D. Donnison, J. Benson, P. Leonard, A. Keith-Lucas, D. Walsh, I. T. Ramsey. 320 pp.*

Primary Socialization, Language and Education

General Editor Basil Bernstein

Adlam, Diana S., *with the assistance of Geoffrey Turner and Lesley Lineker.* Code in Context. *About 272 pp.*

Bernstein, Basil. Class, Codes and Control. *3 volumes.*
1. *Theoretical Studies Towards a Sociology of Language. 254 pp.*
2. *Applied Studies Towards a Sociology of Language. 377 pp.*
3. ● *Towards a Theory of Educatiomal Transmission. 167 pp.*

Brandis, W., and **Bernstein, B.** Selection and Control. *176 pp.*

Brandis, Walter, and **Henderson, Dorothy.** Social Class, Language and Communication. *288 pp.*

Cook-Gumperz, Jenny. Social Control and Socialization. *A Study of Class Differences in the Language of Maternal Control. 290 pp.*

● **Gahagan, D. M.,** and **G. A.** Talk Reform. *Exploration in Language for Infant School Children. 160 pp.*

Hawkins, P. R. Social Class, the Nominal Group and Verbal Strategies. *About 220 pp.*

Robinson, W. P., and **Rackstraw, Susan D. A.** A Question of Answers. *2 volumes. 192 pp. and 180 pp.*

Turner, Geoffrey J., and **Mohan, Bernard A.** A Linguistic Description and Computer Programme for Children's Speech. *208 pp.*

Reports of the Institute of Community Studies

● **Cartwright, Ann.** Parents and Family Planning Services. *306 pp.*
Patients and their Doctors. *A Study of General Practice. 304 pp.*

Dench, Geoff. Maltese in London. *A Case-study in the Erosion of Ethnic Consciousness. 302 pp.*

● **Jackson, Brian.** Streaming: *an Education System in Miniature. 168 pp.*

Jackson, Brian, and **Marsden, Dennis.** Education and the Working Class: *Some General Themes raised by a Study of 88 Working-class Children in a Northern Industrial City. 268 pp. 2 folders.*

Marris, Peter. The Experience of Higher Education. *232 pp. 27 tables.*
Loss and Change. *192 pp.*

Marris, Peter, and **Rein, Martin.** Dilemmas of Social Reform. *Poverty and Community Action in the United States. 256 pp.*

Marris, Peter, and **Somerset, Anthony.** African Businessmen. *A Study of Entrepreneurship and Development in Kenya. 256 pp.*

Mills, Richard. Young Outsiders: *a Study in Alternative Communities. 216 pp.*

Runciman, W. G. Relative Deprivation and Social Justice. *A Study of Attitudes to Social Inequality in Twentieth-Century England. 352 pp.*

Willmott, Peter. Adolescent Boys in East London. *230 pp.*

Willmott, Peter, and **Young, Michael.** Family and Class in a London Suburb. *202 pp. 47 tables.*

Young, Michael. Innovation and Research in Education. *192 pp.*

● **Young, Michael,** and **McGeeney, Patrick.** Learning Begins at Home. *A Study of a Junior School and its Parents. 128 pp.*

Young, Michael, and **Willmott, Peter.** Family and Kinship in East London. *Foreword by Richard M. Titmuss. 252 pp. 39 tables.*

The Symmetrical Family. *410 pp.*

Reports of the Institute for Social Studies in Medical Care

Cartwright, Ann, Hockey, Lisbeth, and **Anderson, John L.** Life Before Death. *310 pp.*

Dunnell, Karen, and **Cartwright, Ann.** Medicine Takers, Prescribers and Hoarders. *190 pp.*

Medicine, Illness and Society

General Editor W. M. Williams

Robinson, David. The Process of Becoming Ill. *142 pp.*

Stacey, Margaret, *et al.* Hospitals, Children and Their Families. *The Report of a Pilot Study. 202 pp.*

Stimson, G. V., and **Webb, B.** Going to See the Doctor. *The Consultation Process in General Practice. 155 pp.*

Monographs in Social Theory

General Editor Arthur Brittan

● **Barnes, B.** Scientific Knowledge and Sociological Theory. *192 pp.*

Bauman, Zygmunt. Culture as Praxis. *204 pp.*

● **Dixon, Keith.** Sociological Theory. *Pretence and Possibility. 142 pp.*

Meltzer, B. N., Petras, J. W., and **Reynolds, L. T.** Symbolic Interactionism. *Genesis, Varieties and Criticisms. 144 pp.*

● **Smith, Anthony D.** The Concept of Social Change. *A Critique of the Functionalist Theory of Social Change. 208 pp.*

Routledge Social Science Journals

The British Journal of Sociology. *Editor – Angus Stewart; Associate Editor – Leslie Sklair. Vol. 1, No. 1 – March 1950 and Quarterly. Roy. 8vo. All back issues available. An international journal publishing original papers in the field of sociology and related areas.*

Community Work. *Edited by David Jones and Marjorie Mayo. 1973. Published annually.*

Economy and Society. *Vol. 1, No. 1. February 1972 and Quarterly. Metric Roy. 8vo. A journal for all social scientists covering sociology, philosophy, anthropology, economics and history. All back numbers available.*

Religion. Journal of Religion and Religions. *Chairman of Editorial Board, Ninian Smart. Vol. 1, No. 1, Spring 1971. A journal with an interdisciplinary approach to the study of the phenomena of religion. All back numbers available.*

Year Book of Social Policy in Britain, The. *Edited by Kathleen Jones. 1971. Published annually.*

Social and Psychological Aspects of Medical Practice

Editor Trevor Silverstone

Lader, Malcolm. Psychophysiology of Mental Illness. *280 pp.*

● **Silverstone, Trevor,** and **Turner, Paul.** Drug Treatment in Psychiatry. *232 pp.*

Printed in Great Britain by
Lowe & Brydone Printers Limited, Thetford, Norfolk